# MINOANS

The Wilmington Giant
*The quest for a lost myth*

The Knossos Labyrinth
*A new view of the 'Palace of Minos' at Knossos*

The Stonehenge People
*An exploration of life in neolithic Britain 4700–2000 BC*

# MINOANS

## Life in Bronze Age Crete

## RODNEY CASTLEDEN

*Illustrated by the author*

London and New York

First published 1990 by Routledge
11 New Fetter Lane, London EC4P 4EE
29 West 35th Street, New York NY 10001

Photoset by Rowland Phototypesetting Ltd,
Bury St Edmunds, Suffolk
Printed in Great Britain by
Richard Clay Ltd, Bungay, Suffolk

*British Library Cataloguing in Publication Data*
Castleden, Rodney
Minoans: life in bronze age crete.
1. Minoan civilisation
I. Title
939'.18
ISBN 0–415–04070–1

*Library of Congress Cataloging in Publication Data*
Castleden, Rodney
Minoans: life in Bronze Age Crete / by Rodney Castleden.
p. cm.
Includes bibliographical references.
1. Minoans—Social life and customs. 2. Crete (Greece)—Social
life and customs. I. Title.
DF220.3.C37 1991 90-32407
ISBN 0-415-04070-1

*For Michael Tippett*

Thou buildest upon the bosom of darkness, out of the fantastic imagery of the brain, cities and temples beyond the art of Phidias and Praxiteles – beyond the splendour of Babylon and Hekatompylos: and from the anarchy of dreaming sleep, callest into sunny light the faces of long-buried beauties.
(Thomas de Quincey, *Confessions of an English Opium Eater*, 1821)

# Contents

# List of illustrations

CHAPTER TITLE ILLUSTRATIONS

# Acknowledgements

I should like to thank Mr Brian McGregor, the Librarian at the Ashmolean Library in Oxford, for allowing me access to the books and journals in his care, and John and Celia Clarke for their hospitality during my visits to Oxford. Joan Newey offered useful advice on translations from the Greek, and conversations with Eileen Smith gave me some ideas on the lack of Minoan literature.

Doreena and Keith of John Proctor Travel expertly organized specially-tailored transport and accommodation arrangements for both the 1988 and 1989 visits to Crete, which enabled me to cover a lot of ground. I am especially indebted to Kit, who came with me on both occasions, and was keen to explore even the most inaccessible and elusive Minoan sites.

I am grateful to Chris Pearce and Andrew Wheatcroft at Routledge for making the publication process so smooth and straightforward, and to Countess Anne Romanov for proof-reading the text and for her invaluable help with the library research.

The book functions as a sequel and companion volume to *The Knossos Labyrinth*: whereas the latter focuses on the single most important monument produced by the culture, *Minoans* provides the background on the people, an account of the culture itself. The large bronze age building known as the 'Palace of Minos' at Knossos is generally acknowledged as the principal 'marker' for the Minoan civilization. A radical re-interpretation of that building's function necessitates nothing less than a re-evaluation of the civilization: hence the need for this book. A good deal of the material for *Minoans* was gathered, almost by the way, during the research for the earlier book. As a result, all the people who helped me in the preparation of *The Knossos Labyrinth* must be acknowledged here too: Dr Tzedakis, the Director of Heraklion Museum, Karambinis Emanolis, Custodian of Knossos, John and Trudy Urmson, Angelika Schönborn, Ann Brown, Diana Cooke, and Professor Peter Warren of the Department of Ancient History and Classical Archaeology at Bristol.

R. C.
Brighton

# 1
# Introduction

Hail, son of Kronos,
Welcome, greatest Kouros,
Mighty of brightness,
Here now present, leading your spirits,
Come for the year to Dikte
And rejoice in this ode,
Which we strike on the strings, as we
Blend it with the sound of pipes, as we
Chant our song, standing round
This your well-walled altar.
(Hymn of the Kouretes to Diktaian Zeus. From Palaikastro,
*c.* 250 AD, but representing a much earlier tradition)

In the short time that has elapsed since Sir Arthur Evans effectively rediscovered the Minoans in the early 1900s, the people of bronze age Crete have become familiar figures in our mental landscape of European prehistory. We have come to accept as established and defined a whole string of cultural traits that go to make up the 'Minoan personality'. The Minoans were elegant, graceful people who took an innocent pleasure in displaying their own physical beauty; they were lithe, athletic and enjoyed boxing, wrestling, and bull-leaping; they were intensely refined aesthetes, surrounding themselves with sophisticated architecture and beautiful objects; they were nature-lovers, commissioning frescoes of landscapes full of flowers, birds, and butterflies; they were collectively strong, too, with fleets controlling the seas surrounding Crete, so minimizing the danger of attack by would-be invaders; they were lovers of peace, the inhabitants of each city-state living in harmony with their neighbours; they were ruled by a great and powerful king of Knossos called Minos.

But how far does the work of subsequent archaeologists in Crete support this widely held view of the Minoans? It is appropriate, as we approach the centenary of Evans' historic 1900 excavation, to take stock of the evidence. It may well be that we need to revise our image of the Minoans in the light of that evidence.

Until about a hundred years ago, it was customary to see the history of the Aegean world as beginning with the First Olympiad of 776 BC. Although it was recognized that the region was inhabited before that date, all the events of that earlier period were regarded as lost beyond retrieval and any references to them treated as pure legend. The heroes and heroines of Greek folklore and myth were tossed aside by scholars: they were as unhistorical as the gods and goddesses.

In the wake of Schliemann's and Evans' discoveries at Troy, Mycenae, Tiryns and Knossos, there was a tendency for historians to swing to the opposite extreme. The historical reality of Troy seemed to prove the existence of Priam, that of Mycenae Agamemnon, that of Knossos Minos. Bury (1951), for instance, accepted such figures as Perseus, Minos, Jason, Theseus, and even Heracles as historically real people, pointing out in support of this position that the Greeks themselves believed in their reality and that (in Homer, for example) they were given fairly consistent biographies and pedigrees. But this extreme position is fraught with difficulties. The Greeks not only believed in Theseus and Jason: they believed in Prometheus too – Prometheus, the creator of mankind – and put the time of his existence at around 1600 BC. Since we know that the Minoans built the *second* temple at Knossos some one hundred years before this date and we also know that the Minoan civilization had been developing for a thousand years, there is no possibility that the Greek idea of Prometheus could have been historically correct.

Modern historians and prehistorians take the more moderate view that these emblematic figures were folk-heroes, symbolically representing remote but powerfully significant events all but lost to the Aegean folk-memory. Impressive events in the communal past, such as changes of dynasty, the arrival of waves of foreign settlers, wars, invasions, migrations, were summarized in the epic life events of the folk-heroes. Some may turn out to have been real people, and finding their homes by means of archaeological excavation may persuade us that we have discovered the people themselves, but they may well not have been the figures presented to us by the Greeks. Discovering the Knossos Labyrinth implied to Sir Arthur Evans and many who followed his line of thinking that King Minos too had been traced, though this is not the case. Even if a kingly burial had been discovered by archaeologists at Knossos, which significantly it has not, we could still not be sure that the corpse was that of the majestic and tyrannical ruler of the Minoan sea-empire presented to us in Greek legend. Eratosthenes' dating puts the Trojan War at 1183 BC and King Minos into the third generation before that. Minos' floruit was thus, in the Greek view, around 1260 BC – about a hundred years after the date generally agreed by archaeologists for the abandonment of his alleged palace at Knossos. As Thomson (1949) says, it may be better to accept the general substance of the Greek stories, or at any rate to bear them in mind, and let the dates go; certainly the Greeks foreshortened the time-scale for the early events in Aegean prehistory.

Archaeology has added a new dimension to our view of the Aegean. Instead of beginning with the First Olympiad, we now have a much longer perspective revealing a complex cultural evolution stretching back two thousand years further. We have a picture of a prehistoric preamble which is finely detailed and becomes increasingly so with each new archaeological dig. The most startling result of Aegean archaeology during the last hundred years has been the discovery of a complete, original, and previously unsuspected civilization which existed before the Homeric age. The Minoan civilization had all kinds of repercussions on the development of the Greek culture which developed later, yet, extraordinarily, the historians of the fifth century BC, Herodotus and Thucydides, had comparatively little to say about the culture or history of Crete. Why was it that the glittering originality of Minoan Crete vanished from the Greek consciousness within a few centuries of its demise? Was it that the Greeks were too proud of their own civilization to acknowledge the existence of an earlier civilization, one that rivalled or surpassed their own? Or was it that the Minoan civilization had been so totally destroyed that they were unaware of its character?

Certainly the Greeks inherited some strange tales and a large amount of cult activity from the Minoans, but they seem to have been unconscious of their true origins. It may be, as Thomson suggests, that the post-Minoan invasion of Crete and Greece by Dorians from the north cut Crete off from mainland Greece and that when the eastern Mediterranean recovered from this trauma the Greeks resumed trade with Egypt and the Levant direct, without landing on Crete. Whatever the explanation, there is a strange discontinuity at the end of the Minoan civilization; it was as if a door closed on it, only to be opened again after three thousand years.

Minoan Crete may be seen as a cradle of civilization on a level with the Nile, Indus, Tigris, and Euphrates valleys. Arguments are sometimes advanced that the Minoans borrowed much of their culture from Egypt, Syria, or Anatolia, but theirs was a very distinctive culture, however it was assembled or generated, and certainly distinctive enough for us to treat it as an original creation. It could be argued that the Minoan art of fresco painting was borrowed from Egypt, and it may be so, but the artistic effects and even the subject matter are very different; it is clear that the Minoans developed the art in a way that was strongly characteristic of their own personality, making it an integral part of their own culture. So it was with many other cultural elements, and to such an extent that we get, even from fragments of artefacts, a strong sense of the Minoans' personality. After reviewing all the many elements of the culture in the opening chapters, we will come to a discussion of this Minoan personality, utilizing the latest archaeological evidence from Crete in order to achieve the clearest picture. It is possible to gain access to the everyday life of the Minoans and also, to a surprising extent, to their emotional and spiritual world too.

The Cretan bronze age was an extended period of cultural growth, beginning in about 3000 BC and ending in about 1000 BC. During this long period there were many changes and we need to be aware that when we identify particular traits as 'Minoan' we are often thinking of the culture as it was at its peak, in the three centuries preceding the abandonment of the Knossos Labyrinth in 1380 BC. But this pinnacle was reached after a millennium of evolution. From the outset there was an ambitious pattern of trade by land and sea, and complex bartering negotiations with numerous foreign neighbours as far afield as Egypt. Civilization in Egypt was at that stage in advance of the Cretan culture and it may well be that contacts with a more advanced culture stimulated the Cretans. Contacts with Anatolia gave the Cretans access to crafts, artefacts, materials and ideas that had come from Mesopotamia, and these too had their effect in stimulating development; the idea of using sealstones, for instance, seems to have been developed from a few samples imported from the east.

Gradually, during the Early Minoan period (3000–2200 BC), the Cretans evolved all the characteristics that we think of as being distinctively Minoan. Only the 'palaces' remained unbuilt. The 'palace' society (c. 2000–1380 BC) was clearly very advanced in its orderly and bureaucratic organization, showing a strongly rational and practical side with highly developed craft technologies, and yet it also possessed all the imaginative power and childlike freshness of a very young culture. This combination of skill, power, and freshness is exemplified in the frescoes and crafted cult objects, many of which seem to spring from a pervasive religious feeling. Towards the end of the Late Minoan Period (the end of the second millennium BC), religion seems to have dwindled to a rigid and sterile formula for appeasing the deities of what must have seemed an increasingly hostile cosmos. Nevertheless, at the zenith, during the heyday of the so-called 'palaces', the religious life of the Minoans was rich and vibrant. There were moments, quite frequent to judge from the artwork, when gods and men and, more importantly, goddesses and priestesses, were brought together in astonishing unions. In epiphanies of startling drama, men, women, birds, and even pillars and boulders were transformed into deities; gods and goddesses appeared and walked among worshipping mortals, exalted but humanized and accessible.

This religious zeal, amounting to intoxication and possibly actually enhanced by alcohol and opium, is expressed in a wide range of art objects; the frescoes decorating shrines and sanctuaries, the cult vessels, the religious scenes on the sealstones are all executed to the very highest technical and artistic standards. Again and again when we look at objects such as the

Mallia bee-pendant or the Boston Goddess, we sense that the Minoan craftsmen were over-achieving, extending their crafts almost beyond the technical limits of the age. In the virtuosic handling of clay, bronze, and many kinds of stone, they surpassed themselves and we may sometimes feel that the spirit of the age was adventurously romantic rather than pre-classical. The proud figures of the men in the frescoes may look to us like overreachers, vain and perhaps vainglorious; perhaps the idea of *hubris*, vanity in the face of the gods, had not yet evolved and this was still an age of innocent self-pride.

The images of men and women, warriors, worshippers and priestesses give us evidence of their appearance and also of the way they saw themselves, which is every bit as important. Assembling a picture of the Minoans is complicated a little by uncertainty about the authenticity of some of the art objects, especially those not found in modern excavations. No one knows for certain where the beautiful ivory statuette known as the Boston Goddess came from; it seems likely that it was robbed from a surface layer in the ruins of the East Wing of the Knossos Labyrinth, and in terms of materials, shape, and the techniques used in making it, it is characteristically Minoan, and therefore probably genuine. The Ring of Minos, given its known findspot at the site where the Temple Tomb was later unearthed, and given its style and content, is also taken here to be an authentic Minoan ring (see Chapter 6 and Figure 39). Nilsson's objection (1949) that the picture on it is derivative and that it could have been composed from a knowledge of three or four other cult scenes is unconvincing. Significantly, the scene on the Ring of Minos is consistent with what we are learning of Minoan cult activities, and is therefore likely to be genuine.

The Ring of Nestor is another matter. Although many of the elements in its composition appear to be Minoan, they have been assembled in a peculiar way, as four scenes quartered by a 'Tree of Life'. It shows, according to the Evans interpretation, a couple being initiated into the mysteries of the otherworld, where the Tree of Life has its roots: the two people appear before a goddess and an enthroned griffin. The initiation is followed by resurrection and the couple's return to the world of the living. In this case, Nilsson's reasons for doubting the ring's authenticity are well founded. Nowhere else, for instance, is a griffin shown enthroned. Often a griffin or a pair of griffins are attendant on a standing or seated goddess, but it is inexplicable for the roles to be reversed. Another scene shows a lion enthroned on a sacrificial table; this too is incongruous, and suggests that the craftsman who made the ring did not know what the table was for. Although the vocabulary is Minoan, the syntax is not. The Ring of Nestor is therefore treated as a fake and consequently not referred to in later chapters as evidence of the Minoan belief-system.

The Minoans and their civilization have been written about before, but there is a pressing reason for reviewing them now. In *The Knossos Labyrinth*

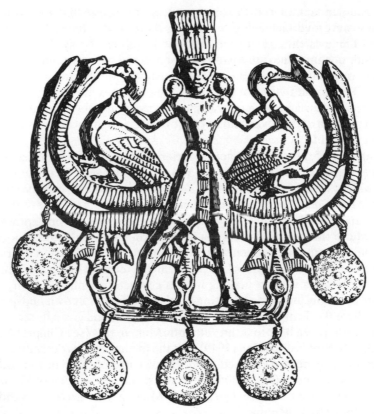

*Figure 1*  The Aigina Treasure Pendant. Found on Aegina, near Athens, but almost
certainly a Minoan masterpiece made in Crete between 1700 and 1600 BC

(Castleden 1989), the nature and purpose of the so-called 'Palace of Minos'
at Knossos were called into question and an array of arguments was
presented for treating the building as a bronze age temple-complex. It was
shown, for example, that the distribution of findspots of religious cult
equipment round the building indicates that a very large area of it must have
been given over to cult activity.

When comparisons are made between Minoan Crete and pharaonic Egypt
or Hittite Anatolia or the cultures of Mesopotamia, interpreting the 'palace'
at Knossos as a temple – and, by implication, the other Cretan 'palaces' as
temples too – seems quite natural. The Hittite capital, Hattusa, possessed
several temples, the largest of which was in many ways similar to the
contemporary Knossos Labyrinth. As Professor Alexiou has pointed out,
there was a broad similarity between the social and economic conditions
prevailing in Minoan Crete and those in the Mesopotamian and Anatolian
cultures. It follows that if the Hittite and Sumerian temples were large

buildings, focal to the societies and economies of their cities and territories, Minoan society might have developed in a similar way. The problem seems to lie in the existence of extensive store-rooms in the Minoan palace-temples, implying a major redistribution role in the economy, but this need not preclude a fundamentally religious role for the building. In ancient Egypt it was normally the kings who dominated trade, but temple-priests were nevertheless also engaged in trade. It seems to have been particularly during periods of weak royal control that the temples engaged in large-scale trade. A priest of Ammon, for example, travelled to Byblos with gold and silver to buy timber to build a sacred ship; after some haggling, the Prince of Byblos delivered timber in return for gold, silver and raiment. There seems little room for doubt that the Knossos Labyrinth played a central role in the economic life of the surrounding central Cretan territory, and that its priests and priestesses were involved in foreign trade, the organization of public works and the allocation of rations to workers, as well as playing a central role in ceremonial and religious life – just like the temples of the east.

Trade went on at a surprisingly ambitious scale, exclusively by barter. Fourteenth-century BC correspondence regarding barter has been found at Amarna in Egypt; Pharaoh sent 'presents' of gold to the king of Babylon and received gifts of horses and lapis lazuli in return. The king of Alasia (= Cyprus) offered 500 bronze talents in exchange for silver, clothing, beds and war chariots. There are even records of trade with the Minoans themselves, 'gifts from the Princes (or leaders) of the Land of Keftiu and of the isles which are in the midst of the sea'. These were probably direct exports to Egypt of manufactured goods from the Cretan temples. In return the Egyptians sent gifts of gold, ivory, cloth, stone vessels containing perfume, chariots (probably in kits) and probably monkeys and Nubian slaves.

The economic aspects of the Minoan culture have become fairly clearly established, but interpreting the largest buildings in the Minoan towns as temples rather than palaces shifts the culture's centre of gravity very significantly. It is for this very specific reason that we need to take a fresh look at the Minoan civilization.

Most of the representational art surviving from the Minoan period has come from the temples and should be treated as religious art. In the past we have tended to assume that because women are regularly depicted bare-breasted in the 'palace' frescoes they were disrobed in this way in their normal everyday lives. If such representations are seen as religious art and the women are seen as priestesses, temple attendants, dancers, or even goddesses, the earlier assumption is seen to be unwarranted; it may well be that women uncovered their breasts only during acts of religious worship. The temple art of the Minoans may depict ritual, ceremonial, and mytho-logical scenes to the exclusion of secular elements. It is hard to tell, but Minoan temple art may be as unrelated to the realities of everyday life in bronze age Crete as Edward Burne-Jones' stained glass saints were to the East London of the Whitechapel murders.

That important reservation apart, the art of the temples can tell us a great deal about the Minoans, their view of the world and their ritual preoccupations.

Interpreting the 'palaces' as temples in no way diminishes the interest which they hold for us. It rectifies an anomaly – a sophisticated bronze age society without temples was a strange beast indeed – and it adds a new dimension in the form of a powerful and highly organized priesthood. There is also the still-unanswered question, raised in *The Knossos Labyrinth*, about the location of the real palaces. If the Minoans had kings, where did they live? Have their dwellings not been discovered, or simply not recognized?

Inevitably and rightly, the preoccupation with palace-temples will continue, but it is important to remember that it was only in the later part of Minoan history, from 1900 BC onwards, that temples dominated. There were significant periods before and after when there seem to have been no large temple centres, and we need to attend to those phases too. As with many aspects of the Minoan civilization, this is well known among archaeologists, but often overlooked by the tourist and the general reader. One purpose of this book is to rectify that and make available to the general reader some of the results of modern archaeology, so that he or she may develop a well-rounded picture of the Minoans, their way of life, their beliefs and their quite remarkable achievements.

The Minoans are credited with sensing, perhaps for the first time, that a pleasurable afterlife was to come – with, in effect, inventing or discovering Elysium. We may well come to believe, as Pindar was much later to write of those who had gone before to the Elysian Fields, that

> For them the sun shines at full strength, while we here walk in night.
> The plains around their city are red with roses
> And shaded by incense trees heavy with golden fruit.
> And some enjoy horses and wrestling, or table games and the lyre,
> And near them blossoms a flower of perfect joy.
> Perfumes always hover above the land
> From the frankincense strewn in deep-shining fire of the gods' altars . . .

# 2
# The people

My lords, we have had our fill of the good things we have shared, and of the banquet's boon companion, the harp. Let us go out of doors now and try our hands at various sports, so that when our guest has reached his house he can tell his friends that at boxing, wrestling, jumping and running there is no one who could beat us. . . . We can run fast and we are first-rate seamen. But the things in which we take a perennial delight are the feast, the lyre, the dance, clean linen in plenty, a hot bath and our beds.

(Homer, *Odyssey*, Book 8)

### APPEARANCE AND DRESS

Although the Minoan civilization had its origins as long as five thousand years ago and had come to an end by 1000 BC, we nevertheless have a very clear idea of what the Minoan people looked like. There are in the region of a hundred statuettes in stone, metal and clay, showing us ordinary Minoans worshipping. There are also representations of Minoans on sealstones and decorative metalwork, as well as in the best-known medium of all, the frescoes. Among these, there is plenty of evidence of the sort of clothes they wore and of their general appearance or, to be more precise, of the way in which the Minoans liked to see themselves.

The Minoans depicted themselves as straight-nosed (often with a high bridge), and with large almond-shaped eyes. They had conspicuous eyebrows and long, wavy black hair falling in curling locks to their shoulders and sometimes to their waists. Their tanned bodies were athletic and tense with nervous energy; their arms, shoulders and thighs were strong and muscular, their waists and lower legs slim and lithe. It is above all a physically attractive type that we are shown, graceful whether in repose or engaged in energetic activity, and graceful in a rather self-conscious, theatrical way: it is the grace of a matador or a ballet dancer.

Whether the majority of Minoans actually possessed these characteristics is another matter. Perhaps we should see them as goals or ideals against which individual Minoans were measured. Perhaps, alternatively, it is only the young Minoans that are depicted. In Crete today, even millennia later, after many other races have passed through, the stereotypes of Minoan beauty can still be seen in young men and women in their teens and twenties with all the characteristics of the people in the frescoes. One of the bronze figurines of worshippers shows a rather portly man in a loincloth, making the gesture of adoration, fist to forehead: but this departure from the lithe, athletic and above all youthful norm is unusual.

In classical Greece too an ideal of human physical perfection was held up for admiration, and for a particular purpose; the city-state needed strong young men to defend and preserve it, so there was a strong practical need to encourage the development of strong, healthy male bodies. In Minoan Crete a similar impulse may have lain behind the perfect male figures, but the existence of ideals of female beauty must have had a different purpose: no mortal female warriors are shown. It may be that there was a religious motive; only perfect female (and perhaps male) forms could become the incarnation of a deity (see Chapter 6). Wherever possible, the Minoans' fashions in clothes, jewellery and face-painting were designed to accentuate the bodily characteristics that were specially favoured. The very fact that the

*Figure 2*  A Minoan worshipper. This fine bronze figurine illustrates the Minoan ideal of youthful manhood

men often wore very skimpy clothes revealing as much of their physique as possible indicates their intense love of physical beauty.

Precisely who the Minoans were is an unanswered question. It seems likely that the native neolithic people of Crete interbred with small numbers of immigrants from mainland Greece and Anatolia to produce the Minoan population, but how distinct the Minoans were is unclear. Studies of Minoan skulls and skeletons from cemeteries at Mavro Spilio and Palaikastro show that there were variations among individuals, but not such as to imply any difference of racial type within the population. When the Minoan bones are compared with those of a sample of twelve hundred modern Cretans (quoted by Faure 1973), there is very little difference: overall, the Cretan physical type has not changed significantly.

There was, however, a very significant difference in appearance because of their clothes. The Minoans' main cloth-making fibre was wool. Spinning and weaving were well-established cottage industries by the beginning of the bronze age: clay spindle whorls and loom weights are found at a great many Minoan sites. The wooden upright looms on which the cloth was produced have not survived, but there is a stone in the Agia Varvara house at Mallia with two slots which may well have held a loom's upright posts. Wool is known to have been available from the many references to flocks of sheep on the clay tablets at Knossos; possibly woollen cloth was one of the Minoans' main exports.

Traces of linen were found in an Early Minoan I tomb at Mochlos. This may have been produced in Minoan Crete, but in view of its early date it may be better explained as an import from Egypt. Possibly silk was produced in Crete: it is known to have been produced in Cos, just to the north-east of Crete, after the Minoan civilization collapsed. Animal furs and skins were used to make garments for rituals (see Chapter 6), although leather was no doubt used for making sandals and boots for everyday wear.

In the Early and Middle Minoan Periods (see Appendix D for chronology), men nearly always wore a loincloth, either rolled and tucked round the waist or held up by a belt. There were several different styles of loincloth and it may be that they were fashionable at different times or in different areas. Sometimes the loincloth was folded out on each side to cover the upper thighs. Sometimes it was simply wrapped round like a mini-skirt. From this it was a straightforward development to turn the skirt or kilt into a pair of shorts by sewing the centre at the front and back together between the legs. The Lion Hunt Dagger (Figure 10), made in Crete although found at Mycenae, clearly shows Minoan hunters wearing patterned shorts; the third hunter from the left in particular is shown to have shorts made in two layers, a curious parallel with the flounced or layered skirts worn by the women. The archer depicted on a carved steatite jar from the Knossos area is shown wearing similar shorts.

The codpiece was another enduring feature of male attire. The early design was a straight and narrow genital-guard held up by a belt: it was often worn without a loincloth. A fragment of a steatite rhyton showing a wrestler's naked back and buttocks clearly shows the way the G-string of the codpiece, a narrow strip of cloth, passed between the legs and up between the man's buttocks. After 1700 BC the codpiece was developed into a more exaggerated feature. Wider and more prominent, it was often worn with a kilt made of a stiff material. The kilt left the codpiece exposed, covering the front of the thigh but rising to expose the side of the thigh: the 'tail' was somehow made to curl back. It is a garment like this that the harvesters on the Harvesters Vase from Agia Triadha are wearing. Other kilts were fairly long at the back, sloping up towards the exposed codpiece at the front.

By 1500 BC the codpiece was not always exposed. Several representations of men from this time show them wearing kilts but no codpieces. From 1500 BC a new, bulkier kilt was introduced and, for a time, it seems that both old and new styles were worn. The new kilt had a hem that sloped down from back to front and reached the knees; the codpiece was replaced by a decorative beaded tassel, which was worn rather like a Scottish sporran (Figure 1). It is possible that the new type of kilt originated in the Knossos area, since most of the early representations of it come from Mallia and Knossos: the tribute-bearers in the Procession and Cupbearer Frescoes at Knossos are classic examples (Figure 57).

The Minoans were known as far afield as ancient Egypt and their likenesses were painted on some of the tomb interiors at Thebes by Egyptian artists. The envoys from the Aegean who visited Thebes around 1450–1470 were described in the Tomb of Rekhmire, a vizier who died in 1450 BC, as 'Princes of the Land of Keftiu and of the isles which are in the midst of the sea'. Keftiu was Crete. The isles were presumably the Aegean islands to the north of Crete, the Cyclades. Since at that time – or at any rate until the time of the great eruption of Thera in 1470 BC – the Minoans had colonies and trading stations in the southern Aegean, it may well have been possible for them to boast to the Egyptians that they *ruled* the Aegean, although the truth may have been rather different (see Chapter 5). Perhaps the Egyptians misunderstood the subtlety of the situation.

The Rekhmire paintings show the envoys wearing patterned kilts similar to those on the Procession Fresco, without codpieces, with the hemline sloping down towards the front. Cleaning revealed that this representation is an overpainting and that underneath it are the older style kilts, *with* codpieces and with the hemline sloping *up* towards the front. This reflects the Egyptian view that the Minoans had significantly changed their appearance in successive embassies: the Egyptian artist only recorded the change of fashion that he had observed. The wall paintings in the Tomb of Senmut at Thebes, dating to around 1500 BC, simply show the older style of kilt, which had decorative braid along the hem and on the broad belt.

Sometimes it is argued that the arrival of the long kilt in Crete signalled the arrival of 'Mycenean conquerors' in Crete, but this is not the only possible interpretation. Both short and long kilts were to find their way to mainland Greece. A man in a Pylian fresco (Lang 1969) dating to around 1400 BC is shown wearing the short kilt and codpiece and we would scarcely expect to cite this as evidence of a Minoan conquest of Pylos at that time. There were simply changes of fashion, washing, like the gentle Mediterranean tides, back and forth across the Aegean coastlands.

Women's fashions, though covering more of the body than male attire, nevertheless showed an equal interest in display. Their clothes are not the clothes of women kept in purdah, but of women who expect to take the centre of the social stage. Generally, designs accentuated full hips, slender wasp-waists and prominent breasts; in fact the most conspicuous and best-known feature of Minoan attire is that it usually left the breasts exposed.

At the time of the first temples, women wore long robe-like dresses held in at the waist by girdles wound twice round and tied in a knot, leaving the girdle-ends hanging down in front. The dress tops, which were sometimes separate bodices, had short and fairly tight sleeves, rather in the style of a modern T-shirt, but with a deep slit at the front right down to the navel. This gave two options. The bodice front could be arranged to cover the breasts, leaving only the cleavage showing, which I suspect was the normal practice; alternatively, it could be pulled sideways, deliberately to display the breasts, as was the custom during religious ceremonies. Often the bodice rose to a high peak at the back of the neck.

The Snake Goddess statuette, which shows how a priestess dressed for a religious ceremony to transform herself into a deity, shows some extra garments. She has a wide belt to accentuate her slender waist and from it, descending at the front and back, is an elaborately embroidered double apron, which may be a sacral garment worn only by priestesses. Underneath this she wears a heavy flounced skirt made of seven overlapping layers of

*Figure 3* A woman's head-dress, about 1900 BC. Head from a clay figurine

material, each layer composed of different coloured and patterned cloth in 12–15 centimetre squares to make a very striking check pattern.

This style was evidently a very enduring one. It appears on an early ivory seal from Knossos and continued in use through both the temple periods. By 1550 the layered skirts began to develop a marked 'V' in front, which may indicate that a new way of tying on the overskirt was being tried out. It is clear from a careful scrutiny of the figurines and frescoes, including those from Thera, that the flounced skirt was tied on as a kind of kilt and that often – perhaps usually – a long flared underskirt was worn as well. The rather complex textures visible in the dresses on the Arkhanes and Isopata gold rings can be better understood in terms of an ankle-length underskirt and a knee- or calf-length layered overskirt.

An assumption is often made that the heavy flounced skirt was normal to female attire, but this is by no means certain: its use may have been restricted to religious ceremonies. How the priestesses managed to dance in them is hard to imagine, but this is shown in several rings and frescoes.

As for footwear, people often went unshod, particularly indoors or if participating in a religious ceremony. The use of slabs of soft gypsum for stairs and floors in the Knossos Labyrinth, a material which could not have withstood heavy wear, supports the idea that priestesses, attendants and worshippers went barefoot, much as in many temples of the present day. Sometimes sandals were worn. There are ivories which show their design in detail, and it has been suggested that the word 'sandal' may even be derived from a Minoan word: the Greek word 'sandalon' seems to have had a pre-Greek origin. Calf-length leather boots were probably the standard outdoor footwear for men. There is good reason to suppose that the upper parts of at least some boots were either of very soft leather or even woollen fabric.

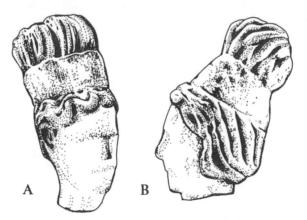

*Figure 4* Heads from female figurines, showing hair-styles. Woman A has used a band of cloth to pile her hair up vertically. Woman B has used a similar band to push the hair-pile back towards the crown of her head

The 'prince' on the Chieftain Cup from Agia Triadha is wearing boots, but his shins are bandaged up with puttees; this practice may have been a precaution to protect the very soft leather, or to make them warmer, or to prevent stones and other debris falling into the boots, or to hold them on more securely – it is hard to judge which. Curiously, the officer reporting to the prince has boots without puttees. Rank seems not to be the explanation, since the boxers on the Boxer Vase are also shown wearing puttees. On a detail of style, the boots nearly always have pointed, turned-up toes.

Men often went hatless, and it is a little surprising that their styles of headgear were mostly unadventurous: it is an area of missed opportunities. When they wore hats, they had wide flat caps or caps with short, thick rolled brims. Women on the other hand went in for a wide variety of hat styles. In the first temple period, they often wore high, pointed hats, possibly made necessary by their hair-style, although we must not overlook the bronze *male* worshipper from Katsamba who is also wearing a tall pointed hat. From 1700 onwards, women's hats became more and more outlandish. Some of the headgear may have been ceremonial in nature and not intended for everyday use.

Both women and men usually had very long dark-brown or black hair falling to the shoulders and below, with curling locks hanging down each side of the face in front of the ears. But some men are shown with short hair, and it may have been felt that it was more appropriate, perhaps even essential for safety, for men in certain occupations to have their hair cut relatively short. This is to an extent borne out by the Chieftain Cup. The 'prince' has the beautiful long flowing locks that we might expect of a leisured aristocrat, but the officer reporting to him has short hair and seems to have a broad diadem or visor across the front of his head: this may have had the purely practical purpose of keeping the hair off his face. The hunters on the Lion Hunt Dagger also have short hair, and it may have been customary for soldiers – if indeed there were regular soldiers – to have their hair short. In the circumstances, it seems extraordinary that the bull-leapers had long hair, which must have made their vaulting and somersaulting even more difficult to bring off successfully; but bull-leaping was a religious rite, and there was some ritual reason why the bull-leaping teams – boys and girls alike – wore their hair long.

Men were usually clean-shaven, but at least some had moustaches and beards, such as the man shown on the plaque from Agios Onoufrios, dating to about 2000 BC. This may have been a matter of personal preference or of social group: perhaps instead there were certain localities where beards were preferred. Small bronze blades were used as razors (Figure 5D). For a time they were leaf-shaped, although in the Late Minoan III Period an Egyptian type of razor shaped like a small chopper became fashionable. Tweezers too were used for removing hair and possibly shaping the eyebrows which, as the frescoes clearly show, were regarded as a very important

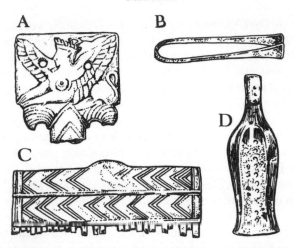

*Figure 5* Cosmetic implements. A: fragment of carved ivory mirror handle from Knossos. B: bronze tweezers. C: ivory comb, with all its teeth broken. D: bronze two-edged razor

facial feature – and there is no reason to suppose that Minoan men were any less concerned about the beauty of their appearance than Minoan women.

The pigments used to colour the face and eyes were evidently ground on specially made rectangular stone palettes and later in stone bowls. The priestess known as 'La Parisienne' is obviously wearing heavy make-up (Figure 46). The eye is enlarged and emphatic and the arc of the eyebrow is exaggerated; some sort of black eye-liner must have been used to create this impression. The lips too have been emphasized with rouge. To help with this beautification, the Minoans used mirrors of polished bronze, just as their Egyptian contemporaries did, held on handles of wood or ivory. The long hair must have required careful combing and it is assumed that to begin with the Minoans used wooden combs: ivory combs did not appear in Crete until around 1500 BC (Figure 5C).

Both women and men – even the scantily-clad men – wore jewellery. The Minoans reveal their love of physical beauty in many ways, but to an exceptional degree in their addiction to jewellery. They decorated themselves with gold-topped hairpins, earrings that were often large and elaborate – sometimes double and triple earrings were worn – armlets, wristlets and anklets, fancy beaded collars and necklaces made of copper, silver, gold or semi-precious stones.

Some of the early communal tombs at Mochlos yielded silver or gold diadems which may have originated as functional hairbands to keep the long hair off the face. There were also gold flowers and leaves mounted on the tops of gold pins, which were used as hair ornaments; oddly enough, this was a feature that was to become simpler in the Late Minoan Period.

The Aegina Treasure, now in the British Museum, is Minoan work, probably dating to around 1600 BC and generally thought to have been stolen from burials at Mallia. It includes a remarkable gold pendant which was probably worn as a pectoral. It shows the Master of Animals wearing a long kilt with a large beaded tassel at the front, large single earrings that are almost the diameter of his face and an extraordinary head-dress apparently made of two tiers of feathers mounted vertically in a crown; he also wears armlets and wristlets. Whether Minoan priests or kings ever dressed up like this is not known, but it is quite possible that they did as a preliminary to transforming themselves into deities. Another extraordinary jewel from the Aegina Treasure is probably an earring rather than a pectoral, since it is reversible. It has two greyhounds and two monkeys within the ring and, hanging from it, alternating pendants consisting of gold discs and gold birds, which are apparently owls.

The overall picture is one of remarkable richness and inventiveness. The Minoan style is unmistakable, original and intensely sensual. There is a delight in the sheer physical beauty of the human body – all the rest is there to emphasize it – and a delight in the beauty of jewels, coloured textiles, feathers, cosmetics and gold. In all this it would be easy to overlook detail,

*Figure 6* Minoan fabric designs, as shown on garments on the frescoes

but the Minoans were careful to make even the smallest detail of a garment interesting to look at. The frescoes show a great variety of fabric patterns, many of them intricate, interlocked repeating patterns in many colours (Figure 6). Some of the fabric patterns may have been woven, some hand-printed with wooden blocks; others may have been produced by a mixture of techniques, with embroidery and beads sewn onto a printed or woven pattern.

ARMS AND ARMOUR

To judge from the available evidence, which is far from complete, the towns of bronze age Crete were not fortified. As yet no traces have been found of city walls or defensive towers at Knossos or at any of the other Minoan centres. We may be lulled by this into believing that life on Minoan Crete was entirely peaceful. In fact many of the sites were destroyed by burning and we have no way of knowing whether those fires were accidental, starting as a result of carelessness, or deliberate acts of arson by an enemy, or precipitated by a convulsive earthquake upsetting lamps and domestic hearths. The archaeological evidence is often ambiguous. On the other hand, destruction in about 1700 BC seems to have been very widespread and yet there was cultural continuity after the event: it seems much more likely that *these* destructions were the result of an earthquake rather than war or invasion.

Even so, we should not rule out the possibility – likelihood, even – of warfare between one Cretan city-state and another. It is known from documentation (e.g. Diodorus Siculus Book XVI and Polybius IX) that the Cretan city-states of the third and fourth centuries BC were at war with each other constantly, struggling for supremacy. Bitter fighting over long periods may leave no archaeological trace. We also know that the Minoans were equipped for war. Linear B tablets mention tunics reinforced with bronze, and the Minoans probably had their own version of the corslet, to judge from the tunic ideograms. Bronze helmets were made in eight pieces: four to make the conical crown with its mount for a horsehair or feathered plume, two cheek-pieces which hung down in front of the ears, and two other pieces which may have protected the back of the neck; one such helmet was found at Sanatorion near Knossos (Figure 7D). Similarly shaped helmets were also made out of boar's tusks, just as depicted in an ivory plaque of a warrior's head from Arkhanes and as described by Homer on the Cretan hero Meriones. A socket on the helmet's crown was a mount for a crest or plume. Remains of a Minoan boar's tusk helmet were found in a tomb at the Zafer Papoura cemetery at Knossos (Figure 7C).

The Lion Hunt Dagger from Shaft Grave IV at Mycenae, dating to around 1550 and produced in Crete, shows three shield shapes: the figure-of-eight shape which appears in Knossian frescoes, rectangular and rectangular with

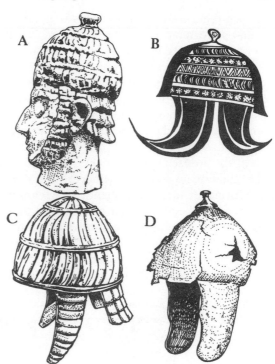

Figure 7 Minoan helmets.
A: ivory plaque from a stool
at Arkhanes. B: helmet used
as a decorative motif on a
3-handled amphora at
Katsamba, about 1400 BC.
C: boar's tooth helmet found
at Knossos (reconstructed).
D: bronze helmet found at
Knossos (unreconstructed)

a curved raised section on the top (Figure 10). These shields were light and made of cattle hides stretched over wooden frames, with at least one handle-strap on the back. The hair was left on the hides, presumably for the sake of the texture and pattern and perhaps also for totemic reasons. The lion hunters are shown with their shields hung over one shoulder, the handle-strap over their heads, to free both hands for spear-throwing. Shields are never mentioned on archive tablets, unlike other items of weaponry, which suggests that every man was allowed, and probably expected, to keep and maintain his own shield.

The Minoans had daggers and swords, some of them richly decorated. At Mallia a beautiful matching set of sword and dagger was found. The sword handle was covered in gold sheet decorated top and bottom with an incised herringbone design, the pommel being fashioned out of a large piece of rock crystal. Since the sword and dagger were found close to a ceremonial leopard-axe, it may be that all these weapons from the Mallia temple had a ceremonial rather than a military use. A pair of long, rapier-like swords with rounded hilts was also found in the Mallia temple, buried, perhaps as a deliberate foundation offering, below the latest paved floor in the north-west quarter. They are of a type which is known to have been in use by 1500 BC and which is also found in Mycenean shaft graves. One of the sword-hilts was richly decorated with a circular gold sheet showing a short-haired acrobat performing a somersault (Figure 29). It is possible that some of the acrobats performed gymnastic feats with swords, perhaps doing handstands and somersaults over swords planted point-upwards in the ground.

A plain and functional hilt on a short sword from the Zafer Papoura cemetery is interesting because of its laminated construction. The bronze of the blade and hand-guard continues through the centre of the hilt and pommel as a central layer, which must have given it far greater strength than some of the ornamental swords. Shaped ivory plates were riveted to each side of the bronze sheet to thicken the handle and make it comfortable to hold; additional pieces of bone were stuck on to the outside of the ivory plates to make the rounded shape of the pommel. Functional and tough, this may well have been a standard design for a 'working' sword.

One of the finest pieces of Minoan weaponry to have survived in Crete is the sword from the so-called Chieftain's Tomb at Knossos. The sword hilt is superb, with a delicately worked detailed pattern covering the whole surface of the gold-plated handle and a carefully turned piece of agate for a pommel.

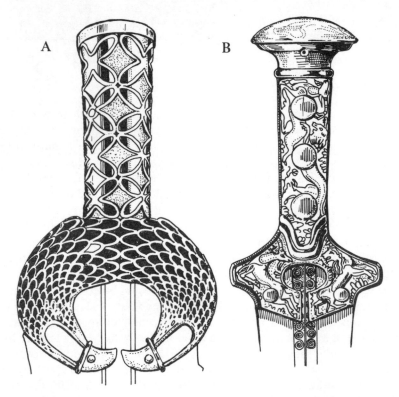

*Figure 8* Bronze dagger hilts. A: bronze, gold-plated, inlaid with pieces of lapis lazuli and rock crystal. B: bronze, gold-plated, with polished agate pommel

The design consists of a lion hunting and bringing down a goat in a mountain landscape – a classic struggle scene – edged with a border of running spirals. Some very fine Minoan gold sword hilts were found at Mycenae. One clasped the top of the blade with two eagles' heads, and the gold plate was patterned with scale-like depressions soldered to hold inlays of lapis lazuli (Figure 8).

Some of the Minoan daggers exported to mainland Greece and probably Anatolia had bronze blades decorated with inlays of gold and silver against a background of black niello. The Lion Hunt Dagger is the finest of these, with a scene on one side of five Minoan hunters facing a charging lion, while two other lions run away towards the dagger point. The hunters are armed with spears, shields and a bow. On the other side a lion seizes a gazelle, while four other gazelles escape. These superb Minoan daggers and swords were undoubtedly highly prized in the ancient world. A tablet found far away at Mari in Mesopotamia mentions a weapon adorned with lapis lazuli and gold and describes it as 'Caphtorite'. The Egyptians called Crete 'Kefti', 'Keftiu' or 'the land of the Keftiu', while in the Near East Crete was known as 'Caphtor': it is as Caphtor that ancient Crete appears in the Old Testament. 'Caphtorite' clearly means 'Cretan'. The similarity of the words 'Caphtor', 'Caphtorite' and 'Keftiu' strongly implies that the Minoans themselves used something like the word 'Kaftor' as a name for their homeland.

The Minoans used chariots in battle. The shape of their chariots is clearly shown in the ideogram for 'chariot' on the Linear B tablets. The Minoan chariot was the same as the Mycenaean chariot depicted on a fresco at Pylos (Figure 9B). It had a lightweight body, with sides and front possibly made of wickerwork or layers of hide on a wooden frame, and two simple four-spoked wheels mounted on a central axle. A wooden bar or frame extended forwards between the two ponies who drew the chariot along. It seems from the detailed descriptions of chariot spare-parts at Pylos as if the aristocracy had chariots equipped with special wheels; they are described as 'Followers' wheels'. Whether these had extra fittings such as silver inlays on the spokes or were painted a different colour is not known.

The earliest renderings of these very lightweight and probably fast war chariots appear on sealstones of the New Temple Period. Professor Stylianos Alexiou suggests that both the chariot and the horse were introduced from Egypt; they had been introduced to Egypt by the Hyksos kings who came from Asia, and contact between Hyksos Egypt and Knossos has been proved from other finds. Certainly the development of Minoan technology was in many ways stimulated by contacts with other cultures.

SOCIAL STRUCTURE

In spite of the abundance of artefacts, images and even inscriptions from the Cretan bronze age, it is still very difficult to reconstruct the society with any

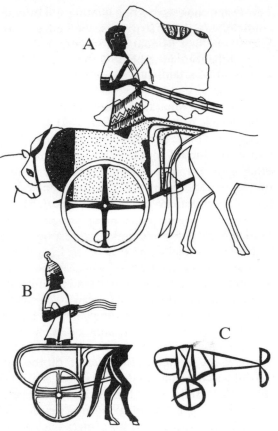

*Figure 9* Chariots.
A: reconstruction from fresco
fragments in the Knossos
Labyrinth. B: fresco from
Pylos showing winged chariot
of common Minoan-Mycenean
type. C: chariot symbol on a
Linear B tablet from the
Knossos Labyrinth

confidence. The Linear B tablets offer fleeting glimpses of deities, officials
and bureaucrats from the fourteenth century. Since some of the officials'
titles have been found at Pylos on mainland Greece as well as at Knossos, it
may be fair to assume provisionally that Minoan society had a rather similar
structure to that of Pylos.

A few tablet references imply the existence of a king or Wanax at both
Pylos and Knossos, but little more than this can be said. The adjective 'royal'
is used of certain craftsmen – a royal fuller and a royal potter at Pylos – and
even of certain textiles and pottery at Knossos. There is no mention of a king
or of the adjective 'royal' at Mycenae at all. Sometimes the word 'king' was
used for a deity such as Poseidon, so we cannot be sure, even where the word
occurs, that a secular king existed. Evans and his supporters, identifying the
large buildings at Knossos, Phaistos, Mallia and Zakro as royal palaces,
took these as tacit evidence for the existence of powerful and grandiose
dynastic kings. But if we interpret the palaces as temples and are unable to
identify alternative sites for kings' residences, the *prima facie* case for kings
is significantly weakened.

However sparingly, the word 'royal' was nevertheless used at Knossos, so we should perhaps assume that there was a king of Knossos, even if he was a fairly shadowy, background figure dominated by the priesthood and by other officials. The great temple centres of Knossos, Phaistos, Mallia and Zakro were certainly major administrative, economic, and political centres and it is likely that each had its own ruler. The classical Greek tradition had it that Minos co-ruled Crete with his brothers Rhadamanthys and Sarpedon; King Minos became associated with Knossos, King Rhadamanthys with Phaistos and King Sarpedon with Mallia. It is likely that Middle Minoan Crete was a loose confederation of city-states, each with its own ruler and often with its own great temple-complex. After the destructions of 1470 BC, only the temple at Knossos was rebuilt, and this implies political as well as religious centralization in the New Temple Period; at this time, the power of Knossos seems to have extended across the whole of central Crete, with perhaps only the western and eastern extremities remaining independent of the Knossian rulers.

At Knossos, one tablet lists the names of men attached to two officials who are given the title qa-si-re-wi-ja. This may be the word 'guasileus', later to become the Homeric word 'basileus', an alternative title for a king. In Minoan-Mycenean times, the guasileus seems to have been a less exalted figure than a king, but still an important figure, perhaps a local chief. Tablet As 1516 from Knossos speaks of the Guasileus of a place ending in -ti-jo (possibly pa-i-ti-jo, Phaistos) and a retinue or an offering of twenty-three men. The tablet speaks of the Guasileus of Sitia (se-to-i-ja) and his retinue or offering of twelve or more men. Whether these chiefs were officials acting under a king or in effect kinglets in their own right is unclear. On the whole it looks as if they were local leaders, less important than the relatively small number of kings; each lesser centre, like Agii Theodhori, Kanli Kastelli, Arkhanes, and Pyrgos-Myrtos, probably had its own Guasileus.

It is at this point that we begin to notice some differences between the social hierarchies of Knossos and Pylos. Whilst the Guasileus at Knossos was an important figure, at Pylos he seems to have been little more than a foreman or supervisor. Conversely, an official called the ra-wa-ke-ja was regarded as a person of high status at Pylos, whereas at Knossos he was treated as merely the equal of the Guasileus (Hooker 1987). Clearly, we need to be cautious in drawing too close a parallel between the two social structures.

In the Early Minoan Period, to judge from burial practices, society was structured mainly round clans or extended families. It may be that as the urban centres evolved and became foci of wealth, certain families emerged as wealthier and more successful commercially than others and that the Guasileus emerged from these rich families. It would certainly make sense for progressive economic and social differentiation to result in the emergence of individual social leaders. The clans remained important right into the

Old Temple Period, and this may have been partly thanks to the clan-focus supplied by the person of the Guasileus.

The most outstanding leader, though, was in a stratum above the Guasileus. He was the Lawagetas, literally 'the leader of the people'. In later Greek, for instance in the *Iliad*, the word translated as 'people' often refers to 'the people arrayed for battle' or 'the war host', so some have understandably assumed that this Minoan-Mycenean title designates the commander of the army. But the tablets do not confirm this interpretation. There is nothing, apart from the much later connotation accruing to the word 'people', to connect the Lawagetas with the command of the army. He may have been the leader of the people in a political rather than a military sense, a kind of prime minister under the Wanax or possibly even a president, if the Wanax was a ceremonial figure-head with circumscribed powers. There is really too little evidence to go on, but what we have is compatible with a Wanax who was a monarch with very limited secular power, a constitutional monarch who formed a charismatic focus for public ceremony, and a Lawagetas who was the effective secular ruler.

At Pylos, the Lawagetas' estates were significantly smaller than the king's, though he had tradesmen attached or allocated to him. The title 'Lawagetas' is found at Knossos, but only on tablet fragments, so it is very difficult to find out anything about him. Chadwick (1976) thinks that tablet E1569 may give the size of his estate, which is comparable to that of his peer at Pylos. Lydia Baumbach (1983) believes that the broken tablet As 1516 may have been headed 'Lawagetas of Knossos': it gives a list of thirty-one men's names, men who may have constituted the Lawagetas' retinue.

In terms of land ownership, the Telestai were as important as the Lawagetas. There seem to have been several of these. At one time Chadwick thought they had a cult role, but he has come round to the view that they were simply men who owned large tracts of land and therefore had become politically powerful. But the telestes in later Greek times had associations with cult and ritual, so it may be wiser to assume provisionally that the Minoan and Mycenean telestai were also major religious leaders.

Another official who had a religious role of some kind was the Klawiphoros. This 'key-bearer', known from Pylos, was often and perhaps always a woman. In classical Greece, 'key-holder' was a synonym for priestess, so it may well have been that the Minoan and Mycenean key-bearers were also priestesses. Given the size and elaborateness of the Minoan temples and the very large number of cult objects produced, we should expect that priests, priestesses and other religious leaders were prominent in the social hierarchy.

Surrounding the Pylian Wanax was an important group of courtiers known as Hequetai (e-qe-ta in the tablets) or 'Followers'. These noblemen presumably formed an entourage for the leader, providing him with support, security and company, and who probably also functioned as senior administrators and military commanders. Followers also appear at Knossos, for example on a badly damaged tablet (tablet B 1055) which seems to list Knossian Followers; one Follower came from Exos, according to tablet Am 821. But here too we must exercise caution in assuming that Knossian and Pylian Followers enjoyed equally high status. According to the tablets, the Followers at Pylos had slaves, special clothes and wheels, i.e. chariots, which implies either high status or a military role or both. The Knossian Followers, according to J. T. Hooker, had a supervisory role in, for example, textile production, which certainly implies a less exalted status. On the other hand, the distinction made in the tablets between 'cloth for export' and 'cloth to do with the Followers' could be interpreted differently: it may be that certain cloth was reserved for use in making garments for the aristocracy because of its high quality. Nevertheless, whatever conclusion we draw, it will have to be cautious and provisional.

It is not known how many Followers there were at Knossos or at any of the other centres on Crete; they may have formed an elite corps, a mobile fighting force, or each may have commanded a regiment. The Followers were probably town-based and Chadwick suggests that, as a group, they could have been a threat to the king's (or leader's) power; he further suggests that the second class of grandees, the rural landowners, acted as a check on them. Equally, the Followers may have acted on the king's (or leader's) behalf sometimes in counteracting any tendency for a Land-holder to behave independently of the central administration.

Another group of rural officials, the Koreters or Governors, existed at Pylos, and may also have existed in Crete. It is not clear how the role of the Koreter differed from that of the Guasileus, but it may be that the Koreter was an official appointed by the central administration and allocated to a district, whereas the Guasileus emerged as it were dynastically out of the district's clan system. The district Governors or Superintendents had deputies called, among other things, Prokoreters: the Minoans were great bureaucrats.

Of the great mass of ordinary people, little is known. The lower classes were, on the whole, not the concern of the tablet scribes; masons are mentioned in the Knossos tablets, but few other trades-people. Professor Willetts (1969) reflects that the society of classical Crete had three lower classes. There were free citizens, and then two classes of serfs, one with some rights, though not the right to possess arms, the other with no rights and these were the chattel slaves. This three-tiered lower class may have been inherited from the Minoans, although there is no reason to think so, except that Aristotle made a passing reference to the laws of Minos still being in force among Cretan serfs. Certainly some slaves at Knossos were bought and sold; the phrase 'he bought' crops up in four places in tablets listing men and women by name, which is strongly suggestive of slavery. 'Women' and their children are mentioned on the tablets too, without any reference to menfolk, implying slavery and absent males. The male slaves were probably removed to work elsewhere, possibly to reduce slave solidarity, possibly to reduce morale, possibly to supply a work-force for the Minoan galleys. We know that Minoan ships were rowed as well as sailed (see Chapter 5) from the fresco evidence; we also know from the Pylos tablets that as many as 600 rowers were required for a fleet. The 'women' were probably on their own because their men were deployed at sea, as galley slaves.

At Knossos, a fragmentary fresco shows a white (i.e. Caucasian) officer exercising a troop of black soldiers at the double. The negroes are probably Nubian slaves given to the Minoans by the Egyptians in exchange for manufactured goods such as pottery and metalwork. At Pylos, slaves were listed in order to make calculations for rations. It seems that significant numbers of the Pylian slaves were servants of a deity and therefore not ordinary slaves at all. It may well be that at Phaistos, Mallia, Zakro and Knossos many slaves became temple servants – and probably considered themselves fortunate.

The very fragmentary evidence from Minoan Crete dating from around 1380 BC harmonizes well with the more complete social picture Chadwick has pieced together from mainland Pylos. What emerges is still indistinct, a suggestion of an extremely complex society with a shadowy, possibly powerless King as its figure-head and the ambiguous figure of the Lawagetas, the Leader of the People, at his side with a troupe of noble Followers; there were also the Telestai, possibly the religious leaders, and Klawiphoroi, the priestesses, controlling the all-important temples where wealth was gathered and redistributed. In the countryside, the Land-holders counterbalanced the urban-based power of the Followers, while the district Governor and his Deputy administrated the land for the King or Leader and the Guasileus satisfied the village clansmen's need for a clan chief and a local identity. Probably the hold of kinship ties, the hold of the clan, diminished with time as new bonds, those of craft specialization, strengthened. The great mass of ordinary people went about their work, some 'free' (whatever that may have meant to a Minoan), some in servitude, and some chattel slaves.

The great public festivals, such as those shown on the Grandstand and Sacred Dance Frescoes at Knossos, played an important part in displaying and reinforcing the social hierarchy. Public ceremonies tend to have this function even in the modern world; a British Coronation, for example, parades, expounds, and confirms the fine detail of social stratification. In classical Greece there were many festivals. Some, such as the Thesmophoria, were exclusively female festivals; others, like the Gymnopaideia of Sparta, were exclusively male; some, like the Athenian Panathenaia, sought to involve the whole community. These were socially oriented festivals. There were also seasonally oriented festivals, which had the rather different role of harmonizing society with nature. It is reasonable, given the fresco

*Figure 10* Design on the Lion Hunt Dagger

evidence, to assume that the Minoans too had a range of festivals and religious ceremonies which contained these various emphases.

In the Theran Naval Festival Fresco, we can see the central, queenly figure of a priestess on a balcony with the sacral horns beside her. Below the town walls a procession of naked, uninitiated youths takes an animal to be sacrificed. Elsewhere there are men in kilts who, Marinatos (1984) believes, may be initiated young people of higher social rank; there are common towns-people in tunics, nobles in long robes and rustics in sheepskins. We do not need to believe that rural farm workers actually wore shaggy hide garments as they went about their work, or that boys normally went naked until their manhood initiation; the fresco artist was simply spelling out the concepts of social stratification and of social unification during the festival. Possibly the Theran artist was deliberately focusing on the appropriate dress for certain rituals. For instance, the priest in the harvest festival on the Harvesters Vase is wearing a symbolically bizarre garment; the boys stripped for their initiation rituals, such as boxing, tests of strength, and head-shaving. The girls had their own ritual which took place indoors, partly in a pier-and-door-partitioned room, partly in a sunken adyton. Possibly they had to draw blood, symbolizing the onset of menstruation. This is shown graphically by the wounded, bleeding girl sitting on a rock in Room 3 of Xeste 3 at Akrotiri; her blood sacrifice is shown again in a different way on the wall over the adyton, where sinister, blood-spattered sacral horns stand forbiddingly on top of a blood-spattered altar.

Individual and small-group initiations probably took place in the temples, where many small and medium-sized chambers were designed and equipped for specialized religious ceremonies. Mark Cameron (1987) made a paper reconstruction of the rooms, apparently on an upper floor of the Knossos Labyrinth, where the Sacred Communion (Camp Stool), Grandstand and Sacred Dance Frescoes were installed; the scale of these frescoes strongly implies that the chambers they decorated were small – perhaps 4 metres square – and therefore used by small groups of people. Both Mark Cameron and Nanno Marinatos (1984) have developed the very important idea that the decorative schemes sign the functions of whole suites of rooms, a crucial idea in establishing the function of the Knossos Labyrinth in particular as a major cult centre.

The mainly small-scale, private and intimate ceremonies of initiation undertaken in the temples enabled people to step as individuals and peer-groups from one social, spiritual and status class to another. The transition from childhood to adulthood was probably marked by a graded series of initiation rites. Gösta Säflund (1987) argues that the strong elements of an initiatory character detected in later Cretan society were probably a survival from the Minoan civilization. Possibly the image on the Chieftain Cup can be interpreted as a herd of boys – they seem to be covering themselves with animal hides – presenting themselves to an older, already-initiated youth on completion of their rite.

Strabo (x, 482) wrote of a later Cretan custom which may also have been a Minoan survival; Strabo himself said that it was 'a tribal feature of great antiquity'. Youths promoted from the herd of boys were then obliged to marry. In other words, marriage too was a rite of passage controlled by the community. Säflund (1987) interprets the Sacred Dance Fresco as the culminating public festival in this initiation sequence, a pre-marriage rally of the promoted girls and boys; he argues, interestingly, that the ritual focus of the fresco is not missing, as received opinion has it, but inherent in the crowd of boys and girls itself. Cameron (1987) added the idea that the sacral knot was a marriage token. These are interesting speculations, but perhaps they read too much into the fragmentary fresco record.

The private, small-scale ceremonies took place within the framework of the larger, public ceremonies. In the Cretan towns, many of the private and public rites must have taken place at the great temples. The inner chambers and adyta of the temples were places where individual and small-group initiations and rites of passage were conducted. The Central and West Courts were places where the large public ceremonies took place. The Grandstand Fresco appears to show a crowd of spectators – Evans estimated 600 onlookers – gathered in the Central Court of the Knossos Labyrinth. The Sacred Dance Fresco appears from the design of the pavement to have been set in the West Court, either at Knossos or at a similarly designed temple. The temples were thus major foci, socially as well as spiritually.

Again and again, women are shown in dominant roles – in the Theran Naval Festival Fresco, and in the Knossos frescoes too. That priestesses were dominant in the temples cannot be doubted – the Grandstand and Sacred Dance Frescoes make their position very plain – and it is left for us to speculate on the possible role of women in society outside the temple. In state affairs, for instance, were women able to take their place as equals alongside men? Or perhaps even as their superiors? There is no hint in the tablets that women held important political positions, but we know that the picture they give is incomplete. The Klawiphoroi, the Key-bearers, were priestesses who may have held some secular position, but what that was and how important it was cannot be gauged. Nevertheless, it is tempting to see the powerless Wanax, with his mainly ceremonial role, living in the shadow of a Labyrinth run by powerful priestesses as an earthly parallel to the Minoan myth of a relatively insignificant male god, Velchanos, who was subordinate to a more powerful goddess.

MINOAN 'HISTORY'

Minoan society grew out of a long period of indigenous cultural development. The neolithic levels under the Knossos Labyrinth are among the deepest in Europe, and contain the remains of many successive settlements. Those layers represent something approaching a 3,000-year-long neolithic preamble to the Minoan civilization. Then, shortly after 3000 BC, there was a rapid surge forwards into the bronze age. Traditionally, this is explained as a result of immigration – large numbers of new people arriving with new ideas – but now there is a tendency to explain change in terms of local native developments. There may have been small numbers of incomers to Crete at this time, as seems likely at all stages in Cretan prehistory, because of the island's situation, but new ideas could have been introduced by social and cultural contact alone.

Ideas and goods arrived from the Cyclades and the practice of burying people in domed round tombs seems to have been imported from Anatolia (see Chapter 6). Sinclair Hood (1971, p. 49) likens Early Minoan Crete to America: with its fermenting mixture of ideas and traditions it was a prehistoric New World. Some of the Early Minoan II pottery (2600–2300 BC) is reminiscent of Syrian ware and the first Minoan seals, produced at this time, are also reminiscent of seals from Syria; these are pointers to trade with the Levant. The Pre-Temple Period of Minoan Crete gives us little evidence of its social and political life, but it is likely that society revolved mainly round the clan.

In 1930 BC, the Old Temple Period began with the building of the first huge labyrinth at Knossos. This was so distinctive a development that it is tempting to attribute it to invaders or migrants bringing in an exotic architectural idea from abroad. But there is no need to postulate invaders from Greece or Anatolia. The maze-like, multi-chambered temples – the so-called 'palaces' – had their native Cretan precursors. There was a cellular multi-room building, albeit much smaller, on the site of the Knossos Labyrinth itself, and a recognizable L-shaped predecessor for the temple plan, complete with central courtyard, was built at Vasiliki in 2600 BC. The big Minoan temples should be seen as resulting from a long period of indigenous development, increasing prosperity and increasingly centralized organization, in religion and in the economy.

The evidence of social and political development in the Old Temple Period (1930–1700 BC) is fragmentary, though it looks as if social classes based on rural or urban roles and divisions based on occupational specialization led to the development of a more stratified society than before. The bonds of the old clan system were beginning to loosen. The growth of towns at this time probably had much to do with the process, and we should see Minoan society developing towards something like the much later city-state system, although in Crete it looks as if the towns lived in relative harmony with each other.

Widespread physical damage brought the Old Temple Period to an end in 1700 BC. Both temple and city at Knossos suffered extensive damage, perhaps more than once. The temple at Phaistos was apparently damaged at the same time by an earthquake, then repaired, only to be destroyed by a catastrophic fire. The destruction at Phaistos was complete; the ruins of the old temple were levelled, the site was filled in and a new temple built on top of the rubble with a different plan. At Monastiraki, a small 'palace' or temple was destroyed by fire at the same time as Knossos and Phaistos. The destructions may not have occurred simultaneously all over Crete, and they may have been due to different causes: nevertheless, the Phaistos evidence apart, the effects of a large-scale earthquake seem sufficient to explain events.

Sinclair Hood (1971) believes that foreign settlers arrived in Crete in 1700 BC in the wake of the temple destructions. He rejects mainland Greeks in favour of Luvians from south-west Anatolia, a people with a language related to that of the Hittites further east. The Beycesultan palace, which may have been the headquarters of one of the Luvian rulers, could conceivably have served as a model for the New Temples on Crete, i.e. the temples built in and after 1700 BC. Arguing against this idea is the fact that the New Temples were very similar in concept and design to the Old Temples, so the use of Beycesultan as a model is unlikely. But arguing in support of a Luvian influx is the appearance of one of the Minoans' distinctive forms of writing, the script known as Linear A. The later Linear B script has been interpreted as a primitive form of Greek. Linear A, which contributed some of its signs to Linear B, was nevertheless not Greek but some other language, yet to be identified. Leonard Palmer (1961) noticed a link between Linear A and the Luvian language, a link which may prove to be very significant. The last word in an inscription on an altar from the Diktaian Cave, using Michael Ventris's values for the syllabic signs, reads 'ja-sa-sa-ra'. This is fairly close to the Luvian title 'Ashassarasmes'. In other Minoan Linear A examples, there is an extra suffix, '-me', which brings the word form even closer to what we must assume was the Luvian original. Therefore, Palmer argues, the title guessed by Evans to be the name of the deity turns out to be the title of the Linear B goddess Potnia ('Lady') in the Luvian language, where it also means 'Lady'. This certainly reinforces the general idea of significant cultural contact between the Minoans and the Arzawa Lands of south-west Anatolia during the Second Temple Period, though it does not necessarily mean that there was any large-scale immigration from Anatolia into Crete.

The rebuilding on a more lavish scale of the Knossos temple following the

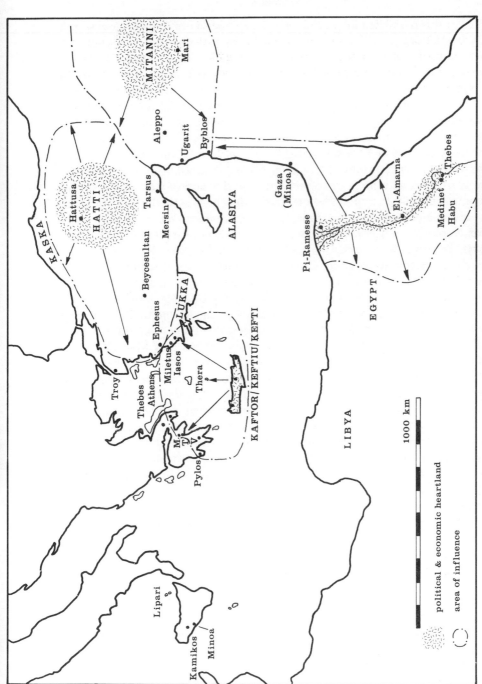

*Figure 11* The Minoan world. The map shows the cultural heartlands of the Minoans and their neighbours in the middle of the second millennium BC (stippled), together with their areas of influence (arrows and dot-and-dash line). The Minoans' activities were not confined to their 'area of influence' as defined on the map; there is archaeological evidence that they traded with Hatti, Mitanni and Egypt as well

disaster was paralleled in Anatolia by the rebuilding of the war-devastated city of Hattusa by Tabarna, the Great King of the Hittites. It would be interesting to know whether diplomatic or trading relations existed between the Minoans and Hittites; both cultures were at their zenith at this time. In Egypt, the central power structure disintegrated as the Semitic Hyksos people invaded Egypt from the Near East. Some form of relationship was maintained between Hyksos Egypt and Minoan Crete: Hyksos artefacts have been found in the Knossos Labyrinth.

The New Temple Period (1700–1470 BC) was to be the most exuberant phase of Minoan civilization, producing the most elaborate architecture, the finest frescoes and the most sophisticated and beautiful works of art. The population grew to a point where the island may actually have become overpopulated. The remedy then, as in later times, was to found over-seas colonies (see Chapter 5). These colonies were established across the southern Aegean and some may even have been on the Greek mainland, which seems to have become strongly 'Minoanized' at this time. There is every possibility that this process of Minoanization was mainly the result of consumer demand, because the Minoans were producing goods that were extremely attractive and of the highest quality. The legend of Theseus, the tribute-children and the Minotaur may suggest that there was a time, before the classical period, when Greek cities like Athens and Mycenae were tributary to Crete, but the legend may conceal a rather different folk-memory. It may have been a sore point with the classical Greeks that once there had been a time when they were culturally inferior to their neighbours on Crete; the Minoans' cultural and therefore trading superiority may, to a proud race, have *felt* like political subjugation. It may have been this subjective and exaggerated view which found its way into the folklore.

There is more evidence of the Minoan social structure from the New Temple Period. Women emerged as dominant figures in ceremonial contexts, and society as a whole had become much more strongly stratified. Social classes were now more important than the clans as the towns came to dominate the organization of rural areas. The government may have been more or less theocratic, with priestesses and other religious officials occupying positions of importance. One peculiarity of Minoan society, even at this zenith stage, is that it shows no sign whatever of personal ambition. There are, in the archaeological record, no signs at all of boastful, self-aggrandizing rulers or viziers, which is a striking contrast to the situation that prevailed in contemporary Egypt or Anatolia.

The New Temple Period came to an abrupt end with the catastrophic Thera eruption of 1470 BC. The precise date is still a matter of controversy, but the most likely scenario is a long series of premonitory earthquakes and minor eruptions beginning in about 1500 BC and culminating in a caldera eruption of enormous violence in 1470 BC. Thera is 120 kilometres north of Crete, but major earthquakes with their epicentres on Thera would have caused significant damage to Knossos and other Minoan sites on Crete. The final eruption would have been experienced as a multiple disaster at the Minoan sites. The initial damage to walls and foundations by blast and earthquake was followed by a towering tsunami, or 'tidal' wave, which would have washed across the northern coastal lowlands, destroying the principal Minoan harbour towns of Katsamba, Amnisos, Agii Theodhori and possibly quays at Kytaiton, Kydonia and Mallia too. A link between the Thera eruption and events in Crete is very plausible; in AD 1650, volcanic activity on Thera was responsible for earthquakes and tsunamis in Crete, though on a much smaller scale than envisaged in the prehistoric eruption.

After the waters of the 1470 tsunami receded, a great cloud of white ash blown south-eastwards by the wind covered the whole of central and eastern Crete, blotting out the sun and then settling over the landscape; on the sea-bed 120 kilometres south-east of Thera it is still 78 centimetres thick. Knossos and Mallia were not directly downwind at the time of the eruption, but the ashfall there must have been 20–30 centimetres thick, and half that amount would have been enough to put the farmland out of production for several years and paralyse the Minoan economy.

The archaeological evidence is patchy, but the town of Palaikastro at the eastern end of Crete was apparently destroyed in about 1470 BC. Some houses were repaired, but others were so badly damaged that the new houses built on their ruined foundations had a completely different alignment. There is evidence of disaster at Zakro, Mochlos and Pseira, which were never rebuilt. Knossos was extensively damaged by earthquake in 1470 BC and also somewhat earlier, presumably in the long premonitory series of earthquakes.

The Thera eruption must have been an appalling experience for the Minoans. The massive earthquake, the blasting bull-roar of Thera exploding, the darkening skies, the tsunamis and the silent rain of white ash must have reduced them to terror and despair. The interruption to food production created an economic crisis. The unparalleled unleashing of the cosmic forces may have precipitated a religious crisis. The reduced importance of the peak sanctuaries in the period following the Thera eruption may reflect a loss of faith in the god Poseidon or in the ritual procedures designed to propitiate him.

There is evidence at Zakro of a large-scale ritual of appeasement in about 1470 BC; on a hill above the Minoan town a large deposit of Late Minoan I pottery was discovered in a votive pit. Similarly, at Niru Khani, in the large house or temple near the shore, a deposit of votive cups with pieces of volcanic pumice (apparently collected after the Thera eruption) was found secreted under the threshold of a shrine; possibly it was placed there as a re-foundation or reconsecration deposit after the building was repaired.

Some commentators, Sinclair Hood among them, place the Thera eruption earlier, towards the year 1500 BC, attributing the disastrous collapse of

Minoan civilization several decades later to some other cause. It is nevertheless compatible with what we know of large-scale caldera eruptions to
suppose that the Thera eruption was a long-drawn-out series of events
beginning in 1500 and culminating in 1470; we therefore need not look for
any external reasons for the serious weakening of the Minoan economy in
the years immediately following 1470. Certainly there seems to have been a
shift of cultural and political balances in the Aegean from this time on. Hood
(1971, p. 58) sees war as the reason for the destruction and permanent
abandonment of the eastern towns of Zakro, Pseira and Mochlos, but it
seems reasonable to attribute these events to the Thera eruption.

After Thera, the Minoan economy was reconstructed, but it was not the
same as before. Many sites were too badly damaged to rebuild. The Phaistos
temple was reoccupied and a new residential building (sometimes called a
Mycenaen megaron) was raised at Agia Triadha. The Knossos Labyrinth
was systematically repaired and redecorated and became the principal
religious focus of Minoan Crete. The severe damage and the economic,
political, and social crisis that followed directly from it accentuated a
tendency towards centralization. Thera led directly to a focus on Knossos as
a capital city, an administrative centre for the greater part of Crete, and a
major cult centre.

Nicolas Platon (1968) and others believe that it was at this time that people
from mainland Greece, often called 'Myceneans' for convenience, invaded a
weakened and disoriented Crete, and succeeded in conquering it. It would
have been relatively easy for them to do so at this time; we can imagine that a
great many ships of the Minoan fleet, whether merchantmen or war galleys,
were sunk either at sea or at anchor in the many harbours along the north
coast; we can imagine also that the normal efficiency of Minoan bureaucracy
and communications had broken down. Physically weakened by food short-
ages as well, the Minoans would have been easy prey to an envious
neighbour who had been waiting for his opportunity to strike. Alternatively,
Myceneans may have taken over peacefully at Knossos, perhaps as a result
of a dynastic marriage between Cretan and mainland royal houses. Nevertheless, as I have argued elsewhere (1989, pp. 153–6), the case for a
Mycenean take-over in Crete in 1470 has not been conclusively developed. It
is an open question still, and we should not assume that Mycenean invaders
were in control at Knossos as early as 1470.

The period which followed, the Late Temple Period (1470–1380 BC), was
one of partial recovery, but to a rather formal, highly centralized and
bureaucratic system with Knossos as the leading city of Crete. Later in
Crete's history, Knossos was to become the leading city again; the recorded
chronicle of the classical period opens with the capture of the hill-top city of
Lyttos by the Knossian army in 343 BC: in 250 BC, after a long power struggle,
Knossos once again dominated the whole of Crete. In the Late Temple
Period, many of the artistic influences seem to be Mycenean, and the

implication is that the mainland culture had become the dominant one, even though it was still Cretan artists who executed much of the finest artwork and metalwork, on mainland sites as well as on Crete. The adoption of Linear B Greek as the scribal language has been taken by many as proof that the Greeks controlled Crete, but it may be that this reflects a preference for Greek as the Aegean *lingua franca*, the language of officialdom, administration and trade: it does not prove that Greeks ruled at Knossos.

1380 BC was a major turning-point for Minoan civilization. It was the date when the Knossos Labyrinth was devastated by fire and abandoned, never to be rebuilt, never to be repaired, never to be fully reoccupied. The fire may have been the result of an accident – perhaps an overturned hearth or lamp – but if so the temple would surely have been rebuilt, as it was after the 1700 and 1470 destructions. The 1380 fire seems to have been a deliberate act of arson. In fact *this* may have been the time when the Myceneans invaded. The so-called Palace of Kadmos at Thebes was sacked at the same time as the Knossos Labyrinth; we may see both as part of a process of expansion and domination by which thirteenth-century Mycenae appears to have become the capital of an empire extending across most of the Aegean.

There was no sign at Knossos that the fire had been associated with an earthquake – no heavy blocks of masonry were displaced, for instance, as they were in earlier destructions – so some human agency is likely to have been to blame. If not Mycenean soldiers – the likeliest scapegoats – then who else? As suggested earlier, Minoan Crete evolved towards a cellular structure of separate but closely harmonized city-states. It is quite possible that rivalries and disputes developed between them and it may well be that Knossos was sacked by some envious neighbour, perhaps even the people of Kydonia. Another possibility is that the city-states of the New Temple Period which had been assimilated into the greatly expanded Knossos territory of the Late Temple Period resented the hegemony of Knossos. It may be that the people of Phaistos and Mallia, for example, were discontented with their lot and rose up against Knossos. The New Temple phase, with five or more separate temple centres, was a period of relative autonomy; the Late Temple phase had become unacceptably over-centralized to the point of provoking insurrection. Invasion, war, or revolution? The evidence is very inconclusive as yet, so we must leave this, like so many other major 'historic' events in the prehistoric period, as an open question.

The three hundred years which followed the abandonment of the Knossos Labyrinth, the Post-Temple Period (1380–1100 BC), are among the least known of Minoan prehistory. There was a shift of emphasis, with many of the new settlements located inland and some of the old settlements abandoned. It was as if, with the rise of the Mycenean trading empire, the Minoans started to turn away from the sea, narrowing their horizons to the shores of their own island. At the same time the culture flourished, though without the large and spectacular range of artefacts produced in the great days of the temples. Homer tells us that King Idomeneus of Crete sent a fleet of 80 ships to join those of Nestor king of Pylos and Agamemnon king of Mycenae at the siege of Troy, which may have happened towards 1250 BC. This was an unsettled time in the Aegean when, it is believed, waves of Central European peoples invaded mainland Greece, threatening and destroying some of the established Mycenean centres.

Around 1200 BC many Minoan sites were burnt and abandoned. There were many changes, apparently produced by the arrival of refugees from Mycenae and the other mainland cities, which were invaded at this time. The Cretan culture continued to have some recognizably Minoan traits – the potters, for instance, continued to make bell-shaped idols of the goddesses with their hands upraised – but there were many changes under way as a result of repeated contacts with other cultures. It was a complex and gradual evolution away from the Minoan civilization of the temple periods and towards a more purely Greek culture. The *Odyssey*, written down in the eighth century BC, speaks with plausible accuracy of a Crete populated by several peoples speaking several languages. 'There, one language mingles with another. In it are Achaeans, great-hearted native Eteocretans, Kydonians and Dorians in three tribes and noble Pelasgians.'

The Pelasgians were a mysterious people, thought to have originated on the far shores of the Black Sea, filtering west and southwards into the Aegean. There is little archaeological evidence of them on Crete. Willetts (1969) says that 'Larisa' was one of their characteristic place-names. According to Strabo, Cretan Larisa was absorbed by Hierapytna (modern Ierapetra) and there was a tradition that Gortyn too had once been called Larisa; these may give us clues to the parts of Crete where the Pelasgians settled, although it is not known when they arrived or in what numbers.

Strabo, in his commentary on the above-quoted passage of Homer, says that it is reasonable to assume from other sources that the Eteocretans and Kydonians were native to Crete and the Dorians incomers. The Dorians occupied, amongst other areas, the extreme east of the island, east of the town of Praisos. The Praisians, with their temple of Diktaian Zeus and their ancient cults, were clearly native Cretans who had close connections with the old Minoan culture. They somehow kept their ancient and distinct language alive until the third century BC. Several inscriptions in this 'Eteocretan' language have survived, written using letters of the Greek alphabet; if these can be deciphered, we may gain access to at least one of the non-Greek ancient languages once spoken on Crete. Of the Achaeans, of course, much more is known. The Achaeans were the Myceneans – whether conquerors, settlers, or refugees.

The three tribes of Dorians were the people who came to Crete right at the end of the bronze age and, in effect, brought the Minoan period to its close. It was in about 1200 or 1150 BC that Hellenic tribes from the north-west (Dorians, Aetolians, Phocians, and Locrians), tribes who had until now stayed outside the Minoan-Mycenean sphere, surged south into Greece. Mycenae and Tiryns fell; Pylos had fallen already; a little later, the Dorians who had occupied the Peloponnese may have sailed to Crete to bring the now-decaying Cretan civilization to an end. According to Ivor Nixon (1968), the Dorian occupation of Crete may have come about in a different and more complex way, with a migration eastwards through Thrace into Phrygia, then southwards into Lydia and Caria in Anatolia before returning westwards by way of Rhodes and Crete to attack the Peloponnese from the sea. The final push through the south Aegean happened, Nixon believes, after an abortive attack on Egypt, the invasions by the 'Peoples of the Sea' recorded by the Egyptians in about 1190 BC. There is a tradition that the Philistines originated as Cretans; the Book of Jeremiah (47:4) says, 'for the Lord will spoil the Philistines, the remnant of the country of Caphtor.' Caphtor was Crete. There is a close resemblance between Philistine pottery and that of Late Helladic IIIC pottery from Argolis and Attica, too. It is possible that a Cretan contingent joined the 'Peoples of the Sea' confederation to destroy the Hittite empire and invade Egypt. The Egyptians list the Philistines, as 'Pulesati', among the invaders. Defeated and falling back to the north in disarray, remnants of the Sea Peoples may well have resettled in south-west Palestine.

On Crete itself, only a few stragglers managed to keep the Minoan way of life going, and then only in remote mountain refuges such as Karfi, high up in Lasithi, only in a decadent form, and only for a short time. A dark, barbaric period enveloped the close of the Minoan age as a new culture slowly crystallized out of the long struggle for supremacy, the severe and martial civilization of the Dorian cities. Ovid writes of the Minoan age as a time lost in legend, full of wisdom and wealth, fantasy and romance, but he also infers a period of fear and waning power towards the end: 'When Minos was in his prime, his very name had terrified great nations: but now he was weak and very much afraid of Miletus, the son of Deione and Apollo, for the latter was young and strong' (*Metamorphoses*, 9).

# 3
# Life in the countryside

Often at night along the mountain tops,
When gods are revelling by torchlight,
You come carrying a great jar
(Like the ones shepherds use, but of heavy gold).
You fill the jar with milk
Drawn from a lioness and make a great cheese,
Unbroken and gleaming white.

(Alcman, Spartan lyricist, *c*. 630 BC)

## RURAL SETTLEMENT

The Minoan towns depended to a very great extent upon the large tracts of countryside around them for food, labour and other resources: they relied on them for material and political support. Today we tend to focus on the towns and in particular on the glamorous and mysterious life of the 'palaces', but it is important to understand the rural background which sustained them.

A hundred years ago, the rural villages of Crete were mostly small settlements of 150 to 200 people. Paul Faure (1973) speculates that this was the likely size of the Minoan villages too. Then, as now, thousands of small villages nestled among the olive groves and vineyards. There were smaller settlements too: hamlets of perhaps three or four houses and isolated farms, many of which have inevitably disappeared leaving little or no trace. Henri van Effenterre (1983) points out that no centre of Minoan economy has been discovered between Mallia and Gournia: it looks as if this whole area was a pattern of small-scale settlements – villages, hamlets, and farmsteads.

The original Minoan settlement pattern can never be fully recovered, even though new settlement sites continually come to light, but an impression can be gained of the original pattern from some pilot studies. J. L. Bintliff's (1977) study of transhumance patterns in central Crete implies a ring of villages on the hillsides half-way up the slopes of Mount Ida, at altitudes varying between 400 and 900 metres above sea-level and grouped round the high summer pastures of the Nida Plain. Peter Warren's (1982) study of the coastline round the Gulf of Mirabello revealed a scatter of small settlements from Kalo Horio eastwards to Pseira and Mochlos. Some were close together, implying small territories. Kalo Horio, Kopranes and Priniatikos Pyrgos were about 2 kilometres apart, which suggests that each had a territory or estate with a 1-kilometre radius. The spacing of Gournia, Pakhyammos and Vasiliki further along the coast suggests estates of a similar size there too. We may infer from this that a typical rural estate had an area of 3–4 square kilometres. Whether this size prevailed elsewhere is uncertain; possibly on higher sites with less fertile soils and steeper slopes the villages commanded larger estates.

At over 600 metres on a southward-pointing spur to the east of the Mount Juktas ridge, are the remains of Vathypetro. This substantial and apparently

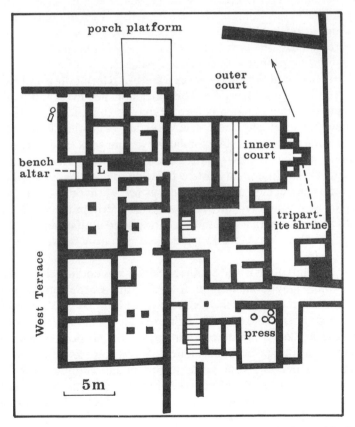

*Figure 12* Vathypetro. An ambiguous Minoan building which changed its function during its period of use in the sixteenth century BC. L = a small chamber at the end of a corridor, with a drain passing under its floor: interpreted here as a lavatory

isolated building, with its spectacular view towards the south and west, has been described as a country house or manor house, or even a mini-palace. Although it had some function as a religious cult centre, we should probably think of it as being, in its final phase at least, a farmhouse and industrial centre. Thought to have been built around 1580 BC, and probably never completed, Vathypetro was severely damaged in about 1550, possibly by an earthquake. It has been suggested that the original plan was an approximation to the Knossos Labyrinth, but on a much-reduced scale (Figure 12).

The lower walls of stone blocks supported an upper storey of brick. There was a small West Court and a 'Central' Court to the east of the completed West Wing. Those who like to see the building as an uncompleted mini-palace imagine that an East Wing would have been built across on the far side of the 'Central' Court. On the other hand, this space was apparently occupied by a major structure, identified recently as a tripartite shrine. To the east of the Three-Columned Portico, across a small courtyard only 4 metres wide, stood an elaborate symmetrical structure with a central recess and square plinths on each side. This arrangement makes the design distinctly different from that of any of the palaces.

The South Sector of the building was rebuilt as a farmhouse and industrial centre after the 1550 destruction. This does not, however, tell us that the building had the same function before. It may be that the original structure was designed as a temple; there are, after all, two other known Minoan temples in the area, commanding similar views: the peak sanctuary on one of the summits and the Anemospilia temple on the northern slope of Mount Juktas. The Three-Columned Portico fronting the small courtyard and the Tripartite Shrine suggest a ritual function for Vathypetro. The benched recess in the west front may have been a shrine. Perhaps the whole building started off as a temple. In its later phase, from 1550 until its final destruction in 1470 BC, Vathypetro seems to have been primarily an agricultural and industrial centre.

One of the main rooms in the Southern Sector was equipped with a wine or oil press. Many clay loom weights found in the same room suggest that weaving went on there, or in the room above. In the West Wing there were sixteen storage jars. In the West Court were found the remains of a large oil press and basin (Plate 1). In other rooms pieces of clay potters' wheels were found, indicating that pottery was made at Vathypetro as well.

The picture emerging from Vathypetro, though complex and far from definitively resolved, is of a Minoan country house with its own domestic shrines, acting as a collecting place for farm produce and as an industrial centre, manufacturing pottery and cloth, making wine or olive oil or possibly both. Sinclair Hood (1983) suggests that Vathypetro may have been the summer residence of the king of Arkhanes. That may be the case, but it seems at least equally likely that it functioned as an autonomous country house, the seat of a rural landowner. Possibly it also functioned as a rural religious centre in the initial stages, before it was ruined and remodelled.

Perhaps more typical was the Minoan village between Kouse and Sira, about an hour's walk south of Phaistos, in hills at 120 metres. A stone farmhouse excavated there had a 6-metre square living room with a beaten earth floor, a wooden pillar supporting the ceiling beams and a low window, perhaps originally glazed with a sheet of translucent parchment. Grain, olives, and wine were stored along the walls. A wooden bench may have served as a seat or a bed. The six smaller rooms ranged along two sides of the farmhouse may have been store-rooms and bedrooms. Paul Faure suggests that one may have been a retiring room for women, but (see Chapter 2), there is no reason to suppose that women retired into the background at any level of society. There was neither kitchen nor stable. Food was evidently cooked in the open air, and donkeys were probably housed in a rough mudbrick shelter built against one of the outside walls.

The Kouse farmhouse yielded a range of tools, but no religious objects and no bronze cauldron. Apparently only rich Minoans owned cauldrons. On the other hand, this house was neither poor nor primitive; it represents the ordinary rural dwelling of the Minoans, fairly comfortable, well-built and durable. It had apparently stood for some 300 years before burning down in about 1500 BC.

Three substantial houses survive from the village of Tylissos, 15 kilometres to the west of Knossos (Figure 13 and Plate 2). The houses date from the end of the Middle Minoan period and Late Minoan I, although there were earlier houses on the same site; some of their remains can be seen in the south-west corner of the site. House A consisted of two wings separated by a partly roofed courtyard. An angled passage led into this paved entrance court; on the west and north sides of the court was an L-shaped peristyle: a window lit the staircase leading upwards on the western side. North of the peristyle are two large store-rooms, each with two pillars supporting an upper floor. Fallen fragments of painted plaster in the store-rooms imply that there were important rooms above them, possibly a refectory. The rooms west of the store-rooms may have been kitchens. Some of the storage jars still *in situ* have holes near their bases: they are also set up on plinths suggesting that they were tapped for liquids, possibly wine but more likely oil.

The passage leading south from the peristyle court connects the North Wing with the South Wing. The main room in the South Wing had two rectangular paved inset panels in its floor and its own adyton, an unusually deep one, with perhaps six steps descending very steeply out of the main room. The hall with its paved floor and double doors opened on to a colonnaded light-well, which also had a window in its west wall. A portico to the north of the light-well leads to a pillar crypt with a pyramidal stand for a double-axe. Reached from the pillar crypt are two small sacristies. It was in

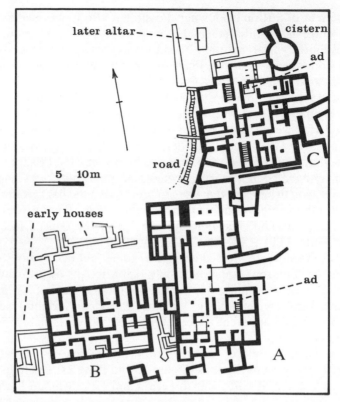

*Figure 13* Plan of Tylissos. The earlier houses date from around 2000 BC, and the three later houses (A, B, and C) date from 1700–1500 BC. The cistern dates from 1400 BC or later, and the altar and its precinct from the Greek occupation in the classical period. It is a site with a long and complex history. ad = adyton

this area that the three huge cauldrons were found – a chance find which led to the discovery of Minoan Tylissos and its excavation by Hazzidakis in 1902–13. The store-rooms also yielded an important find of Linear A tablets. Tylissos is actually named – as tu-ri-so – in the later Linear B archive tablets at Knossos.

The collection of small rooms in the south-west corner, with its short passage connecting it with the principal room and its own private staircase, has suggested parallels with the alleged women's quarters or 'queen's apartments' in the temples.

All things considered, House A must have been a very comfortable villa: 35 metres by 18 metres, and at least two storeys high, it offered generous accommodation for a family. Paul Faure suggests that the first floors of all three houses were occupied by different families. The layout of House A implies that it could possibly have functioned as two entirely separate houses.

House B stood immediately to the west of House A and House C only a short distance to the north-east. An unusual feature of the site is the big circular cistern which overlaps the walls of House C and was presumably built after the demolition of the house in Late Minoan III. Water flowed from a spring, through a sediment trap and along a stone conduit into the cistern. An adyton opens out of House C's principal room, but this sunken rectangle is unusually public in having three doors opening into it, when one is the norm elsewhere. House B has no adyton, no room with pier-and-door partition, and no obvious main room; it is probable that this house had a different function from the others.

Seven kilometres west of Tylissos, and set in spectacular hill country, there was another Late Minoan village, Sklavokampos. Not much of it survives and the one substantial house that has been excavated was only discovered by chance during road-building. The Sklavokampos villa was more crudely built than those at Tylissos and its floors were apparently unpaved. The pottery was nevertheless of good quality and the seal impressions found there show that the people who lived there had contacts that spread extensively across Crete. One seal impression showing a bull-leaping scene has been found at Zakro, Gournia and Agia Triadha as well as at Sklavokampos. It may be that the Minoans who lived at Sklavokampos traded with travelling merchants who were part of a widespread trading system.

The living quarters were in the north-east corner of the house. To the west were the porticoed entrance and store-rooms. In the centre was a courtyard, one of the earliest examples of an atrium, with what were probably the servants' quarters ranged round its western and southern sides. The Sklavokampos house was fairly roughly finished. It had, it seems, no frescoes, no gypsum veneers, although its walls were fitted with timber frames and the building as a whole was well planned. The quality of the Minoans' rural dwellings varied quite considerably, but most of those excavated so far show a degree of sophistication and planning. It is unlikely that caves were ever regarded as suitable accommodation in the Minoan period.

### AGRICULTURE AND FOOD PRODUCTION

One of the signs in the Minoan script was a plough. In the eighth century BC, Hesiod described a primitive type of plough that consisted of little more than a stout forked branch, a type which was still in use in the Roman period. The Minoan plough, as shown in the script-sign, seems to have been a little more complicated, with a handle made of two additional pieces of wood, probably bound together with leather thongs; it was drawn by pairs of oxen or donkeys. Ploughing was an important act, fundamental to food production, and may have been accompanied by rituals.

A remarkable series of clay tablets from Knossos, the Ch series, gives us the names of some of the ox-drivers and their oxen. The oxen were given simple descriptive names: Black, Dusky, Noisy, Fair, Red, Sandy, Dapple or Spotty, White-foot, White-muzzle, and Red-rump.

After the ploughing, the grain was sown. Some millet may have been grown, though no evidence of it has yet been found. Richer cereals were apparently preferred – wheat, soft wheat, spelt and barley. Barley and wheat seem to have been equally plentiful at this time. Although separate signs were available for wheat and barley, the clay tablets often record only 'grain', which makes it difficult to tell which cereal was intended. Sometimes it is possible to infer which was meant by the size of the ration. A basic ration was 2 'T' units per month in one grain, 3.75 'T' in the other. It seems reasonable to assume that the two rations were of equal nutritional value, so the smaller one must be wheat, the larger barley.

On the mainland, at Mycenean Pylos, the sizes of estates were not measured in units of land area but according to the quantity of seed-corn they required, a practice that survives into modern times in some Greek islands. The grain harvest at the village of Tylissos was recorded at Knossos as being 261 units of wheat, or 19.5 tonnes, which was probably produced on an estate of about 10 hectares or less. Lyktos, in the last harvest recorded at Knossos, produced 247 units or 18.3 tonnes, and Lato produced 31 units or 2.3 tonnes. The highest figure is for Dawos, which was apparently in the plain of Messara; the tablet was broken off, but the figure was in excess of 10,000 units or 788 tonnes of grain. The figure is quite high, but not surprisingly so, given the extent and fertility of the plain (Chadwick 1976).

The bronze age Cretan farmers equipped themselves with axe-adzes as all-purpose tools. These bronze implements had shaft holes for mounting on wooden handles. The axe blade was used for cutting down trees and bushes and clearing undergrowth, the adze for hoeing and weeding. Single-bladed axes and double-axes were also used for land clearance. The early shaft holes were round, but they were later made oval to prevent the head from twisting round on the handle.

Some of the ripened grain may have been picked by hand, just as it was until recently in upland fields on Crete. But simple sickles made of pieces of wood armed with 'teeth' of obsidian or flint are known from the neolithic period and bronze sickles were made in the Minoan period. The Minoans harvested some of their grain with sickles. How the threshing was done is not known. Today, grain is threshed with a wooden sledge with chips of flint fixed into its base; this is dragged round a circular paved threshing floor by oxen. Similar sleds similarly armed may have been used by the Minoans, but so far no threshing floors have been positively identified. It is possible that the circular platforms excavated by Peter Warren in the Minoan town of Knossos were threshing floors rather than dancing floors, as Warren himself has suggested (1984). Two of the circular platforms he excavated were about 3 metres in diameter, the third was 8 metres.

After threshing, the grain was winnowed, probably by flinging it up into the air so that the chaff blew away in the breeze, leaving the grain to fall to the ground – the method still used in Crete today. The Harvester Vase, a stone libation vessel found at Agia Triadha, may show winnowing forks. A group of exultant farm workers is shown singing and dancing in procession with a priest, a musician and a trio of singers; several of the farm workers carry what appear to be winnowing forks on their shoulders.

Groups of large cylindrical pits at the temples have been interpreted as granaries. In the south-west corner of the temple at Mallia are two rows of four circular granaries, each about 4.5 metres in diameter. Each granary was built of rough masonry and lined with plaster. Professor Graham (1987) speculates that the central stump, which survives in several, was originally a pillar extending upwards to support the highest point of a corbelled dome. The excavators thought the structures were cisterns, but Graham thinks they were granaries. It is possible that the three cylindrical stone-lined pits or *kouloures* in the West Court at Knossos and the two similar pits in the West Court at Phaistos were also granaries.

Besides cereals, the Minoans were growing vetch, chick peas, pigeon peas, cultivated peas, sesame, hemp, flax and castor oil plants in their fields. Large areas were given over to vineyards. The vine may have been native to Crete. Grape pips were found at the early settlement at Fournou Korifi, and in Middle Minoan storage jars at Monastiraki and Phaistos. These pips may represent the remains of raisins rather than signs of wine production; some grapes were almost certainly dried in the autumn sun in order to store them for winter food. On the other hand, wine had been produced from grapes for a long time in the eastern Mediterranean region: there was wine production in Egypt not long after 3000 BC, so there is no reason why Cretans should have been without wine even at the beginning of the bronze age. The Egyptians had both light and dark grapes to produce white and red wines; the Cretans too probably produced both, just as they do today. In historic times, it has been the Cretan red wine that was particularly well known; the province of Malemvizi to the west of Knossos is said to have given its name to Malmsey, the popular red wine that was exported to England in the middle ages.

The Knossos archive tablets contain references to vines. One, Gv 863, refers to 420 vines and 104 fig trees. Wine was not, it seems from the archives, on any ordinary ration lists: it may have been regarded as something of a luxury and generally used abstemiously. Tablet Gm 840 shows the product of the last vintage to be gathered into Knossos under the aegis of the temple priestesses, and it is a very large quantity. The total of the entries amounts to over 14,000 litres. On the other hand, the redistributed output from the Knossos temple is very small. The only inferences that can be made from this are that the archive is incomplete or that most of the wine received was consumed in the temple. The latter seems very likely, given the sort of religious ceremonies that were conducted there: libations and sacred communions would account for the consumption of large quantities of wine.

Another major crop was the olive. It was of fundamental importance in Crete as in other Mediterranean lands. The main problem with the olive tree is that it bears a heavy crop only in alternate years and that the trees of a whole district tend to be in phase. On the other hand, the fruit can easily be stored in jars and the pressed oil keeps well too. Olive oil was used for cooking, washing, lighting and possibly as a body oil. Paul Faure (1973) writes of two forms, the wild olive and the cultivated olive. Chadwick (1976) disputes this on the grounds that the wild olives are of too low a quality to have been a significant element in the Minoan economy; he suggests instead that the two sorts of olive referred to in the tablets were olives picked at two distinct states of ripeness.

The olive harvest was the last and longest of the year, starting in November and going on until the beginning of March. The olives were probably beaten from the trees with sticks, just as they are today, then soaked in water, crushed in wooden mortars or presses, and the resulting pulp put into a settling tank. Various sorts of presses that could have been used in wine-making or oil-pressing have been found in rural dwellings, together with mortars and pestles. After some time in the settling tank, the oil rose to the surface and the water was drained off through a spout at the base of the vessel. Large clay jars with spouts at the base are known from each Minoan period. An installation at Vathypetro, which includes a spouted jar of this type, has been interpreted as a wine press, but it could equally have been for separating olive oil.

Olive stones were found at Fournou Korifi and in a well at Knossos dating back to the Early Minoan I period: a cup of olive stones was found at the temple of Zakro. The Knossos tablets document olive production levels; the Dawos area, in the Messara plain, is recorded as producing about 9,000 litres of olives.

Fig trees were also grown. Like the olive tree, the fig appears to have been regarded as sacred by the Minoans. One of the Knossos tablets refers to an estate with 1,770 fig trees. Chadwick rightly surmises that the picked fruit was dried in the sun and stored for the winter: figs, like olives, were probably eaten all the year round. Other fruits were consumed as well. Quinces and pears may have been indigenous to Crete. Kydonia, the name of the principal Minoan city in the west of Crete, actually means 'quince' in Greek, and was sometimes, for example in Aristophanes, applied metaphorically to the plump, round breasts of a girl; it is possible that the word carried the same meanings in the Minoan language, since many words were borrowed from older languages (Newey 1989). The well-watered plain behind the site of Kydonia, now replaced and obscured by modern Khania, is still a major fruit-growing area, though now it is given over mainly to the orange, brought in during the middle ages. Almond trees were probably exploited, then as now, for their nuts.

Palms were probably not native to Crete, but they were introduced very early, and were certainly in Crete in the Minoan period. Evans identified one of the earliest script signs as a palm branch and there are lots of images of palms on sealstones and vases from Middle Minoan II (about 1900 BC) onwards. Hood feels that the date palm was sacred: later on it became associated with Apollo, who himself was probably a pre-Greek god.

Livestock farming was a major element in the Minoan economy. In the New Temple Period, according to Nicolas Platon (1968), there is much evidence of large-scale breeding of cattle, sheep, goats, and pigs. There were domestic goats in Minoan Crete and it is suggested, by Hood (1971), that the wild goats of bezoar stock (the agrimi or Cretan ibex) may really be feral, i.e. descendants of Minoan domestic goats that escaped or were deliberately turned loose back in the bronze age. The creatures so carefully depicted by Minoan artists, creatures with long horns knobbed at intervals, look very similar to the modern wild goats, yet they are often shown in domesticated situations, such as drawing goat-carts or sitting on the roof of a temple. At the same time, similar-looking goats were portrayed leaping through mountainous landscapes or being chased by hunters; in other words, in the Minoan period there was little difference between the wild and the domesticated goat.

No doubt flocks of goats and sheep were driven back and forth by herdsmen, wintering on the low ground and spending the summers on the high pastures. Paul Faure (1973) believes that the shepherds' dwellings in the high pasture became surrounded by mystique, and that they served as places of initiation. Faure draws on the substantial and very peculiar folklore which surrounded shepherds in the later, classical period. The shepherds' folklore includes strange three-eyed giants, the Triametes, who were both cunning and cruel: the third eye, on the nape of the neck, looked backwards. The man-eating Triametes were a Cretan variation on the cyclops Polyphemus. Odysseus' experience with the cyclops represents a bronze age initiation in which the young shepherd became a mortal master of animals. Some of the caves high in the mountains have a sinister reputation; they are places where you can throw the beasts of your enemy if you wish to take revenge on him for some wrong. Faure speculates that many of the deeply entrenched rural customs of Crete may be Minoan in origin, but it would be rash to assume this.

There are cave drawings in the Vernofeto Cave at Kato Pervolakia (Sitia district) which indicate that the cave was used for rituals of pastoral magic. Goats are shown, one being netted. A crouching female, possibly a priestess or goddess, holds a bow and arrow with her arms upraised: a dog is near her. Below is a fishing scene, with three men in three boats casting nets for several different sorts of seafood, including octopus, dolphin and starfish. It is one of the clearest examples of sympathetic magic in ancient Crete and is thought to date from around 1400 BC.

But to return to the sheep. A clay dish found in the Minoan town of Palaikastro contains a model of a flock of sheep with their shepherd. The Knossos tablets add documentary evidence by listing very large numbers of sheep. The total mentioned for the Labyrinth's final year, around 1380 BC, runs to about 100,000 sheep. The numbers of lambs are carefully noted, presumably so as to keep a check on the ever-changing strength of the flocks. The tablets record target figures for flocks and for wool production. The target is one unit of wool, about 3 kilograms, for every four sheep, or about 750 grams per sheep, which agrees with the quantity of wool expected from sheep in the medieval period. Breeding flocks yielded less because lambs produce no wool in their first spring. The tablets give the names of 'sheep officials' or owners, who are presumably not the shepherds. A second name on some of the tablets seems to indicate a dedication to either a deity or a named citizen.

J. L. Bintliff (1977) has reconstructed the likely seasonal movements of flocks in central Crete. There were Minoan farming villages at Sphakia, Anogeia, Kroussonas, Gergeri, Zaros, Vorizou and Kamares. From these, flocks were taken up in the spring to graze on the Nida Plain, with the peak shrine and sacred caves of Mount Ida probably developing as a ritual focus later. After spending the summer on the Nida Plain the flocks moved down to spend the winter on the low hills in the Phaistos area. There is a clear association between the migration to the high summer pastures and the development of the peak sanctuaries and high caves as cult centres.

Pigs were apparently domesticated in Crete as early as the neolithic period. In Minoan times they were widely distributed but in fairly low numbers. At Knossos, single pigs were being offered in tribute, probably as special offerings for sacrifice.

Cattle were reared from neolithic times too. Their bones, along with those of sheep and goats, were recovered from the earliest neolithic level at Knossos. The Cretan cattle, introduced into the island by the same generation of neolithic occupants who built the first village at Knossos, were brought in from elsewhere, a breed apparently descended from the giant long-horned *Bos primigenius*. The cattle may have been kept principally for their milk rather than for their meat. They also served as draught animals, and their skins were used to make the large figure-of-eight shields carried by warriors and hunters.

Cattle featured in the bull games, a major religious rite. It seems that the bulls were sometimes sacrificed after the games, but there is no direct or necessary connection between the two rites. Bull-leaping and -grappling evidently started very early in Crete, whereas most of the evidence of cattle sacrifice comes from the fourteenth century BC, and then often in connection with funerary rites. The bulls used for the bull games are shown on the

*Figure 14* A terracotta bull, showing the
Minoans' love of pattern and – I think – sense
of humour

frescoes as having dappled hides, implying that they were domesticated, not
wild, but their behaviour may well have been fairly unmanageable if they
were allowed to live in a semi-wild state. The scene of bull capture on one of
the Vaphio cups shows how dangerous netting one of these half-wild beasts
could be.

Dogs are known to have existed in Minoan Crete. The handles on some
Early Minoan stone pot lids are shaped like relaxing dogs. It seems that the
dogs were used mainly in hunting. At Pylos, the term 'hunters' literally
means 'dog-leaders', proving that dogs were used in this way. On a sealstone apparently dating to Middle Minoan III, a collared dog is shown
barking at a goat cornered on the rock above. A chalcedony seal with gold
end-mounts found in a Late Minoan tomb at Knossos shows a dog of mythic
size wearing an embossed collar. Evans suggested that this was a sacred dog,
reminiscent of those described at the classical temple of Diktynna, a goddess
with a pre-Greek name and pre-Greek origins; it seems that a Minoan
goddess, called Diktynna, had sacred dogs in her service on the rugged
headland of Spatha, to the west of the Minoan city of Kydonia.

John Chadwick (1976) regrets that he sees no evidence of cats, but Sinclair
Hood (1971) suggests that some of the Minoan sealstones do show cats. One
very finely carved Middle Minoan seal has a cat-like symbol engraved on it;
Evans proposed that the cat may have been the personal badge of a Cretan

prince, which seems to be going too far. Another seal shows a cat attacking a group of water-birds. Domestic cats had been trained to hunt wildfowl in the marshes, and it may be that they were introduced to Crete from Egypt for the same purpose. An inlaid dagger from Mycenae, but probably made by a Cretan, shows golden cats again stalking water-birds, with fish and clumps of papyrus.

It is not certain whether the Minoans had chickens. The people of the Indus valley civilization were domesticating fowl by the year 2000 BC, but there is no mention of them in Egypt until the early fifteenth century BC, when they are mentioned elliptically as 'the birds that give birth every day'. The chicken may have been introduced to Crete at about this time: a clay vase from Agia Triadha looks rather like a caricature of a chicken.

Cats and dogs were used to help in hunting, and the wild mountain sides of Minoan Crete were rich in game of all kinds. In addition to the water-birds and wild goats already mentioned, there were deer and wild boar. The boar were dangerous wild animals and were doubtless hunted as a pest mainly, but their meat was probably welcome too. Their tusks are found among kitchen refuse, both at Knossos and elsewhere on Crete.

It is possible that lions prowled there too. They were still in existence in Macedonia in the fifth century BC, so they may well have existed on Minoan Crete. Lions were often shown on Early Minoan and later sealstones. On Late Minoan seals they are often shown attacking other animals such as wild deer or cattle. Lions would have been regarded as a destructive menace, devourers of cattle, game and men, and pursuing and killing them a test of a warrior's skill and courage. The best-known Mycenean dagger shows a pride of lions being hunted by men with shields, spears and bows; even though it was found in one of the shaft graves at Mycenae, it was probably made by a Cretan craftsman, and may conceivably show a scene on Crete. Lions are shown as sacred animals, attendant upon Minoan deities. One seal shows a lion walking along beside an armed goddess, and evidently accompanying rather than stalking her; another, apparently its pair, shows a lioness walking beside a god armed with a spear and a square shield.

Monkeys may have found their way, like cats, from Egypt. They appear in several wall paintings dating to the sixteenth century BC at Knossos and Akrotiri; the fossilized head of a monkey was identified – although it may have been a stone – among the debris of the fifteenth-century eruptions on Thera. Nevertheless, monkeys do appear in Minoan art and, significantly, they are painted blue, according to the contemporary Egyptian convention.. They were also included in Middle Minoan jewellery and appear on Early Minoan seals: some of the early sealstones even have monkeys carved in the round as handles. The monkey may have been a sacred animal (see Chapter 6), but it may also have been caught for its meat, as it still is in the equatorial forests.

Wild birds were probably also part of the Minoans' diet. As we have seen, cats may have been used to stalk and catch them, as shown on Late Minoan seals. Partridges and hoopoes may have been caught for food as well; these two birds appear in a frieze painted round the walls of one of the chambers of the Pilgrim Hostel at Knossos. Hoopoes are still summer visitors to Crete and Evans believed that they were regarded as a special delicacy in the eastern Mediterranean region in the Minoan period. Set against this, though, is the Jewish prohibition against eating the hoopoe, under the name 'lapwing', on the grounds that it is unclean. A law of this kind suggests an ancient prejudice against eating the hoopoe in the Levant at least. Perhaps we should not be so quick to read the frieze at the Pilgrim Hostel as a menu.

Even so, the natural environment of ancient Crete brimmed with food. Bees were important in the Minoan economy, as the honey they produced was the main source of sugar. Egyptian bees were kept in horizontal clay cylinders with a flight hole at one end and a larger smoke hole at the other. When the honey was to be extracted, smoke was blown in to clear the tube of bees. As yet, no clay beehives have been found, or at any rate recognized, from Minoan Crete. Hood suggests that the honey of wild bees may have been gathered from rocky clefts or hollow trees, but it may be that hives were built partly or wholly of wood and that they have simply not survived in the archaeological record. Some containers seem to have been made in the shape of modern hives; it is possible that one of the symbols of the Phaistos Disc (Evans' symbol number 7) shows the shape of a Minoan beehive.

The bee was used as a decorative motif. The famous gold pendant found at Mallia seems to show a pair of bees kissing. It has been proposed that it may be a pair of wasps fighting instead, on the grounds that the insects look more like wasps or hornets; on the other hand the Egyptians, with whom the Minoans shared many conventions, tended to portray bees in this way, so it is a difficult image to interpret (Figure 28).

Archive tablets at Knossos record offerings of honey to the goddess Eleuthia, so it seems likely that some of the large storage jars at Knossos were used to store honey. One of the many legends surrounding the Knossos Labyrinth is the story of Glaukos, a son of King Minos who, while exploring the labyrinth's cellars, fell into a huge jar of honey and drowned.

This story may be taken as a half-memory of a time when jars of honey were used to embalm the dead in Crete. Herodotus mentions that in Babylon the dead were buried in honey, and the body of Alexander was embalmed in this way before being taken on its long journey to Alexandria for burial. Even so, there is no evidence at all, *pace* Wunderlich (1975), that the Minoans embalmed their dead with honey or anything else. More to the point is a mention in the bronze age archive at Pylos that the wine was 'honeyed'. Honey does make a very pleasant additive to alcoholic drinks, especially mulled wine, and we may assume that at least some of the distinctively flavoured Cretan honey stored at Knossos would have been stirred into wine for consumption in the sanctuaries.

The Cretan hillsides still burgeon with herbs, shrubs and trees which can make their contribution as food sources, and this must also have been true in the Minoan period. Coriander has always been a common cooking spice. The very similar Mycenean Greek word for it was 'koriadnon', which may be the word the Minoans themselves used. Large quantities of coriander passed through Knossos. A total of more than 7,500 litres was issued, although the receipts recorded were far less. Chadwick (1976) says it is a mystery how the books were balanced, but there is no reason to suppose that the surviving archive, as picked from the badly eroded ruins at Knossos, is complete. Whether the coriander was gathered from the wild or grown domestically is unclear, but it was produced on a large scale. One reference at Pylos records 576 litres of coriander in a list given by a senior official to a perfume-maker. This tells us that coriander was used as an ingredient in perfume manufacture. It also tells us that in the Minoan-Mycenean world the scent of coriander was regarded as attractive – an indication of a change of tastes.

Other likely herbs and spices include cumin, fennel, sesame, celery, mint, garden cress and safflower. The cyperus mentioned at Knossos may have been *Cyperus rotundus*, a species which yields a fragrant oil which could have been used as a hair- or body-oil. Finally, there is the pistacia tree mentioned in the Knossos tablets. The word 'ki-ta-no' in the tablets has been reconstructed as 'kritanos', an alternative name for the turpentine tree, *Pistacia terebinthos*. Enormous quantities of pistachio nuts passed through the store-rooms of the Knossos Labyrinth; they seem to have been as popular with the Minoans as they are among modern-day Greeks.

There are those who would have us believe that the Minoans plundered this horn of plenty, that they over-exploited the island's economic capacity. Soil depletion and soil erosion have been common problems throughout the Mediterranean region, but it is difficult, given the lack of evidence, to be sure how far these processes were important in Crete in the Minoan period. John Seymour and Herbert Girardet (1986) argue that a change-over in burial customs, between 1700 and 1400 BC, from the use of wooden coffins to the use of clay larnakes shows that timber supplies had declined; this in turn is made to prove, by implication, that there was significant deforestation on Crete. One problem with this rather facile reasoning, which seems not to have been based on any Cretan palaeo-environmental evidence, is that we have no reason to believe that burial in wooden coffins was ever common in Crete – even before 1700 BC.

On the other hand, we have the evidence of the temples. It must be admitted that the building and maintenance of the temples, between 2000 and 1380 BC, involved the use of enormous quantities of large timbers, particularly for rafters, ceiling beams and the hundreds of tapered columns which the Minoan architects deployed. Since the only large temple to remain in use in 1400 BC was the Knossos Labyrinth, and that was abandoned after a serious fire in 1380 BC, we might infer that the Minoans had simply run out of timber. Certainly the depletion of Cretan cedar forests would have made it very difficult for the Knossians to replace all the burnt columns, and this may have been a contributory factor in their abrupt abandonment of the temple concept; the traditional style of Minoan temple-architecture, with its mock forests of columns and pillars, was simply no longer possible.

Seymour and Girardet maintain that the Minoan civilization in effect weakened and destroyed itself by poor land management. Deforestation wiped out the supply of timber, and also exposed the hillslope soils to rapid erosion, so that agricultural production was reduced as well. A *coup de grâce*, they argue, may have been delivered by the Thera eruption, but the civilization was already destroying itself from within. As we saw in the last chapter, the Thera eruption did not deliver a death blow to the civilization; however surprising it may be, the civilization recovered from it. There may nevertheless be some truth in the Seymour and Girardet view, to the extent that the forests were probably reduced in area and timber-production capacity as time elapsed, and the farmland too probably became less productive. Indeed, these processes may help to explain the gradual waning of the bronze age Cretan culture in the centuries between 1400 and 1000 BC.

<br>

RURAL SHRINES

*The peak sanctuaries*

Religion played a major role in the Minoan way of life, both in the towns and in the countryside. There were some easily recognizable built sanctuaries, as well as other cult centres that are far less easily identified.

The 'house' at Niru Khani has always, ever since it was excavated in 1918–19 by Xanthoudides, been the subject of controversy. Was it a country mansion as Graham (1987) suggests, or the only surviving large house in a harbour town that extended all the way along the shore to Agii Theodhori? Or was it, as Xanthoudides and Evans thought, the headquarters as well as the residence of a High Priest? Three of its rooms contained a total of about fifty clay altars neatly stacked in piles; another room contained four large stone sanctuary lamps; in another, four very large ritual double-axes made of thin bronze sheets were found. The walls were frescoed and one fresco fragment showed a sacral knot, a religious symbol. The courtyard to the east was clearly intended for religious rites: remains of sacral horns were found there together with a niche designed to receive them and, nearby, a kind of tripartite altar.

The Niru Khani temple, if we can provisionally call the building that, was evidently an important centre for religious ritual. The large number of religious objects found suggests that the building may have been, as Evans proposed, a centre for the manufacture of votive objects. Niru Khani may have been an important rural religious centre. It is nevertheless possible that other buildings stood round it along the shore, which lies only a few metres away. Minoan harbour works have been found half a kilometre away at Agii Theodhori. Whether this adds up to a port is questionable: too much of the evidence is missing.

More unambiguously rural are the peak sanctuaries, consisting of temples and sacred enclosures on the lower and more accessible rocky mountain tops, which were often riven by fissures and clefts. These places were always dramatically situated, bare and windswept. The sanctuaries varied in height from only 215 to 1,100 metres above sea-level, so the surrounding vegetation varied considerably. Petsophas, one of the lower sanctuaries, was in the zone of evergreen Mediterranean vegetation in which vines were cultivated. From 350 to 650 metres there were oak woods and maquis, although the olive could be cultivated right up into this zone; it was here that most of the peak sanctuaries were built. The highest sanctuary of all, Karfi (1,158 metres above the Mediterranean), is in the high summer grazing zone: there are still evergreen shrubs and some oaks at this altitude, although the landscape is more open.

The sanctuaries differed from each other in their appearance, but the votive offerings and other trappings of the cult were uniform; in other words their function was the same, even though the buildings may have looked different. The exposed position meant strong winds and few trees, but short shrubs, flowers and herbs grew in profusion in the rock crevices. The Zakro rhyton shows a wild, rocky site with an elaborately carved or painted shrine standing in front of a summit; a flight of altar-strewn paved terraces designed for cult activities descends before it, the temenos or sacred precinct. Walls and balustrades are crowned with sacral horns. One of the altars carries an offering of two branches, possibly torn from a sacred tree. The façade of the sanctuary is embellished by tall masts or pylons anchored to the wall by substantial square brackets. A rhyton fragment found on the Gypsades Hill at Knossos shows a sanctuary of very similar shape, again with bracketed masts (Figure 15). The Gypsades rhyton differs in showing a worshipper stooping in front of the sanctuary to set down a basket or large bowl.

Both the rhytons show the façade divided into three parts. The middle section is shown broader and higher than the flanking sections. The lower flanking sections are surmounted by sacral horns. The design may well contain a resonance of the tripartite form seen in the major shrine in the Central Court at Knossos. The façades were apparently designed to be backdrops for ceremonies, cult dances, processions and possibly religious-theatrical performances.

Solitary, raised to the skies, exposed to the wind, silent but for the sounds of birds and wild goats, the peaks must have seemed places that were propitious for meetings with the gods. A range of devotional activity is implied in the various types of altar found or depicted: long, step-like altars, rectangular table-like altars, fire altars, incurved or waisted altars and natural stones functioning as altars. It seems likely that there were cult images or statues in the sanctuaries. Rutkowski (1986) interprets the curious rendering of the peak itself on the Zakro rhyton as an aniconic representation of the goddess, like the enshrined baetyls shown on some of the gold ring scenes. Clay cult statues or wooden xoana with clay feet and elaborate robes were probably installed in the shrines within the temple. Some of the statues or figurines were apparently votives, i.e. brought to the deity as offerings by pilgrims, but the larger ones were probably part of the sacred furniture of the temples. Two large statues have been discovered at Kophinas; others, discovered at Plagia, were said to have been 0.7 metres high but they were destroyed before that could be verified. On Mount Juktas, the clay curls of a large-scale human figure were discovered, though the exact findspot is not known.

The peak sanctuaries must have been elaborately furnished, though little now survives. There were movable sacrificial tables, stone ladles or lamps, libation vessels, including one from Kophinas in the shape of a bull's head, kernoi, pottery, small balls of crystal or steatite (probably used in connection with prayers). The many clay figurines are 10 or 20 centimetres high. Typically, they are of women in bell-shaped dresses, with jackets which expose the breasts, and with high head-dresses; the hats are fantastic and widely varying (Figure 3). There are also male figures wearing loincloths. Almost all the figures stand erect, with their hands raised in a gesture of supplication, fist to forehead in salutation (or perhaps to shield mortal eyes from the dazzling apparition of the deity), but some have their hands drawn back to the collar bones. The dedication of a figurine of the worshipper in an

*Figure 15*  A Minoan worshipper leaves offerings at a peak sanctuary

attitude of prayer and adoration signified the worshipper's continuing presence and continuing worship at the sanctuary; the figurine was a surrogate for a worshipper (Figures 2 and 30).

The Minoans went up to the peak sanctuaries to plead with and worship the deities who controlled the heavens. The pastoralists moving about among the high pastures in particular would have used these temples to intercede with the weather gods who controlled the lives and well-being of both people and livestock. The supplicating attitudes of the figurines tell us that prayers and pleas were offered. Large numbers of cattle models, especially bulls, and clay models of oxen, sheep and rams imply that the herds and flocks were being offered to the gods' protection.

Clay figurines of beetles have also been found in the peak sanctuary sites. Rutkowski thinks that they are intended to represent the scaraboid species *Copris hispanus*, which digs holes to bury sheep droppings; it may be relevant that small balls of clay, which may represent sheep droppings, have been found at peak sanctuaries too. The copris never acquired the same importance or status in Crete as the scarab in Egypt, but it was evidently thought to have some magical or religious significance. Where there were copris beetles, there were sheep. Perhaps the copris was seen as a messenger of the protecting deity, perhaps even as a theophany of the goddess.

Pilgrims such as nomadic shepherds might have visited the peak sanctuaries informally at any time, but large-scale ceremonies probably only happened at certain times, perhaps twice a year. As the worshippers arrived they placed their offerings inside the temenos, in front of the shrine. To judge from the later Greek festivals, large-scale and elaborate rituals followed; a priest placed the offerings on an altar, bonfires were lit, lambs were sacrificed and consumed at a feast. There was dancing and singing in honour of the deity, who was called up by blowing on triton shells. Pilgrims threw votives into the pyre embers. Afterwards, the ashes were swept up together with the votive offerings and kept in special repositories, usually a rock cleft. On Mount Juktas, this was a deep fissure in the rock to the west of the temple.

The Minoans clearly believed, in common with many other peoples in Africa, Asia and Europe, that deities lived on the mountain tops, or at least made appearances there. From their own habitations, the Minoans saw the mountain tops as intimately and supernaturally connected with the vagaries of weather. As rain clouds descended, the summits vanished; as they reappeared, the rain clouds lifted. Sometimes the shape of a mountain suggested supernatural properties. From Ghazi and Tylissos, the Mount Juktas ridge looks like the face of a reclining, supine giant; we can be sure that the rural peasants of Minoan Ghazi noticed it, just as the later Cretans did. Buondelmonti, visiting Crete in the fifteenth century, reported the views of the medieval Cretan peasants: 'The mountain is shaped like a human face. On the forehead . . . is the temple of Jupiter, while on the nose are three churches. . . . To the south, more or less facing Ida, is the chin.'

Minoans were venerating their gods on mountain tops a century or two before they started building large temples on the lowlands. The peak sanctuaries seem to have appeared rather suddenly in about 2100 or 2200 BC. As we have seen, most of them were situated on low peaks, at 400–800 metres, and they all have easy paths leading up to them, easy at any rate for habitual hill-dwellers, from nearby Minoan settlements. In most cases the peak sanctuary was less than an hour's walk from a Minoan village and surrounded by pasturage. They were places which must often have been visited by shepherds, and we should see the development of the peak cult as a natural outgrowth of the pastoral economy. Just at the time the lowlands were becoming urbanized and the first great temples were being planned, a major shift in the Minoan economic and social system was taking place. The lowland centres needed more food: pressure increased on the outlying, marginal areas to produce more cattle and sheep, and supernatural help was invoked.

The best-known of the peak sanctuaries is the one on Mount Juktas. Its temenos walls were apparently well preserved until the nineteenth century, and the precinct within has been investigated periodically: new discoveries are still being made there. In 1837, Pashley described the site, apparently for the first time:

> I found considerable remains of ancient walls. The construction is chiefly of very large stones, among which a good many small ones were inter-mixed. These fragments seem to offer a good specimen of the so-called first cyclopean style. . . . No more than 50 paces are occupied by the actually existing remains. It is, however, evident that the old walls extended all round the summit, except where, as on its western side, it is a nearly perpendicular precipice.

Now, most of the perimeter wall is so degraded that it is unrecognizable. Originally, the 740-metre-long wall was 3 metres wide and probably 4 metres high; built in the Middle Minoan IA period, around 2100 BC, it was probably repaired intermittently until the Late Minoan period, around 1470 BC. The massiveness of the walling has led some to suggest that the place functioned as a refuge in times of danger. At the same time, structures built for cult purposes are often redundantly massive; one could cite examples such as Stonehenge, the Pyramids, or the Egyptian temples. Possibly there was a need to express on a large scale in stone the majesty and power of the divinity.

At some stage, possibly shortly after the temenos wall was completed, the temple was built inside it. The temple, a long narrow rectangular building, separated off a small area of the precinct close to the cliff edge (Plate 3). The rock rises steeply up a dramatic ramp before plunging down towards the west: this area was the focus of the ritual activity, with a large rectangular altar, a pyre, and the jagged entrance to a sacred cave. In this vertical cleft, which has been excavated to a depth of 10 metres, large numbers of small clay votives, fragments of offering tables and bronze figurines were found. The site also yielded thirty cult double-axes.

The little temple itself consisted of a row of five compartments, each of which may have functioned as a separate shrine. Their west-facing entrances were probably screened from general view by a wall. The shrines were decorated with painted plaster and probably supported an upper storey. As I have suggested in *The Knossos Labyrinth*, the upper storey probably consisted of a tripartite shrine.

Juktas is special because of its well documented if poorly preserved temenos wall. It is special because the discovery of its sacred cleft emphatically connected the peak sanctuary and cave sanctuary cults as parts of the same religious system. It is also special because it was said by the ancient Cretans to be the burial-place of Zeus: a piece of folklore which earned Cretans an undeserved reputation as liars in the ancient world. But most of all it is special because it is the peak sanctuary which served Knossos, the principal city of Minoan Crete, and whose temple came to dominate the religious life of much of the island. Juktas, a presiding presence high on the southern skyline when viewed from Knossos, was an integral part of the belief-system which developed in the Knossos Labyrinth.

Tylissos had its own peak sanctuary; it was discovered in 1962 on one of the summits of Mount Pyrgos. It stood at 685 metres, some 90 metres lower than the Mount Juktas sanctuary. Like Juktas, it had a stone-built temple within a terraced temenos, and there were many Middle Minoan clay votive offerings: there were even caves a little way down from the summit which may have been used in connection with the sanctuary.

The town of Palaikastro in eastern Crete was evidently served by Petsophas which, at 215 metres above sea-level, was one of the lowest of the peak sanctuaries. It was excavated in 1903 by J. L. Myres, who found many clay figurines dating from every period of the Minoan civilization. There were some large copris beetle figurines, inscribed offering tables, lamps and bronze daggers that may have been used for sacrifices. As reconstructed by Rutkowski, the temple was a two-storey tripartite shrine somewhat similar to Juktas, and also built close to a steep drop. The walls of the ruined sanctuary still remain, commanding a spectacular view across the rocky hillside and the sea.

A final example is the sanctuary of Kophinas, discovered in 1955. In Minoan times, this served a scatter of rural villages, especially in the area round the present-day village of Kapetaniana. A 9-metre section of its long temenos wall survives: originally it ran round a more or less rectangular precinct some 80 metres by 30. This was unusually large. Pyrgos and Juktas were large, but the usual size for a temenos was under 600 square metres.

The sanctuary site, in use in the Middle Minoan and later, yielded a variety of cult objects including clay and bronze votive offerings. There were significant quantities of pottery as well, which was unusual; apart from Kophinas, only the peak sanctuaries at Koumasa and Juktas produced large quantities of pottery. The sanctuaries clearly varied a good deal in details of design and proportion, but the associations of site, perimeter wall, small temple, altars and votives are recognizable enough.

It is also evident from the thirty-five sanctuary sites that have been positively identified (see Appendix B) that worship at peak sanctuaries was a widespread and integral part of the Minoan rural belief-system – one which accompanied and was to an extent taken over by economic, political, and religious developments down on the plains.

## The cave sanctuaries

The Minoans also worshipped their gods and goddesses in the depths of the earth. The practice of worshipping in caves may have begun as a result of the practice of cave burial. The most important burial cave is at Pyrgos near the Minoan harbour at Agii Theodhori and the Niru temple. It contained hundreds of interments. Some people were buried there in clay coffins: some were buried with grave goods of stone idols, Early Minoan vases and bronze daggers. The use of caves for burial went on right through the Minoan period and it may be that this was because of an association with ancient habitations, although some of the caves used for burial and worship can never have been used as dwellings; the sacred caves at Kamares and Mount Ida are often blocked by snow until midsummer. The explanation is probably simpler. The Minoans used caves for worship and burial because of their mysterious and other-worldly atmosphere. One has only to descend into the magnificent caverns of Psychro or Skotino to sense the awe that the Minoan pilgrims too must have felt. They are places apart, like no other, places where deities might yet dwell.

Some cave sanctuaries were centres of worship well before the great temples were built in the towns; votive ivory figurines were left in the Trapeza Cave high in Lasithi in these Pre-Temple days. The caves were visited once the temples were built, too; pilgrims from Phaistos in the days of the Old Temple made their way up the southern slopes of Mount Ida as far as Kamares, where offerings were left in pottery vessels in the Kamares Cave. Some caves, like the Cave of Eileithyia at Amnisos, continued as centres of worship long after the temples had fallen.

It is important to recognize that the Minoans did not regard all caves as sacred. Of the two thousand caves in Crete, perhaps as few as thirty-five were used by the Minoans for religious purposes: of those, only sixteen or so were definitely used as cult places (see Appendix A). The selection of a cave for cult activity depended on whether it fulfilled certain requirements: a

mysterious and awe-inspiring interior with fantastically shaped rock formations, including stalagmites and stalactites, together with rock pools
where holy water might be collected. Our knowledge of the cave sanctuaries
is incomplete; not one of the caves has been completely excavated and
documented.

Some of the caves, such as the Hermes Grotto at Patsos and the cave at
Mavro Spilio at Knossos, are simple rock shelters. Some are relatively
simple one-chamber caverns, like the Cave of Eileithyia at Amnisos and the
Arkalochori Cave. Skotino is rather more complex, its plan dividing into
four compartments linked end to end to make a chain 160 metres long
overall. Skotino ranked among the most important cave sanctuaries, as the
sacred cave of Knossos. Four hours' walk east of Knossos, on a level plateau
and visible only from close at hand, is a large hollow formed either by
solution or by cave-collapse; the cave entrance opens from the south side of
this wooded dell (Plate 4). Paul Faure believes that Evans was wrong in
identifying the large building at Knossos, the House of the Double-Axe, as
the Labyrinth: he considers the Skotino Cave to be the Labyrinth. There
seems to be no reason to go along with this view. Even so, Skotino emerged
as one of the most important cult caves in Minoan Crete.

Skotino has a narrow entrance leading into a large first chamber. Daylit,
94 metres long, 36 metres wide and with a ceiling soaring an impressive 50
metres above the cave floor, it is cathedral-like and awe-inspiring. In its
centre a massive stalagmite formation rears up like some primitive piece of
statuary. The floor slopes unevenly down past this impressive structure. At
the end of it there is a drop into the second chamber, which is 24 metres
long and has a much lower ceiling. The light here is dim and it seems
that this was the focus of the Minoan rituals; remains of sacrifices and
votive offerings including figurines were found in it, close to a natural rock
altar.

The small third chamber, lower and darker still, has several branches
leading off it, one connecting it with a circular fourth chamber. Most of the
cult activity seems to have taken place in the first and second chambers. The
large rock formation in the first chamber is said to look like a bear or a dog. It
really looks more abstract than that, organic perhaps, but in a more general
way. To pilgrims under the influence of alcohol, opium, religious fervour, or
all three, it might have suggested all kinds of monsters, demons, deities.
From one angle it looks like a sphinx. At its innermost end, the stalagmite
formation culminates in a pillar which looks, in the half-light, like an
expressive bearded head, startlingly similar to the images of Zeus made in
the archaic period. Was the image of Zeus perhaps taken from this rock-
image in the shadows of the Skotino Cave?

The ashes of sacrificial pyres and quantities of pottery indicate high levels
of cult activity. The cave itself is huge, impressive and easily reached across
the gentle hill slopes. There seems little doubt that Skotino was the principal

cult place of a large region. It served the rural communities of that region and also the towns, including Knossos.

The sacred cave of Eileithyia at Amnisos was probably also visited by urban as well as Minoans, from Knossos, 5 kilometres away, and from Amnisos itself, directly below it. The cave mouth is hidden behind a fig tree in a hillside gully overlooking the sea and the southern edge of modern Amnisos. The cave is low-ceilinged and its floor extends more or less horizontally into the rock. It has a fairly uncomplicated and open plan broken up only by clusters of stalagmites. One stalagmite was clearly sacred; it had a low wall built round it and it seems to have been treated as an aniconic cult image of the goddess Eleuthia, the Minoan goddess known to have been honoured here. Offerings to Eleuthia were recorded in the Linear B archive at Knossos.

Close at hand outside the cave mouth, Marinatos discovered the remains of a rectangular building. This may have been the house of the sanctuary's custodian or possibly a shrine: Strabo mentions an Eleuthia temple. In the late, post-Minoan period, the Eleuthia sanctuary at Amnisos was famous enough for Homer to be able to refer to it: he expected his readers on the Greek mainland to know of it. It may have started as a centre of worship for a small local community, but later acquired an importance that extended far and wide. Rutkowski (1986) suggests that the cave began as a place of general sanctity and only gradually acquired a very specific association with one particular goddess.

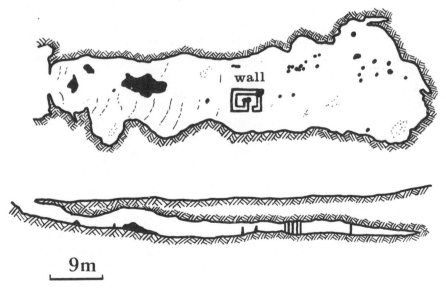

Figure 16  The Cave of Eileithyia: plan (above) and section (below). The black areas represent accretions of stalactite on the cave floor. This was the cave mentioned by Homer, and where the Minoans worshipped the goddess Eleuthia

Extending along the hillside to the west of the cave entrance is a terrace about 10 metres wide, the Square of the Altars: this was a precinct apparently connected with worship at the cave sanctuary. The fissured and weathered surface layer of the rock was laboriously quarried away to produce a smooth and level platform for ceremonies. Six large cubes of living rock, the largest some 3 metres across, were deliberately left at intervals, perhaps for use literally as altars of some kind (Plate 5). A degraded terrace wall leads eastwards from the altars towards a second cave, a well-like shaft 1 metre in diameter, which may have had some ritual function, perhaps for pouring libations; the use of a second shaft may have been necessary since the main cave was small and may often have been congested with pilgrims. Altogether, a considerable area seems to have been deployed for cult activity on this hillside. An isolated altar-cube of the same general shape as those on the Square of the Altars has been preserved further down the hillside to the north-east: it has what seem to be a battered pair of sacral horns on top.

Some of the Minoans' sacred caves have interiors which are more complicated than that of the Eileithyia Cave, maze-like interiors with winding passages and irregularly located side chambers. The Kera Spiliotissa and the Mamelouka Trypa Caves near Khania belong to this type. Another cave near Khania, the Leras Cave, is among the most beautiful on Crete. One group of stalagmites at Leras suggests a group of draped deities standing between the columns of a Minoan temple. The natural rock formations in many of the caves suggest beasts, people or gods; the Cretans of modern times have told travellers of cave rock formations that look like men, animals, or gods – the guides at Psychro still do so – and it is likely that the Minoans saw these likenesses too and may have seen them as significant, as numinous presences.

Water too was a ritual focus at the cave sanctuaries. Towards the back of the lower chamber at Psychro is a small lake of pure water. Its level rises and falls seasonally and at its spring maximum it is 20 metres across. Large numbers of votive offerings were found in the silts flooring the lake, especially close to its shore: bronze figures, rings, pins, sealstones. Rutkowski thinks that the rock pools at the back of the Eileithyia Cave were also regarded as sacred, though without offering any evidence.

The open spaces outside the cave entrances were often used for cult activities such as sacrifices, pyres, dancing and feasting. The terrain varies a good deal. At Skotino there is a wooded dell; at Amnisos there is an open meadow; at Psychro there are rocky mountainsides and a narrow terrace (Plate 6). In front of the Idaian Cave's entrance there is an apron of gently sloping land overlooking the Nida Plain: standing on it is a large altar which was certainly used for cult purposes in later times, although its existence there in Minoan times is uncertain.

The Minoans offered sacrifices of many kinds, both in the sacred caves

themselves and in the open-air precincts near their entrances. They brought
farm produce of all kinds in pottery vessels. Grain was left at the Kamares
Cave. Both domestic and wild animals were sacrificed and burnt. At
Psychro, there is evidence that pilgrims sacrificed oxen, wild goats, sheep,
deer, domestic pigs and wild boar. In other caves, there is evidence that
they left votive gold double-axes, bronze figurines of worshippers and many
other offerings; at Patso, they even deposited the sacral horns which had
probably once adorned the sanctuary's altar.

THE RURAL SYSTEM

The way of life in the rural areas can be presented as a system whose main
temporal components were mixed farming and industrial activities. The
mixed farming or food supply subsystem consisted of arable farming (the
cultivation principally of barley, wheat, olives and vines) and pastoral
farming (the rearing of sheep, goats, cattle and pigs); the gathering of
produce which grew wild (fruit, nuts and herbs) added another element.
Industry can be subdivided into extractive and manufacturing, or primary
and secondary industries. The primary industries included the extraction of
clay, timber, building stone, artefact stone, lime, earths and plants – as raw
materials for the secondary industries. The manufacturing industries included
the making of pottery, tools, votive figurines and idols, loom-weights,
sealstones, textiles, wall plaster and the building trade. Together, all these
activities made up the industrial subsystem.

A third major component was the organization of water supply which, at
some sites, must have occupied a considerable amount of time. The village
of Fournou Korifi, excavated in 1967–8, gives us a great deal of information
about the Early Minoan way of life. With its dry, hilltop site, Fournou Korifi,
or Myrtos as it is often called, must have presented its inhabitants with a
serious problem: presumably they went down the hillsides to gather water at
nearby springs and carried it up to the village in jars or skins.

A fourth component, trade, may have been more important at some
places than others. Most villages had contacts with the larger world outside,
as evidenced by varying quantities of imported goods. At Myrtos, for
example, imported metal objects, stone vessels and obsidian were found.
These small numbers of exotic objects do not, however, indicate long-
distance trading relationships in any modern sense. Some of the exotic goods
may have arrived at Myrtos as a result of many short-distance exchanges, or
as gifts or dowries. Presumably, to compensate, varying quantities of goods
were 'exported' too. In the case of Myrtos, exports may have comprised
pottery or cloth.

A fifth, non-temporal, component was religion. In the bronze age, many
areas of activity which we would now consider to be purely secular were
tinged with religious significance. Artefacts had to be 'charmed' to make

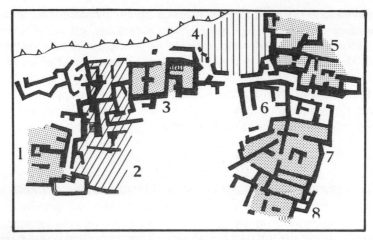

*Figure 17* Plan of the Early Minoan village at Fournou Korifi. Shaded areas 1–8 represent probable household units in use during the second period of occupation

them effective. To make the fields and flocks fertile, deities had to be propitiated and won over to the farmer's cause.

The way of life in the Cretan countryside was an interplay among these separate component activities. At Fournou Korifi, we can see how that interplay produced a village society at a critical stage in the development of Minoan civilization. The village belongs to the third millennium BC, to the period just before urban life evolved on the plains. The first period of occupation, 2600–2400 BC, saw the building of small stone houses in an area that was to become the centre of the village. In the second period, more houses were built so that by the time of the destruction by fire in about 2200 BC the village extended across about 1,250 square metres and consisted of nearly 100 rooms, linking passages and open courtyards (Figure 17).

The little Myrtos village was probably typical of rural Crete at this Pre-Temple or Early Minoan II stage. It is unfortunate that it is the only village so far to have been fully excavated and for which all the finds and precise findspots have been fully published; it is nevertheless likely that Myrtos will prove to be representative. The artefacts found there show that cereals were grown, and sheep, goats, and cattle were reared on the neighbouring slopes; pottery was made, wool was spun and woven, and figurines were made out of clay and stone; agricultural produce was stored in jars, and food was cooked in certain localized areas.

One room dating from the earlier phase, around 2500 BC, was a potter's workshop – the oldest so far known in the Aegean world. In it, eight circular discs were found, flat on one side and convex on the other, their centres worn down by constant turning. They were used for making pottery, turned by the potter's hands, and they precede the introduction of freely rotating, spindle-mounted fast wheels.

A later room in the south-west corner of the village yielded some broken offering vessels and a clay figurine that has become known as the Goddess of Myrtos. The goddess has a stalk-like head and neck, which may connect her with the curious later cult of pillar worship in which the pillar came to stand for the goddess. Her breasts are carefully accentuated, although not in the naturalistic way of the later snake goddess figurines or the priestess frescoes. She carries a water jug of typical Myrtos style, which suggests that she was associated with fertility and abundance. The hatched triangle on the front may represent the pubic triangle, as on other primitive goddess representations, and this would reinforce an interpretation of the figure as a goddess of fertility.

Peter Warren (1972) treats Myrtos as a single large living-complex, identifying specific areas within it as given over to different specialized activities; the implication is that the site functioned as an integrated whole with communal, perhaps clan, decision-making. The Warren view implies that family life was subordinate to that of the tribe or clan, the lack of any differentiation within the settlement suggesting that there was no chief or ruler. Warren puts the population at 100–120.

On the same data, Branigan (reviewing Warren's study in 1975) interprets Myrtos as the mansion of a chief. The cellular structure allows us to interpret the village as a single building if we wish. Todd Whitelaw (1983) has identified about eight household units within the cellular plan, each household unit consisting of a suite of interconnected rooms. A careful examination of the findspots of artefacts shows that each room-cluster incorporated most of the settlement's activities. Each household, in other words, had its own cooking area, its own farm produce storage area, its own wine (or more likely olive oil) storage area, its own area for general domestic activity. Not all of these were actually in use at the time of the destruction and Whitelaw suggests that the plan was the result of a very gradual organic growth through time, perhaps starting with a single nuclear family of 4–6 people and ending with five or six families by 2200 BC. Analyses of floor areas and the numbers of jars for agricultural storage (amphorae and pithoi) both suggested that each household consisted of about five people.

Whitelaw's study implies that Myrtos was a village of only 25–30 people, all living at about the same socio-economic level and grouped in families with a high degree of independence of one another. The key social unit was the nuclear family – a very different conclusion from Warren's, and a more persuasive one. Such a small community as Myrtos could not have survived in complete isolation, which means that at least formal negotiating relationships must have existed to procure mates from other communities, and such meetings may have fulfilled an important social need – a sixth component in the system. The need to procure husbands and wives outside the village may be what is required to explain the exchanges of exotic goods.

At Myrtos, obsidian blades from the island of Melos and stone vessels probably from Mochlos on the north coast of Crete at first sight suggest long-distance trading links. It may instead be that such prized objects were exchanged in elaborate gift-giving ceremonies when marriages between members of different villages were settled. It may also be that some objects were exchanged or given several times over and, in that way, travelled far from their original place of manufacture.

Myrtos was just one of hundreds of rural villages on bronze age Crete and we are entitled to ask whether it was typical or representative of the island as a whole in the Early Minoan period. Todd Whitelaw believes that it was typical and that there are two supporting lines of evidence for believing so. The size of Minoan houses from the very beginning of the Early Minoan Period to the end of the Late Minoan Period implies family units of a similar size to those identified at Myrtos; in other words, the standard unit of the nuclear family, consisting of about five people, seems to have prevailed in Minoan Crete. The numbers of burials in collective tombs seem to support this. Obviously several major, and some might say unwarranted, assumptions have to be made – such as the supposition that a bronze age nuclear family would have yielded twenty bodies per century – but the results are nevertheless very striking. Whitelaw takes a sample of twenty-four tombs and compares the body-counts from them with the estimated period of use. The inference from the sample is that each tomb served 1.17 families. In other words, in death as in life the nuclear family seems to have been the unit of social organization.

When we compare Myrtos on the south coast with Mochlos on the north coast of Crete, we see some significant variations. Both the settlement and the cemetery of Mochlos have been studied extensively, so some interesting links can be made between the large village of some 300 people in the Early Minoan and the social structure implied by the burials. The tombs strongly imply differences in status between families. There are two groups of particularly rich tombs. But Early Minoan Mochlos was a proto-urban settlement and it seems as if, at Mochlos, the Minoans were crossing a threshold. As their villages became towns, social stratification began to evolve. As the settlements became larger, divisions, specialisms and hierarchies began to emerge.

# 4
# Life in the towns

As for walls, it is quite out of date to say, as some do, that cities that lay claim to valour have no need of walls; we have only to look at what has happened to cities that made that boast. Doubtless there is something not quite honourable in seeking safety behind solid walls, but it may happen that the numerical superiority of the attackers is too much for the defenders. If then we are to save our city and avoid the miseries of cruelty and oppression, we must concede that the greatest protection that walls can afford is also the best military measure.

(Aristotle, *Politics*, Book 7, *c*. 340 BC)

## THE DEVELOPMENT OF TOWNS IN CRETE

Towns developed at the same time as the great lowland temples, and are identifiable from about 2000 BC. Sinclair Hood (1971, p. 50) mentions the theory that the temples (though he treats them as palaces) at Knossos and Phaistos were founded by foreign dynasts who invaded Crete at the beginning of the Middle Minoan period; according to this view, urbanization occurred in Crete as a result of the arrival of already-urbanized conquerors. There is evidence of the arrival of migrants at various stages in Crete's prehistory, but it seems too facile to attribute each change in the island's culture to the arrival of a new group of immigrants.

In any case, a study of neolithic Early Minoan buildings very strongly implies that the temples were not an implant but the result of a long period of indigenous development. The first neolithic settlers on the site of Knossos probably lived in wooden huts, of which only the post-holes survive in the archaeological record. By level 9, i.e. by about 6000 BC, Knossian houses were made of mud or mudbrick; some level 9 bricks seem to have been deliberately hardened by firing, which – remarkably – was never again to be the practice in neolithic or bronze age Crete. These houses, the homes of the first pottery makers on Crete, had rectangular rooms and were made without stone footings. Later neolithic houses were normally built on a stone footing and this system – building the lower part of the walls of stone, the upper part of mudbrick – became standard in the bronze age.

A level 3 (middle neolithic) room was preserved a metre or so below the surface of the Central Court at Knossos. It was 5 metres square with a bin made of stone slabs built against the north wall: a similar bin in the north-east corner held a large storage jar. There was a fire-hole in the centre of the room, presumably for warmth in the winter. A 1.8-metre-square platform in the south-east corner is thought to have been a bed. The walls were smoothly plastered.

By the late neolithic, Knossian house plans had become quite elaborate, with square fireplaces set against a wall or in the centre of the room, and with neighbouring dwellings juxtaposed to make a cellular layout familiar in Early Minoan villages such as Fournou Korifi (Myrtos) and the temples that were to be built in the Middle Minoan. It is tempting to see the House on the Hill at Vasiliki as a half-way stage in development between the informal village plans and the rigorously organized plans of the temples. Vasiliki is a cellular arrangement of rectangular chambers disposed round two sides of a courtyard: the temples were larger cellular structures disposed round all four sides of a rectangular courtyard. Obviously, there was a quantum leap of some sort in the development of Minoan culture at the time when the temples were built, just as there was a quantum leap when the towns were built. Even so, the direction of the indigenous developments on Crete during the neolithic and Early Minoan periods is enough to show a continuity into the Middle Minoan.

The quantum leap expressed itself partly in population levels. As we saw in Chapter 3, the population of the village of Fournou Korifi was probably only 25 or 30. Mochlos, one of the smaller towns on the north coast, is estimated (by Todd Whitelaw, 1983) to have had a population ten times greater, living in an estimated fifty-five houses. Early Minoan Phaistos, over one hectare in area, may have had a population of 300–450, Early Minoan Mallia, with its area of 2.58 hectares, had a population of 700–1,000, and Early Minoan Knossos was almost twice as big as Mallia, with a maximum extent of 4.84 hectares and a population estimated to be between 1,300 and 1,900. The towns were thus *much* larger than the rural villages, and they were to expand even more once the temples were built. The town of Knossos had reached a size of not less than 45 hectares by the time its first temple was built in 1930 BC, which would have given it a population of 12,000–18,000.

Vasiliki, with its curious L-shaped half temple on a ship-shaped hill on the Isthmus of Ierapetra, was 20 kilometres north-east of Fournou Korifi and may have served as something of an urban centre for the villagers. Nevertheless, the main centre for the Isthmus of Ierapetra region was to develop not at Vasiliki, but at Gournia, close to the north coast some 6 kilometres north-west of Vasiliki. Gournia (Figure 18) was excavated by the pioneer

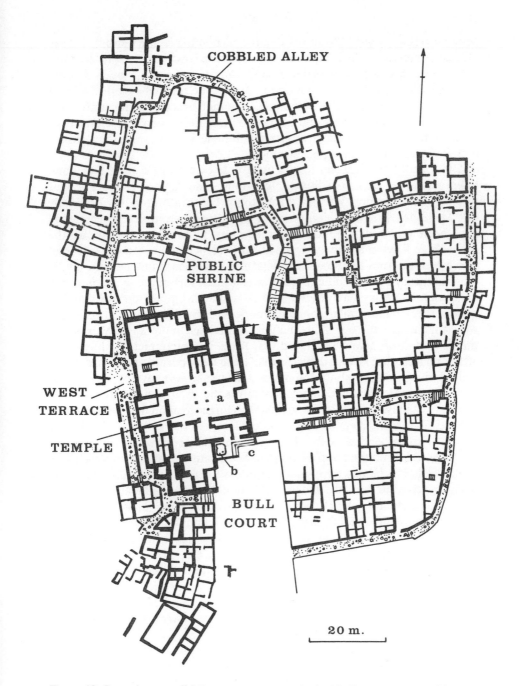

COBBLED ALLEY

PUBLIC
SHRINE

WEST
TERRACE

TEMPLE

BULL
COURT

a

b

c

20 m.

*Figure 18* Gournia, a small Minoan town. a = principal hall or sanctuary, with alternating pairs of piers and columns. b = large stone slab, apparently a sacrificial table. c = L-shaped arrangement of shallow steps

Minoan archaeologist Harriet Boyd at the turn of the century and the entire plan of the town stands completely exposed. Narrow paved streets that are little more than alleys wind informally round a low ridge once densely packed with houses. The town is dominated by the ruins of a modest temple with customary rectangular bull-court, together occupying the south-west quarter of the site. The Gournia houses are quite small, composed of perhaps five small chambers at ground floor level, although they almost certainly had at least one upper storey.

The form of the Minoan town house is known from several ivory and faience plaques depicting house elevations. The faience plaques Evans discovered in the East Wing of the Knossos Labyrinth probably originally fitted together, jigsaw-fashion, to make a picture of a complete town; it may have been a town under attack from invaders, like the town shown on the silver Siege Rhyton found at Mycenae. The faience plaques of the so-called Town Mosaic from Knossos show what the Knossian houses of the seventeenth century BC looked like. There was a small top storey, a room on the flat roof which may have functioned as a sleeping place on hot summer nights: there were similar roof chambers on Egyptian houses too. There were windows on the first floor, though not (at least in the Town Mosaic) on the ground floor. Evans suggested that if the complete picture showed an attack on a city the houses depicted may have been part of an outer defence wall in which no ground-floor doors or windows would have been possible. In fact, several plaques do show doors on the ground floor, though not windows. It may be that having no windows on the ground floor was a simple security feature, a precaution against burglary. An ivory plaque of a slightly later date shows a house with a doorway flanked by narrow slit windows.

The houses, and the temples too, had horizontal beams let into each face of the wall. The beams were linked at intervals by uprights and tie beams; they were fixed to the walls and probably to each other by means of wooden pegs. This technique, which shows clearly in all the house plaques as well as in the remains of the buildings themselves (for example, the north wall of the so-called 'Lobby of the Stone Seat' in the Knossos Labyrinth and in Room 11 of House A at Tylissos), was standard in Minoan Crete (Plate 7). Its original intention is unknown, but it has been suggested that the timber framing gave walls the combination of strength and flexibility needed to withstand earthquakes. The timber bracing was built into stone and rubble walls as well, as can be seen at many points round the Knossos Labyrinth, so it seems likely that earthquake-resistance was the likely purpose.

In major buildings like the temples, dressed stone sawn with long bronze saws was used, particularly for sections of wall that would be seen. At Knossos and Phaistos, an extra refinement in the masonry of the West Fronts was a foundation course of very large blocks: the rest of the wall was stepped back a centimetre or two to make a feature of it. At Mallia, the foundation course projected far enough from the rest of the wall to make a ledge that was wide enough to sit on. The fine masonry extended up to the top of the ground floor, but it seems likely that the upper floors – however many there were – were usually made of mudbricks. Some of these bricks were 50 × 40 × 12 centimetres. Occasionally entire houses were made of mudbrick, but usually the ground floors were stone and the mudbricks were reserved for upper floors and partition walls (Plate 8).

Wooden columns, often painted red, were used on a lavish scale in the temples, though less commonly in smaller buildings. The largest column, which was at Phaistos, had a diameter approaching 1 metre. The columns normally tapered downward, the broad end of the inverted tree trunk supporting the capital and architrave beams. To stop the foot of the column from slipping sideways, the stone base was often given a roughened top or a shallow mortise pit into which a tenon projecting from the foot of the column fitted. The columns were usually smooth and circular in section (Plate 11), but some were ribbed or fluted: some were even given spiral flutes like sticks of barley sugar. The frescoes show us what the colonnades looked like and capitals of varying designs can be inferred from them; some of the stone pedestal lamps seem to be miniature versions of the full-sized timber columns. So far, no large stone capitals have been identified, although a small capital has survived in the house ruins to the south-west of the Knossos Labyrinth. Evans' 'reconstituted' columns at Knossos have a typical cushion-shaped capital, but some were evidently cuboid.

The columns carried hefty ceiling or roof beams, sometimes spanning 5 metres, but usually less. Some of the beams, at the Temple Tomb for instance, were 50 centimetres square in cross-section. It is clear from the lavish way in which timber beams were used, both in houses and temples, that plenty of timber was available in Minoan Crete. The Minoans made flat roofs by laying branches and brushwood across the rafters and adding layers

*Figure 19* The Tripartite Shrine in the Knossos Labyrinth. A reconstruction

of earth and stamped clay on top. No doubt the roofs of the more prestigious buildings were coated with layers of cement.

Interior walls were normally coated with a fine lime plaster. Sometimes, where a richer effect was required, a veneer of thin slabs of veined gypsum was added. Sometimes a fresco was added to the plaster above a gypsum dado. Floors were sometimes plastered, especially in light-wells or court-yards, with small pebbles mixed in with the plaster. Other floors were made of beaten earth, wooden boards or flag stones. Sometimes a chamber was given a floor of mixed materials, with a flagstone edge and a panel of painted plaster, occasionally adorned with a fresco, in the middle.

How far stone was used decoratively is hard to judge. The ruins of the Knossos Labyrinth have yielded some stone friezes carved with rosettes, spirals and half-rosettes carved in relief, but these seem to have been exceptional. At Knossos too the wall and ceiling plaster was in some rooms modelled into relief forms, sometimes abstract, like the spiral reliefs found in the North Sector, sometimes representational, like the Bull Relief from the North Entrance Passage or the Bull-Grappling Fresco from the East Wing.

Ensuring the water supply for the towns during the dry Cretan summers must always have been a problem. The Minoans built cisterns or water tanks

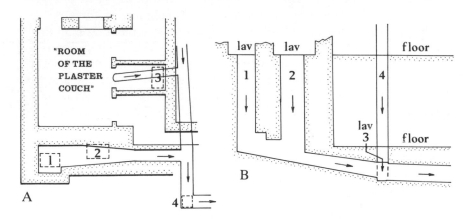

*Figure 20* Three water-closets in the East Wing of the Knossos Labyrinth. A: ground-floor plan of the area Evans called 'the Queen's Toilet'. The large space he called 'the Room of the Plaster Couch' was probably a vestry or robing room. 1: vertical soil pipe from lavatory on first floor. Access to the lavatory was by way of a door from the room directly above the Room of the Plaster Couch. 2: soil pipe from lavatory on first floor. Access to this lavatory was from a room to the south. 3: soil pipe for lavatory on ground floor. 4: rain-water conduit, probably leading from roof. Arrows indicate downward gradient of channels and therefore direction of flow of rain-water and sewage. B: section from west to east. 'lav' indicates location of lavatory

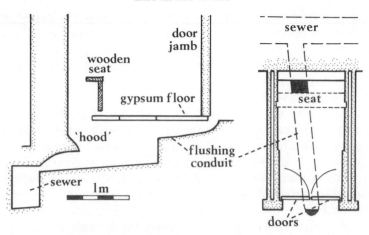

*Figure 21* Detail of ground-floor water-closet in the Labyrinth. Section (left) and plan (right). Detail of lavatory 3 on Figure 20

and lined them with water-resistant plaster. Often these were circular, as at Zakro and Tylissos, with flights of steps leading down into them. Whether the cisterns were purely for water supply or had some ritual function as well is open to question. Certainly the plumbing arrangements in the Minoan towns were elaborate. There were covered stone slab-built drains at Knossos to carry away sewage. The remains at Knossos show clearly how rain-water was led down from the roof by way of light-wells to flush out sewage from three lavatories in the East Wing (Figure 20). The Room of the Plaster Couch was apparently a vestry, robing room or cloakroom: the 'couch' was probably a stand for water ewers. Water was poured through the hole in the floor immediately outside the lavatory door: an under-floor channel linked the hole with the vertical soil pipe under the lavatory seat. The lavatory could thus be flushed even during a rainless summer, either by an attendant outside the lavatory or by the user (Figure 21).

There were also jointed clay pipes, each one a tapering tube with lugs on its sides so that it could be tied to the next. It was an ingenious system, by which the pipes could be laid straight or in curves, not unlike the rubbish chutes used in the building trade today. Evans thought the clay pipes at Knossos were used to bring water into the palace from outside. This would have been very difficult, because the site is on a low hill and some means would have had to be found for overcoming the unfavourable gradients; a siphon effect has been suggested, but that would have involved making the whole length of piping airtight, which seems scarcely credible. An alternative is that the pipes were carried across the valleys from higher ground on the far side by means of high (and now completely vanished) aqueducts.

An elaborate system of rain-water drains can be seen, reconstructed by Evans, at the East Entrance. An open clay channel runs down one side of the labyrinthine staircase. On each landing, a small rectangular settling tank was provided as a sediment trap. More substantial stone drains were fitted into the light-wells, cellars or courtyards known as the Room of the Stone Drainhead and the Court of the Stone Spout. Water travelled along well-made open stone drains 25 metres from the former to the latter, and from there into a vertical soak-away (Plate 9).

The interiors of some houses, shrines and temples were richly decorated with frescoes. The earliest known frescoes date to the time of the second temples, i.e. from 1700 BC onwards. Walls seem to have been painted in flat colour washes even earlier. There are Early Minoan fragments of coloured plaster from Knossos, Vasiliki, and Fournou Korifi; the favoured colour then was a dark red, a colour which, later at any rate, came to symbolize the underworld. From the beginning of the first temples, around 1900 BC, walls were sometimes decorated with simple geometric patterns in white and red. It was only when the new temples were built that pictorial frescoes were attempted.

The Saffron-Gatherer Fresco, found in the Lotus Lamp Sanctuary at Knossos, is reckoned to be one of the earliest. Against a background of dark red we see a blue monkey gathering crocuses into a pot. The head is missing, and Evans originally thought that the figure was that of a boy; it is now seen as a monkey. Blue was the conventional colour for monkeys in ancient Egypt and, apparently, in the Minoan culture too: monkeys in the Minoan frescoes on Thera were also painted blue. The monkey in the Knossos fresco was evidently a pet: it wears a red leather harness.

The art of the fresco painters developed from this beginning over the next 300 years to produce some of the most vivid and original images of the ancient world. The scale varied considerably. Sometimes whole walls were treated, or even whole rooms. Sometimes long narrow friezes were designed to run along the upper part of a wall. Sometimes small panels were painted, apparently so that a sequence of tableaux could be shown. Human figures vary in size from more than life size down to only 3 or 4 centimetres in the so-called Miniature Frescoes.

Most of the frescoes have been found at the Knossos Labyrinth and the 'palace' of Agia Triadha, but it is likely that many other buildings also had frescoes originally. It seems that frescoes were also executed on floors. The Dolphin Fresco in the Dolphin Sanctuary at Knossos may originally have graced the floor of an upper chamber in the East Wing. The floor of a shrine beside the Agia Triadha palace had a similar floor-fresco showing dolphins, octopus and fish.

The technique for producing the Minoan frescoes varied. Some were frescoes in the truest sense: colours were applied to wet plaster and left to sink into it as the plaster dried. Others were painted on to a dry plaster surface. Still others were produced by means of a curious inlay technique. After the initial fresco painting had dried, some areas requiring more detailed work were cut away, and refilled and recoloured with fresh wet plaster. In some set-piece frescoes, life-sized figures of men, bulls, and griffins were moulded in low relief; this seems to have happened in the period 1550–1470 BC, but not later. The famous 'Priest-King Fresco' is of this type.

The colours used for fresco painting were for the most part easily obtained: red ochre, yellow ochre, black (either from charred bone or from carbonaceous shale) and blue (from a copper-tinted glass). An analysis of the paints used on the Agia Triadha sarcophagus shows that some paints had a more exotic origin: the blue seems to be ground lapis lazuli.

Sinclair Hood (1971) says that some of the fresco subjects were secular, but the evidence points increasingly to a pervasive religious content. Even the landscapes, birds and animals may have had a religious significance (see Chapter 6). Landscapes are treated unusually, in frescoes and also in sealstones, as if seen from the air or through a fish-eye lens. Rocks and plants project into the pictures from the top as well as from the bottom, rather like stalactites and stalagmites in a cave. It is a very different approach from that of the ancient Egyptians.

The naturalistic treatment of plants and animals is deceptive: it is often quite inaccurate. The rock-rose, for instance, is given six petals instead of five. Some plants defy identification. The mythic animals are an even stronger reminder that the fresco artists were depicting another world than the everyday one; it is a symbolic world where general concepts such as fecundity were more important than accuracy of detail. A favourite plant in the frescoes is the papyrus, treated in various decorative ways: but the papyrus did not, as far as we know, grow in Crete in the Minoan period, so the frescoes do not factually depict the Cretan landscape. The papyrus may have been a borrowing from Egyptian art which to the Minoans held some symbolic value. Certainly we should not see the Minoan frescoes as simple interior decoration. From the Minoan colony of Thera, where more complete frescoes survive, comes strong evidence that frescoes were indicators of a precise ritual function for a chamber. The position of the frescoes mattered a great deal and also, according to Nanno Marinatos (1984), their visibility: it was important that certain frescoes should only become visible at certain stages in the ritual – hence the pier-and-door partitions.

URBANIZATION IN THE FIRST TEMPLE PERIOD, 1900–1700 BC

One problem in tracing the development of Minoan towns is that the Later Minoan buildings in many cases replaced and obliterated every sign of the Middle Minoan buildings, which in turn effaced Early Minoan buildings. We can see clearly what life was like in Early Minoan Fournou Korifi, because the site was more or less abandoned after that period. Nevertheless, we can

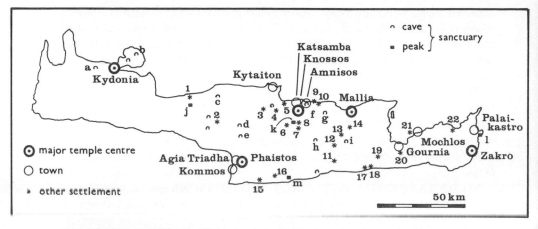

*Figure 22* Map of Minoan Crete. Settlements (other than those named on map):
1 – Rethymnon, 2 – Monastiraki, 3 – Sklavokampos, 4 – Tylissos, 5 – Gazi,
6 – Temenos, 7 – Vathypetro, 8 – Arkhanes, 9 – Agii Theodhori, 10 – Niru Khani,
11 – Vianno, 12 – Erganos, 13 – Plati, 14 – Karfi, 15 – Leben, 16 – Koumasa,
17 – Myrtos Pyrgos, 18 – Fournou Korifi, 19 – Kalamavka, 20 – Vasiliki, 21 – Pseira,
22 – Sitia. Cave sanctuaries: a – Kera Spiliotissa, b – Leras, c – Pankalochori,
d – Idaian Cave, e – Kamares, f – Eileithyia, g – Skotino, h – Arkalochori,
i – Psychro (Diktaian). Peak sanctuaries: j – Vrisinas, k – Juktas, l – Petsophas,
m – Kophinas

gain some insight into Minoan town life in the First Temple period from
boreholes and test pits dug through the ruins of later buildings.

Another problem is the apparent incompleteness of the map of Minoan
Crete (Figure 22). It seems peculiar that Minoan sites are concentrated in
central and eastern Crete, while western Crete is, apparently, relatively
empty. Were there really no major settlements in western Crete other than
Kydonia, Aptera, and Rethymnon? On the evidence, it would seem so, but
it may be that more intensive archaeological prospecting in western Crete
will reveal many more Minoan sites. One that is emerging as a likely temple
centre is Monastiraki, in the Amari valley to the west of Mount Ida. On a low
hill, houses were clustered round an important building with store-rooms,
storage jars, and a collection of seal impressions; it seems logical to interpret
this large building as a temple, even if smaller in scale than the temples found
in other Minoan towns. In the centre of the island, at Knossos and Phaistos,
a Middle Minoan I–II temple also dominated a growing township: at the
eastern end of Crete, the same thing was happening at Zakro.

At this time the agricultural techniques and crafts seen in the Early
Minoan period were developed further. In the Early Minoan, the villages
were oriented principally towards subsistence production. Now, in the
Middle Minoan, they were geared to the production of surpluses. The style,
level of organization and the contents of the urban temples strongly imply

control over a rural hinterland, although the precise nature of that control is a matter for speculation. It may be that the temples, through their bureaucracy, were able to set quotas on production in the rural villages; these may have been specified taxes, or tribute, or they may have been expressed as required offerings. Alternatively, the power of religious belief may have been such that each community gave as much as it could afford. But, however it was organized and expressed, the extensive store-rooms of the temples needed a very large inflow of produce from the rural areas to fill them. At Knossos, the West Magazines of the New Temple (built around 1700 BC) are thought to match closely the area of the store-rooms in the Old Temple (built in 1930 BC). At Phaistos, some of the pithoi and store-rooms from the First Temple Period survive, projecting 5 metres further to the west than the storage area of the later temple, and extending under its West Court.

The large temples, Knossos, Phaistos, Zakro and Mallia, must have depended on an income of agricultural produce from fairly extensive rural hinterlands, from many villages, many estates. On the other hand, small temples like the one at Gournia and those towns, like Palaikastro, which apparently managed without temples, may have organized the agricultural

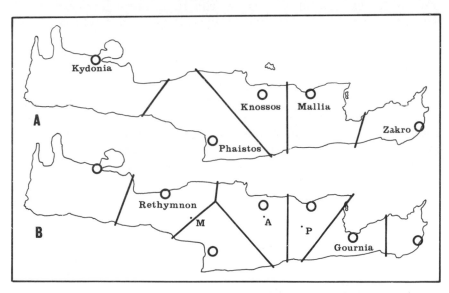

*Figure 23* Major territories centred on urban temples. A: the possible territorial boundaries of the five great temples, applying Thiessen polygons. B: territorial boundaries if Rethymnon and Gournia are added to create territories that are more equal in area. Note that Monastiraki (M), Arkhanes (A) and Plati (P) are also believed to have had temples. If they also commanded territories, the sizes of the territories would become less satisfactory again, with Knossos commanding a rather small territory

production of their own estates near by on a scale that was commensurate with their size and rate of population growth.

A very significant change in the towns of the First or Old Temple Period was the development of the temples as major craft centres. The concentration of craftsmen and skills in the temples had profound effects. Isolating the craftsmen in this way implies that they were, by this time if not before, full-time specialists under temple patronage. Concentrating and juxtaposing the different crafts also had the effect of cross-fertilizing ideas, both artistic and technical, and paving the way for striking and ambitious new developments. Fine pottery was manufactured in the temple workshops, and it was destined to travel far, both in Crete and overseas. But this movement into the temples must not be overstated. There continued to be local craft centres scattered round the island. There must, for example, have been an industry in the Mesara Plain to supply the large numbers of votive figurines that are found in the tombs of that region.

The temple building at Mallia was, as at Knossos, preceded by the development of an important Early Minoan village into a small township. The first temple at Mallia, raised in about 1900 BC, was equipped with storage rooms, but it is clear that other buildings, apparently houses, in the town of Mallia were also equipped with store-rooms. In other words, agricultural produce coming into Mallia was not all destined for the temple: some at least was going into private houses, presumably town houses belonging to the owners of estates in the countryside around Mallia.

Henri van Effenterre (1983) has tried valiantly to reconstruct Mallia's economic pattern, but with no conclusive results. He draws attention to Aristotle's description, in *Politics*, of food gathering and distribution in Crete. Although this seems to refer to a significantly later period, it can be made to relate to Mallia's early economy, in which some surplus food was stored in the larger private houses. Large houses existed in the north-west of the town of Mallia, round the *agora* and in the *Mu* quarter; they had their own store-rooms and their own clay tablet accounts. In other words, at this stage the organization was not completely centralized. There was a mixed economy, with a proportion of the agricultural production routed through the temples and a proportion through the private houses. Aristotle noted a distinction between income from the public land and that from the citizens' private estates.

Henri van Effenterre estimates that, if the population of Mallia was between 5,000 and 10,000, the neighbouring lowland district stretching from Stalis in the west to Milatos in the east would have provided the town with enough olive oil and to spare. This assumes a low consumption level of 15 litres of oil per person per year: in fact the citizens of Mallia may have used significantly more than this. The assumed grain requirement was 3 hecto-litres per head per year. The district has a grain production potential of around 6,000 hectolitres per year, which would not have been adequate to supply Mallia's Minoan population.

The large shortfall may have been met by supplies of grain from outside the immediate district. The most likely tributary area is the Lasithi Plain. It may be that as the town of Mallia grew, it outgrew its local territory and annexed the adjacent Lasithi territory. This is, at any rate, a possible scenario for the New Temple Period. It is nevertheless worth emphasizing that the estimates of population, storage capacity, agricultural yields and food consumption are all based on incomplete evidence; so, interesting though this line of thought may be, no conclusions can be reached yet. We have, for example, no quantified evidence of seafood-gathering or livestock-rearing at Mallia.

## TOWNS IN THE SECOND (NEW) TEMPLE PERIOD, 1700–1470 BC

In 1700 BC, the first temples were destroyed, possibly by earthquakes. The destruction of the temples and the towns round them led directly to a rebuilding programme. It is principally the ruins of the New Temple and Late Temple Periods that we see at Minoan sites today.

In the New Temple Period, the towns remained important foci for large areas. The temples in their turn were elaborated and apparently enlarged: their importance in relation to the towns and the rural hinterlands continued to be at least as great, if not greater. In general, the patterns established in the First Temple Period were maintained. The plans of the towns, for instance, continued to follow the irregular plans established before 1700, but they were extended. Most of the towns were on or near the coast and they exploited their site advantages, capitalizing on their access to sea routes and on the fertile soils of their hinterlands.

Palaikastro in eastern Crete typifies dozens of small Minoan towns. It covered at least 22,000 square metres and possibly twice that area, consisting of rather irregular blocks of houses separated by cobbled streets. The ground-floor rooms were used for storage, cooking and other work: from them stairways rose to the living and sleeping quarters upstairs. Pseira, located on an island close to the north coast, was a similar sort of town – a town without an identifiable temple.

Knossos, Mallia and Zakro belong to a second type of Minoan town: one where the settlement surrounds and is dominated by an important temple. Adjacent to the temple there were further important buildings, some perhaps houses, others perhaps sanctuaries. At Phaistos, Gournia and Myrtos Pyrgos, these intermediate buildings seem to have been absent: instead, a temple or equivalent large building stood on a hill summit, dominating a town quarter of small houses.

The architecture of the great Minoan temples is too large and complex a subject to deal with here, and a discussion of the temples' religious function is reserved for Chapter 6 below. Here, the focus is on the temples' place in the growth of the towns.

At Mallia, the Central Court existed in the First Temple Period, with rooms ranged at least along its western side; as at Phaistos and Knossos, the new temple was apparently preceded by an earlier one on the same site. But the Mallia site (Plates 10 and 11) may prove to be more complicated than this, in view of the fairly recent discovery made to the west of the 'Second Temple' site; there was a large building, at least 1,700 square metres in area, with at least 60 rooms and open light-wells or courts, although no great courtyard, the distinctive feature which typifies the Minoan temple. The large early building dates to the First, or Old, Temple Period and is the best-preserved building of that age so far found in Crete. What its function was and what relationship it bore to the building-complex which then stood on the site of the later temple has yet to be established.

The Phaistos temple rivals the Knossos temple in splendour; although it is smaller and seems, to judge from the remains, to have been decorated less lavishly, it has a spectacular location on a precipitous hilltop offering views across the Mesara Plain to the east and south-east and to Mount Ida in the north. It has many features in common with the Knossos Labyrinth. It was rebuilt in about 1700 BC, although to a significantly different plan and at a

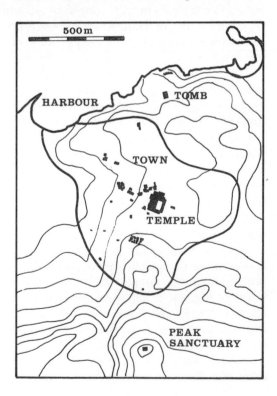

*Figure 24* Mallia. The solid line marks the approximate boundary of the built-up area. The Chrysolakkos tomb seems to have been situated on the outskirts of the town, just like the cemeteries at Knossos. Mallia's peak sanctuary, on the low hill of Prophitis Ilias, is one of the lowest in Crete

higher level, so that the lower wall-courses of the earlier temple and its west façade are still visible on the west side, now that the site has been excavated to the earlier courtyard level. The West Court has a paved entry from the north, but by way of steps down rather than a ramp up. There are two flights of broad steps at right angles to each other, descending to the paved courtyard: the arrangement is reminiscent of the Theatral Area at Knossos, though at Phaistos it is located in the north-east corner of the West Court. There are corridor-like store-rooms in the West Wing, though not as extensive as those at Knossos. There is a bench-lined sanctuary opening out of the west side of the Central Court, but without a throne and without an antechamber or *en suite* lustral basin. A major suite of chambers with pier-and-door partitions, colonnades and light-wells comparable to the so-called 'royal apartments' at Knossos is located in the northern sector, not in the East Wing: it has a lustral area attached to it. There is also a workshop area.

The architectural parallels are numerous and striking enough for us to assume that the large buildings at Phaistos and Knossos had a similar function. If the Knossos Labyrinth was a temple-complex, then so too was the large building at Phaistos. The differences between the two buildings seem to be mainly differences of style and emphasis, not differences of overall purpose. There is, for instance, a showy and large-scale entrance to the Phaistos temple at the north-west corner; at the equivalent point in the Knossos Labyrinth there seems to have been no entrance at all, in spite of the arguments of Arthur Evans and James Walter Graham (see Castleden 1989, pp. 12 and 189). There was also a straight and direct access route by way of a corridor in the middle of the West Wing, whereas at Knossos there was a long and circuitous route by way of the Procession Corridor, which doubles back on itself before arriving at the southern end of the Central Court; the Phaistos entrance seems closer in spirit to the more direct west-east access corridor of the Knossos First Temple. It seems as if the Central Court at Phaistos was rather more public than that at Knossos.

Although it is smaller, Phaistos has an additional court, the Peristyle Court, to the north of the Central Court: there seems to have been no comparable courtyard at Knossos. A peculiarity of Phaistos is its two sets of 'royal apartments', one in the northern sector, one in the East Wing. The existence of the two suites argues strongly against the royal apartment interpretation. The idea that the northern suite was used in summer and the eastern in winter does not convince. A significant difference between Phaistos and Knossos arises because virtually the whole of the first temple at Phaistos was replaced when the site was redeveloped after the 1700 BC destruction: only the Central Court remained. As a result, the new temple was built to a single co-ordinated design, and the site levelled and terraced to allow it to extend over a wider area of the hill summit. It is hard to disentangle the building sequence at Knossos, but the final layout seems not

*Figure 25* The Minoan Temple at Knossos: a reconstruction of the 'ground-floor' plan. 1 – Theatral Area, 2 – North-West Portico, 3 – Initiation Area, with adyton, 4 – Induction Hall and Vestibule, 5 – North-West Entrance Passage, 6 – Lotus Lamp Sanctuary, 7 – West Store-Rooms, 8 – Lower West Wing Corridor, 9 – Throne Sanctuary, 10 – Snake Goddess Sanctuary, 11 – West Pillar Crypt, 12 – East Pillar Crypt, 13 – Tripartite Shrine, 14 – Colonnade of the Priestesses,

to be the result of a single overall plan, but to have grown by accretion and piecemeal development.

The temple at Knossos was, so far as we know, the most ambitious building the Minoans attempted. The overall plan, extending about 140 metres from north to south and the same from east to west, is roughly square; the outer walls have extensions and indents that imply design from the centre outwards. The clean outline of the rectangular Central Court was established first and the sanctuary suites aggregated round it. *The Knossos Labyrinth* (Castleden 1989) gives a detailed account of the temple's design and function. The completed building, as it stood in about 1400 BC, was a sprawling maze of chambers and corridors developed in different places to heights of two, three, or four storeys.

One of the most striking features of the Knossos Labyrinth was the richness of its decorations and ritual equipment. The interior walls were covered with elaborate frescoes depicting scenes from mythology and ritual, scenes of bull-leaping, processions of tribute-bearers and religious emblems, all designed to emphasize the building's religious dedication and to sign the function of individual rooms.

In the Procession Fresco, the fabrics worn by the Minoans were painstakingly covered with grids, apparently marked into the soft plaster with taut string; the resulting grid lines were used by the fresco painters to construct detailed textile patterns (Figure 6). Some of the patterns shown are so elaborate that it seems doubtful that they were woven: some may have been printed with blocks, while others may have been produced by a mixed-medium method, combining printing, embroidery, and appliqué work. Fragmentary and damaged though they are, the Knossos frescoes have yielded a vast amount of information about the world of the Minoans. One miniature fresco fragment shows a woman, perhaps a priestess, leaning

---

15 – Destroyed Sanctuary, 16 – Columnar Shrines, 17 – Cupbearer Sanctuary, 18 – West Porch/Entrance, 19 – West Porch Shrine, 20 – Procession Corridor, 21 – South Terrace, 22 – South-West Porch/Entrance, 23 – Stepped Portico or paved ramp, 24 – South Corridor (at lower level), 25 – Silver Vessels Sanctuary, 26 – South Porch/Entrance, 27 – North Entrance, 28 – South Pillar Hall, 29 – North Entrance Passage, 30 – Service Quarter, 31 – North-East Kamares Pottery Store, 32 – North-East Sanctuary, 33 – East Entrance, 34 – Temple Workshops, 35 – Double-Axe Sanctuary, 36 – Dolphin Sanctuary, 37 – Triton Shell Sanctuary, 38 – Late Dove Goddess Sanctuary, 39 – Monolithic Pillar Crypt, 40 – Pre-Temple buildings, 41 – House or Shrine of the Sacrificed Oxen, 42 – House or Shrine of the Fallen Blocks, 43 – Chancel Screen Sanctuary, 44 – South-East Sanctuary, 45 – Grand Staircase.

Arrows on staircase indicate 'down' direction, asterisks indicate temple repositories, and stippling indicates tell material not quarried away at this level. The winged circle indicates that the site was too badly damaged at the time of excavation for reconstruction to be more than tentative

on a balustrade rail; behind her is a net hanging across a window. Perhaps nets were hung over windows and doorways in the temples to keep out birds, and possibly dragon-flies and locusts.

The cult equipment of the Knossos Labyrinth was also very elaborate, and it demonstrates the extraordinarily high quality of Minoan craftsmanship; all kinds of vessel were used for offerings and ritual, made of pottery, stone, and faience.

The temples were much more than centres of worship. The tribute that poured into the temple store-rooms, dedicated variously to deities and sanctuaries, had to be recorded and redistributed. The clay tablets of the Knossos temple archive record such large quantities of produce that it seems as if the temple was at the very centre of the organization of the Minoan economy. As I have argued elsewhere (1989, pp. 169–71), the temple functioned rather like a great medieval abbey, drawing and re-allocating large revenues from the surrounding area and thereby developing into a major centre of wealth and power.

Some of the pottery found in the temple at Knossos says that it is 'royal', but this may mean no more than 'state' or 'official' or even that the pottery was made by state potters (Haskell 1983). The king is but rarely mentioned even in the archive tablets, where the preoccupation is with lists of offerings and the deities and sanctuaries to which they were dedicated. The implication is that the king was housed elsewhere. There were doubtless all kinds of subtly poised relationships between the royal household and administration on the one hand and the temple priesthood and its administration on the other. It may be that some of the produce offered to the temple for the gods and goddesses was discreetly diverted to the royal household; it may also be, as with many later monarchies, that the royal authority depended on the religious establishment for validation.

The Labyrinth dominates our thinking about Knossos, but it must not be forgotten that the temple was surrounded by a Minoan city, most of which remains unexcavated. Some of it has been disturbed by later developments: the site of the Early Iron Age, classical and Hellenistic city of Knossos overlaps with that of the Minoan city (Hood and Smyth 1981) – but nevertheless much remains to be excavated. The best-known part of the Minoan city is the so-called 'Royal Road' which runs from the Theatral Area at the north-west corner of the temple towards the Bull's Head Sanctuary (or 'Little Palace') 200 metres away to the west-north-west (Plate 12). The road is typical of the Minoan roads of Knossos. There is a central lane 1.4 metres wide, which is made of two lines of large rectangular stone slabs. On each side there are slightly lower and narrower lanes made of smaller unshaped stones. Quite how these three lanes were deployed in Minoan times is not certain, though the differences in level imply that the central lane was kept dry in wet weather by draining to the side lanes. A similar lane design is apparent in the short section of curving roadway which has survived at the

Minoan village of Tylissos, just to the west of House C (Figure 13 and Plate 13). At Tylissos there are also 'sleeping policemen' – slabs crossing the entire roadway and rising some 3 centimetres above its general surface level – but their function is not clear. Was their purpose to debar wheeled vehicles from a congested part of the village, or to slow down and reduce the destructive effects of runoff during torrential rainstorms?

The Royal Road passed through what seems to have been a densely built-up area of the Minoan city. To one side were houses, including the House of the Frescoes, and workshops. The Late Minoan debris of an ivory carver's workshop was found to have been destroyed by fire. On the other side were more houses and a large building tentatively identified as an armoury or arsenal. After running dead straight for about 160 metres, the Royal Road reaches the modern road from Heraklion. At this point the Minoan road reaches a crossroads; the Royal Road continues (underground now) westwards past the south fronts of the Bull's Head Sanctuary and Unexplored Mansion and past more Minoan houses, including the House of the Sacrificed Children, discovered by Peter Warren in 1979. The northern fork, branching off the Royal Road, runs along the east front of the Bull's Head Sanctuary. The road leading south from the crossroads seems to have followed the course of the modern road and may have led to the south-west corner of the Labyrinth's West Court, where a part of an access road has been exposed.

The Knossian roads were laid out in straight sections, but without any overall geometric plan. Curiously, the contrasting paved/cobbled texture of the road surface continues into open courtyard areas round the temple. In the Theatral Area and the West Court, raised linear pathways of well-made slabs pass through open areas of irregular cobbling, and show us clearly the main lines of movement through these courtyards: they emphasize the North Entrance and West Porch of the temple as important destinations.

From the Labyrinth's south-west entrance a paved ramp, now eroded beyond recognition, led down to a bridge over the Vlychia stream; on the south side this was supported on a finely built stone viaduct, which carried the road on south-eastwards along the north front of the Pilgrim Hostel and then southwards between yet more Minoan houses. On the southern edge of the Minoan city, the road passed through a cemetery: the Temple Tomb was the principal building in this area.

Immediately to the north of the temple stood several substantial buildings: the North-East House, North House, North Pillar Hall and Balustrade Sanctuary (or 'Royal Villa'). Further off in that direction, on the site of the modern village of Makroteichos, there were Minoan houses and traces of Minoan houses have been found as far north as Palaiomilo, some 600 metres north of the temple precinct: beyond this area was the northern cemetery of Zafer Papoura. The archaeological evidence is necessarily very incomplete, but it suggests that the temple was at the centre of a town whose built-up area was approximately 1,200 metres from north to south and 800 metres from east to west.

At Zakro, both temple and town have been excavated. The temple is easily identifiable by its long, rectangular Central Court, in this case oriented north-north-east to south-south-west. A large room at its northern end was a kitchen and there was probably a refectory above it, on the first floor. The West Wing contained chambers which Sinclair Hood (1971, p. 66) interprets as state apartments, although they might better be interpreted as sanctuaries; the chambers behind are admitted, by their excavator, Nicolas Platon (1971, p. 257), to be ritual in nature. A collection of cult equipment came from one room and an archive tablet collection from another. From the upper floor of the West Wing came bronze tools, bronze ingots and elephant tusks. It is not clear whether there were actually craft workshops in the West Wing at Zakro but, if so, it seems to be a significant departure from the pattern observed at the other temples, where the votive workshops were in the east, as at Knossos, or north-east, as at Phaistos.

The East Wing rooms have been interpreted by Platon and Hood as royal living quarters, like those at Knossos; a lustral basin is represented as a bathroom connected with these. Nevertheless, there is every reason to see the lustral basin, originally embellished with unequivocally religious frescoes, as a special chthonic shrine. The East Wings of both Knossos and Zakro make better sense interpreted as sanctuaries (see Castleden 1989, pp. 48–51, 90–2).

Steps in the south-east corner of the Central Court led down into a well which was used, at least in the temple's final days, for offerings: there were many small clay vases, one of which still had olives in it when excavated. The alleged royal suite opened onto a colonnade to east and west: that to the east led to a square courtyard with a circular spring chamber in it. A rectangular spring chamber nearby seems to have been accessible only from outside the temple. These may have been used for normal, secular water supply, or they may have had some cult use.

The visible temple remains at Zakro seem to belong entirely to the New Temple Period. Its site was evidently occupied beforehand – the outer walls near the main entrance in the eastern corner extend across the remains of earlier houses – but it is not yet known whether a temple stood there. As at Knossos and Mallia, the temple grew up symbiotically with its adjacent town, but at Zakro we can see the whole urban structure. A paved road ascends the gentle gradient from the east, leading from the now-drowned site of the Minoan harbour, through the lower town to the main gate of the temple. This gate must have been a conspicuous structure, since its footings project some 8 metres from the eastern corner of the temple. Curiously, the Zakro temple is oriented with its corners, not its sides, facing the cardinal compass points: in this respect, it is reminiscent of the early 'proto-temple' at Vasiliki.

The paved road continues westwards past the main temple gate and connects with the road network of the upper town. Another road leads away at right angles to it, in front of the temple gate, and ascends the hillside. A large area of the town has been excavated and left continuously exposed, stretching some 80 metres along the slope and 40 metres up it. The layout is very similar to that of Gournia, with narrow cobbled alleys weaving irregularly among blocks of houses, many of which had rather small chambers, cellars perhaps, on the ground floor. Where it differs significantly from Gournia is in being situated in the bottom of a steep-sided valley instead of on a low hill; in a sense, the Zakro site is the mirror image of that of Gournia. The Gournia temple crowns a hill summit, with a commanding view of the Mediterranean. The Zakro temple lies in the lowest part of the valley, frequently half-submerged by the rising water-table, and threatened by further sea-level rises.

### CRAFT WORKERS IN THE TOWNS

Crafts underwent a long evolution during the Early Minoan, an incubation that prepared the way for major developments in the Middle Minoan temples and towns. We have, for example, the potter's workshop at Fournou Korifi, the carpenter's tool-kit found at Khamaizi and the three almost identical dog-handled schist jars; these instances show a significant degree of craft specialization in the Early Minoan (Branigan 1983).

Most of the evidence we find for full-time craftsmen nevertheless comes from the temples of the Middle and Late Minoan periods, so we should see the main period of craft industries as belonging to an urban society and in particular to the temples within that urban society. There were lapidaries in the temple workshops at Knossos, Mallia and Phaistos, bronze-smiths at Phaistos, seal carvers at Knossos, ivory carvers at Zakro. Craft specialization is often subsidized at the redistribution centre in a chiefdom society, so we should expect to see crafts flourishing in the temple culture of bronze age Crete: we should also expect to see craftsmen gathering in the temples, where the agricultural surpluses and imports were collected and redistributed. From the economic and organizational standpoint, it was very natural for the craftsmen to have become concentrated in workshops in the temples.

At the same time, there were craftsmen working outside the temples. For example, ivory carvers and stone vase makers worked in premises along the Royal Road in Knossos. Whether these craftsmen were independent or worked under the aegis of the temple, which was close at hand, is hard to judge.

Certainly there were part-time specialists operating in settlements like Palaikastro which had no temple, so it was possible for them to work geographically separate from the temple centres. But even there it is hard to be sure that there was no ultimate control from the temples. We know from the temple archives at Knossos that the geographical reach of the administrators was exceptional, so it is possible that ivory carvers in Palaikastro were employed and controlled by the Zakro priests. Concentrations of workshops, such as those along the Knossos Royal Road, in the East Wing of the Knossos Labyrinth, and in the Northern Quarter of Gournia, suggest another possibility – that there were guilds of craft workers. The evidence so far gathered is very inadequate, so we could not be sure, but there does seem to be some tendency to concentrate. Guilds could be the answer, or alternatively some form of temple control: either way, the tablets imply a minutely ordered society.

### Makers of stone vases

In the manufacture of stone vases, the Minoans displayed enormous patience, as well as very high levels of confidence and skill. It was a craft that evolved into an art form, as they attempted more and more ambitious shapes in a widening range of materials. Perhaps the most extraordinary creation was a libation vessel in the form of a shell, yet made out of a block of hard and brittle obsidian. The great majority of the vessels made were simpler. The first stage in making a stone vase was to rough out its external shape: then the interior was hollowed out by a combination of drilling and chiselling. Sometimes a ring of holes was made and the core knocked out, and sometimes a larger solid drill was used instead. The drill might be made of wood or bronze, using sand or emery, imported from Naxos, as an abrasive. The exterior of the vase was then finished and both surfaces, inside and out, were ground smooth with a stone.

The initial idea of making vases out of solid stone was probably a foreign import. Egyptian stone vases reached Crete before the bronze age began; the Cretan industry, which had started as early as 2500 BC, nevertheless post-dated the arrival of these foreign vases. To begin with, the Cretan vases were made out of chlorite or chlorite schist, but the vase makers soon branched out into other materials, favouring especially the relatively soft and easily worked serpentine which can be found in various parts of central and eastern Crete.

By the time the first temples were built, in 1900 BC, craftsmen had the confidence to attempt harder stones which had more attractive colours and textures, such as mottled breccias and orange stalactite. The technique had developed to such an extent by the New Temple Period, beginning in 1700 BC, that vases were being made out of obsidian and rock crystal: for example, the beautiful crystal rhyton from Zakro.

Perhaps the commonest stone vessels were those that were compact in form, like birds' nests, but more ambitious forms were attempted even from the beginning, such as the circular pot-lids with handles in the form of a reclining dog, made, apparently in some numbers, at Mochlos in around

*Figure 26* A stone vase from the
temple at Zakro

2500 BC. Very large numbers of stone vases were deposited as grave goods in the early communal tombs of the Mesara plain; there were some fine examples deposited in early tombs at Mochlos too. Often the earliest jars and vases were decorated with hatched incised triangles and spirals in relief, in much the same style as the cosmetic jars made in the Cyclades: probably the designs were copied from Cycladic models.

Although some of the designs and the technique of vase making were borrowed from abroad, the Minoans developed the technique in a quite extraordinary way. By the time of the first temples, the making of stone vases had become widespread, with the production of buckets, jars, bowls and lamps designed to be used both in the house and the temple. It was in this first temple period that the Minoan vase makers began to tackle hard exotic stones, like the *rosso antico* from the Greek mainland and the white-speckled obsidian from Yiali near Karpathos in the Dodecanese. A typical stone vase maker's workshop from this period has been identified at Mallia.

It was in the period after 1700 BC that the stone vase makers' art reached unparalleled heights. The dark, blue-black serpentine which had been popular before was still used a great deal, but now new materials were tried out as well – alabaster, gypsum, limestone, marble and breccia – and some extremely hard rocks like porphyry. A plain black obsidian which the Minoan craftsmen tried may have come from the Çiftlik area of Cappadocia. The green speckled Spartan basalt used at Knossos came from the south Peloponnese; a store-room in the East Wing of the Knossos Labyrinth held a supply of Spartan basalt blocks at the time of the temple's abandonment in 1380 BC. Some relatively soft Egyptian alabaster was imported and at least forty vases were made from it by Minoan craftsmen. Occasionally, Minoan vase makers took Egyptian vases and adapted them, often painstakingly and with great ingenuity, to suit the tastes of their Minoan masters and mistresses. One, that was eventually exported to Mycenae, had been turned upside down, transforming its mouth into a pedestal base, and its original base had been sawn off and replaced with a moulded rim of gilded bronze; then a pair of wooden handles and a spout were added, completing the transformation of the Egyptian vessel into a Minoan jar.

The relief-picture offering vases or rhytons were probably the most remarkable of the vase makers' creations. They were designed for ritual use and some of them were coated in gold leaf. The Harvester, Boxer, and Chieftain Vases and the Peak Sanctuary Rhyton are all made of a close-grained black steatite and decorated with highly detailed reliefs showing ritual scenes (Figure 56).

By the end of the New Temple Period, the art of making vases out of stone had become a very specialized and rare craft. It had become purely a temple art. The final chapter of the vase makers' story is shrouded in mystery. The art seems to have died out in Crete altogether, yet mysteriously reappeared in Mycenae in the thirteenth century BC; Sinclair Hood (1978) has suggested that after the conquest of Minoan Crete by Myceneans, the finest craftsmen may have been taken by force to the mainland and made to work for new masters.

*Workers in metal*

The existence of metal vases and bowls can be inferred from pottery objects which imitate metal models, sometimes even to the extent of having fake rivets and fake chain-links added. The direct survival of the metal originals has been patchy, but there is evidence of a fairly large-scale metal-working industry in Minoan Crete, producing copper and bronze vessels. A hoard of 153 silver cups and one gold cup found at Tôd in Upper Egypt may have come originally from Minoan workshops; the vessels appear to be Middle Minoan IB work, which was produced in Crete between 2000 and 1900 BC, and were found in an Egyptian deposit which has been dated fairly precisely to about 1920 BC. The Tôd cups were apparently offered as tribute from a Syrian king, perhaps the king of Byblos, which implies that there were complex and long-distance exchanges of goods in the twentieth century BC. Another metal object of Minoan origin, a spouted jug dating from 1850 BC, was found among the grave goods of a prince of Byblos.

Certainly by the year 2000 BC, the tables of the Cretan rulers shone and glittered with drinking cups of gold and silver and, even in the century before the first temples were raised, those rulers were wearing elegant gold ornaments, not imported, but produced by Minoan craft workers.

By 1500 BC, the metal workers of Crete were producing a large range of cooking and storage utensils, including some large cauldrons made by riveting together several bronze sheets: some fine examples were found at

*Figure 27* Bronze objects from a tomb at Zafer Papoura, Knossos. The tripod in the foreground is a portable hearth or offering table made of plaster

Tylissos. Sheet bronze was also used for making armour. Hammered or cast, bronze could be made into tools: single-edged knives for cutting meat, razors, axes, adzes, axe-adzes, double-axes, double-adzes, chisels, sickles, hammers and saws. Throughout the Minoan period, Cretan craftsmen went on making stone axes and maces. Sometimes the workmanship in these archaic stone artefacts was very fine, and it is possible that they were used as insignia of rank, in much the same way as stone maces in the Wessex Culture in southern England; if so, it is curious that the same obsolete tool became associated with rank in two cultures that were geographically so widely separated.

Copper was found in Crete itself, especially in the Asterousi mountains bordering the Mesara plain, and some may have come from Chrysokamino, near the coast east of Pachyammos, but the demand for metal artefacts is likely to have been high enough for imports of copper to be necessary. The most likely foreign source is Cyprus. The bronze was cast in standard ingots that were about 0.9 metres long with inward-curving sides that made them easier to carry on the shoulder, as shown on one of the contemporary Egyptian tomb paintings depicting Minoan emissaries.

Gold was reserved for making ornaments, jewellery (pins, rings and bracelets) and decorative inlays of various kinds. Some of the stone vases were partially coated with gold leaf. Sometimes the ivory figurines of deities

*Figure 28* The Bee or Wasp Pendant
from Mallia

and bull-leapers were given details such as loincloths in gold. The overall
effect of, for example, a group of elaborately dressed and bejewelled
priestesses conducting a rite with carved and gilded cult objects against a
background of inlaid furniture, brightly painted pillars and multi-coloured
frescoes must have been one of dazzling opulence.

The temple goldsmiths at Mallia seem to have been outstanding. The
celebrated Wasp Pendant (Figure 28) came from a rich burial at Mallia, and
it is generally believed that at least some of the Aigina Treasure – found at
Aigina, but of unknown provenance – came from Mallia too. The nature-
god pendant found at Aigina looks very much like Middle Minoan III work,
dating from about 1600 BC; it may have been robbed from the Chrysolakkos
tomb at Mallia in antiquity. The large building to the west of the Mallia
temple yielded a gold-handled dagger with cut-out designs on its hilt, while
the temple itself yielded some magnificent long swords: one of them had a
pommel covered in gold sheet modelled to depict an acrobat (Figure 29).
The swords may have been ceremonial, or they may have been used in an
acrobatic ritual sword dance. The gold used by the Minoan smiths to make

*Figure 29* Acrobat on a gold sword hilt
from the temple at Mallia. Made in about
1550–1500 BC

all these fine objects was imported from the Egyptian gold mines in Sinai, from the Arabian desert and from Anatolia.

The gold cups found in a burial at Vaphio near Sparta on the Greek mainland were probably made by Cretan craftsmen, although Sinclair Hood (1978, p. 167) takes the rather odd position that one of the cups is of Mycenean origin, one of Minoan origin. There are slight stylistic differences in the execution of the relief work, and it may be that one cup is an exotic, a Minoan import, and the other was made by a Mycenean craftsman to make a pair; on balance, I think it more likely that both are Minoan (Figure 51).

A set of silver vessels was found in the Silver Vessels Sanctuary (Evans' South House) at Knossos, but relatively few vases made of precious metals have been found in Crete. This seems to be because temple, villa and tomb sites have been plundered – mainly in antiquity – rather than because of any original dearth. It is possible that a high-status tomb may yet be found entirely intact and that many gold and silver objects remain to be discovered by excavation. Nicolas Platon (1968, pp. 167–8) mentions the remarkable technique, perfected by the Minoan metal workers, by which superbly decorated daggers were produced. The technique, known as damascening, involved the addition of inlays of threads of silver and gold to bronze blades and hilts, and set off by patches or pools of black enamel; the designs depicted hunting scenes (Figure 10). Many artefacts decorated in this way

*Figure 30* Bronze worshipper from Tylissos

have been found in royal tombs on the mainland. Platon is convinced that the technique came from Crete; if that is so, it is likely that at least some damascened daggers await discovery at Minoan sites on Crete.

The bronze workers, in addition to making weapons, tools and utensils, were also producing figurines as votive offerings. Typically, the figurines which they made are 20 centimetres high and depict worshippers in attitudes of adoration, or reclining goats, or cattle. They were cast in solid bronze, apparently by the *cire perdue* method. The original model was made in wax; it was then encased in a clay mould and molten metal poured in through the feet; the hot metal melted the wax and displaced it, filling the mould. The metal filling the pouring hole was usually left untrimmed after it had cooled, so that many of the figurines have a peg under their bases: even the best figures – and some of them (see Figures 2 and 30) are very fine – may seem rather unfinished to modern eyes. The rough, bubbly surface often seen is possibly due to a shortage of tin in the alloy, which meant that the metal did not flow well. Even allowing for this, the surface was left just as it came out of the mould. The explanation may be that the figurines were not intended for use as ornaments but were votives to be left in shrines: they had a symbolic, not an aesthetic, role to play. Many were recovered from dark caves and rock crevices where they were not intended to be seen by mortal eyes.

## Makers of faience

The manufacture of faience objects was another highly specialized craft closely associated with temple worship; many of these objects have a religious significance and were probably made for cult use. The Minoans may have learnt the art of making faience, a glaze technique, from the Egyptians in about 2000 BC. The glaze consisted of a core of crushed quartz grains coated with glass, usually tinted blue or green by adding small amounts of copper compounds; the result was a richly glazed finish. At first, the technique was used for relatively simple objects, such as pendants and beads, but later it was applied to vases, statuettes and plaques.

The most outstanding collection of faience from the Minoan period is the one that was found in the Temple Repositories in the West Wing at Knossos, where cult vases, plaques, and the famous Snake Goddess statuettes were all treated in this way. The miniature faience robes are almost certainly votives standing for full-sized ceremonial robes that were offered to a goddess, either to dress an idol or to dress a priestess for a ceremony in which she somehow became the goddess. In the classical period and earlier it was quite common for statues of goddesses to be annually reinvested with robes. In Book 6 of the *Iliad*, we are told of an embroidered robe carried by a procession of old women to the Trojan Athena. At Athens itself, around the summer solstice, the image of Athena Polis was veiled, taken down, disrobed and washed, before being ceremonially reclothed in a new robe specially woven by the *arrhephoroi*. A similar rite seems to have taken place at the Temple of Artemis at Ephesus. The faience robes tell us that something similar happened in the Knossos Labyrinth too.

The Minoan faience artists achieved very high levels of technical ability. Quite how independent they were of other craftsmen, particularly in the temples, is impossible to judge, but the fact that many objects – and especially the cult objects – required the shared expertise of several different crafts implies collaboration. Potters, faience artists, pot painters, clay figurine makers, stone carvers and the priesthood probably worked closely together, sharing ideas that would glorify their deities.

### Shell and ivory workers

In the New Temple Period (1700–1470 bc), inlays made of shell were applied to wooden chests and other furniture. Often only broken fragments of these inlays survive, and nothing of the item of furniture to which they were attached, so it is difficult to visualize the original effect or even the extent of the shell decoration. A plaque from Agios Onoufrios near Phaistos shows the head of a man with moustache and beard. A rectangular plaque from the Phaistos temple shows, in relief, four animal-headed figures in long robes with tasselled belts; it was originally fixed to a curving surface, probably of wood, by means of nails at the four corners (Figure 49). An irregularly shaped plaque from the Throne Sanctuary at Knossos shows a sheathed dagger hanging from a decorative belt.

The shell used for this decorative work was probably the oyster-like *Spondylus gaederopus*, which is native to the Aegean. The Minoans did not invent the technique of carving shell: it was used earlier, in the Cyclades, for making figurines and bracelets.

The craft of the ivory carvers has attracted more attention. Some of the early ivory seals made on Crete seem to have been strongly influenced by Syrian originals, which suggests that the craft may have been introduced from Syria. Ivory was used, like shell, to decorate wooden boxes and other pieces of furniture. Probably the most spectacular example of this is the large gaming or divination board found in the East Wing of the Knossos Labyrinth: it was covered with plaques of ivory, plated with gold and further decorated with plaques of crystal backed with silver or blue paste. The wooden box to which all these fittings were fixed probably contained the gaming pieces, which were as likely as not also made of ivory. The early temple at Phaistos yielded some small ivory pieces carved in the shape of a bull's leg and a lion's head: the lion's mane was coated in gold.

The temples seem to have had their own ivory carvers, but it is known that ivory carving also went on at Palaikastro, where there was no temple. Some finished ivory plaques were found there, as well as a piece of unworked tusk. Generally, though, ivory seems to have been concentrated in and near the temples. At Zakro, there were ivories shaped like double-axes. In the Silver Vessels Sanctuary at Knossos there was an ivory of a griffin biting a bull's leg.

During the period of the later temples, there was a remarkable output of large ivory figurines at Knossos. The most celebrated of these is the Boston Goddess, a highly detailed representation of the Snake Goddess with details picked out in gold. Some of the figures represent bull-leapers. They have tiny holes drilled in their heads for the insertion of twisted pairs of gold-plated bronze wire to represent tresses of waving hair. They probably had gold loincloths too. It is possible that the bull-leaping figurines belonged to a cult model showing a tableau of bull-leaping. Some at least of the Knossos ivory figurines were made in the workshop beside the Royal Road. The carefully assembled figures, some of them 40 centimetres high when complete, exploited the same colour and texture contrasts between polished gold and carved and polished ivory that were achieved in the large chryselephantine (literally 'gold and ivory') statues of classical Greece.

Some of the smaller ivory pieces are just as impressive as displays of technical skill and aesthetic control. A small cylindrical ivory box found at Katsamba, and dating to 1450–1400 BC, shows a group of men attempting to capture a bull in a wild landscape.

After the (assumed) conquest of Crete by the Myceneans, large quantities of Minoan artworks may have been transported to the mainland. The light, portable ivories would have been particularly attractive as loot. There is some doubt about the provenance of the fine ivory sculpture found at Mycenae, depicting two goddesses and a small boy-god. It was found in a Late Helladic IIIA context, dating to 1400–1300 BC, yet it seems to be of Minoan workmanship or inspiration; it may well have been brought to the mainland by proud Mycenean conquerors as booty.

### Sculptors of statues

The Minoans made large numbers of statuettes in clay, faience, ivory and bronze, but no large-scale stone reliefs and no large statues in any materials have survived. It may be argued from the evidence that the Minoans did not make large statues. Whilst this is possible, it would be odd; the plaster relief frescoes, such as the one at Knossos depicting a temple attendant leading a large beast, show that the Minoans were interested in large-scale modelled representations of people, bulls and mythological animals. The Minoans had the skill to make life-sized statues in stone or wood – or even ivory – if they chose: the elaborately carved stone vases and fragments of high quality frieze work in carved stone show this very clearly. The Minoans also had diplomatic and trading contacts with Egypt, where stone carvers were making representational bas-reliefs and larger-than-life-sized statues.

Both the models and the technical skills were available, so it would be strange if no large statues were attempted. It is possible that some were made but later destroyed or stolen. Ironically, the more striking and distinctive objects are, the more likely it is that they will have been stolen and therefore absent from the archaeological record. Lord Elgin found (and took) two fragments of carved slabs showing reliefs of bulls at Mycenae. They may have come from the inner chamber of the tholos tomb known as the Treasury of Atreus. The subject matter suggests Minoan Crete, but more to the point is the material of which the carving is made: it is gypsum, which is not found near Mycenae, but *is* found on Crete and was used extensively by the Knossians for embellishing their temple. It is thus possible that, just as we are suggesting for some of the other finds at Mycenae, it was taken from Knossos: if so, the implication is that other pieces of statuary and relief carving from Minoan Knossos were also removed – by some Mycenean equivalent of Lord Elgin, perhaps.

Some carved stone heads rather less than half life-size have been found in Crete, for example the Middle Minoan II head (1900–1700 BC) which was found at Monastiriako Kefali. The absence of trunks or limbs to go with the heads implies that they were mounted on clay or wooden bodies which have subsequently disintegrated, probably simple wooden xoana. Other evidence, such as the votive faience robes mentioned earlier, tells us that elaborate dresses were offered to deities and it is probable that statues of deities were clothed in these. If so, the timber structure need have been little more than the simplest type of tailor's dummy. Evidence of clay feet found at the Anemospilia and Mallia temples suggests that the robes were floor length or nearly so, with the feet fitted loosely under the hem. These goddesses were very simple, and may have been armless, like the earliest wooden idols on mainland Greece.

Some bronze and clay fittings imply that there were at least two large statues on Minoan Crete, i.e. life-size or larger. One stood in the Great Goddess Sanctuary in the East Wing of the Knossos Labyrinth: bronze curls from its head were found in the cellars. The other was enshrined at the Mount Juktas peak sanctuary not far away to the south. Hood has suggested that the statue at Knossos may have looked like the snake goddess shown in faience in the Temple Repositories. This is possible, though a simpler rendering without raised arms is more likely. The statues were probably made of cypress wood; it was commented in later times that this was the most suitable material for cult images because it was so long-lasting (Pausanias, VIII; Theophrastus, *Historia Plantarum*, V).

### Seal makers

The locks the Minoans fitted to their doors were little more than wooden bolts with pegs to hold them in place. They were fairly clumsy devices and only offered security from one side: anyone could unlock them from the other side. The seals which the Minoans devised were a simple way of ensuring security. A loop of string or even thread securing a door or a wooden chest could be 'locked' with a lump of clay stamped with the owner's personal seal. The seal might be broken, the string might be cut – but not without the owner discovering later that his privacy had been invaded.

The designs carved on the sealstones were very varied. They often showed scenes from Minoan mythology or religious symbols, which gave the sealing the extra dimension of defence by superstition. Frescoes show that the seals were worn on string or leather thongs looped round the owner's neck or wrist. As such, they functioned as portable signature stamps, identity tags, and possibly even as credit cards. The magico-religious content of many of the seal images makes it likely that their owners treated them as amulets as well. How far down the social scale the possession of seals extended is not known, but the carrying of personal identification tags is exactly what we would expect of such a minutely organized society.

Seals were manufactured at many settlements, both towns and villages. Half-finished seals were even found at the early settlement of Fournou Korifi. There must have been concentrations of seal makers at the great temple centres, serving the larger populations of the towns.

Some seals are cylindrical, and in the earliest period, from 2500 BC onwards, the designs were carved on the flat end, not on the curve as in Syrian and Mesopotamian seals. After some examples of these foreign seals were imported to Crete in the Middle Minoan, some cylinder seals of the eastern type were tried out by Cretan craftsmen, but the standard seal shape in the Early Minoan period was a simple button shape: a very short cylinder with convex ends. This later evolved into a thin lens, with designs on one or both faces. Other shapes were used too, such as cones, prisms, stamps, and even animals and birds.

In the Late Minoan period (after 1600 BC) carved stone seals were replaced to an extent by metal signet rings. These seem to have been designed to be worn on the finger, although the oval design-disc was so big as to be unwieldy; possibly they were normally worn on a string round the neck, or simply reserved for a leisured elite. The signet rings were probably the prerogative of the rich, as they were often made of gold or silver. They were engraved with elaborate scenes of myth and ritual and consequently provide us with valuable information about the Minoans' religious beliefs (see Chapter 6).

Most of the seals were nevertheless made of bone, ivory, steatite, banded agate, or orange carnelian. By the mid-point of the Minoan civilization's development, the seal makers had some quite sophisticated tools at their disposal: cutting wheels, fast-twirling drills and gravers of bronze. They also had magnifying glasses to help them with the extraordinarily fine detail which they worked into the seal images: some lenses were found in a Middle Minoan tomb at Knossos. In fact, many of these images could only have been created with the aid of magnifying glasses. They must have been used by the painter of the bull depicted on the flat side of a crystal plaque found at Knossos. Since the seal carvers needed both hands free for their work, the lenses may have been mounted in some way, either on stands on the work-bench or on something like spectacle frames.

In the New Temple Period, from 1700 BC onwards, the seal carvers achieved their finest work. Designs incorporating fish, birds, bulls, people, gods, goddesses, schematized buildings of various kinds, ships, and elaborate ritual scenes were carved into an astonishing range of materials: ivory, bone, agate, carnelian, haematite, jasper, chalcedony, lapis lazuli and even rock crystal, amethyst and obsidian. The images on the seals reached new heights of sophistication. Before, the individual elements of the design were simply placed side by side. Now, they were combined and synthesized on aesthetic principles which apparently did not always depend on the content of the subject matter, although it is difficult to be certain in an area such as this. What we certainly can see is a tendency towards synthesis and dynamic development, a typical feature of Minoan civilization.

During the Post-Temple Period (1380–1000 BC) the art of seal cutting gradually declined. Invention flagged and a handful of traditional designs was repeated over and over again. Waterfowl and stylized papyrus flowers recur, as do simplified outlines of chariots. The carving had by this time become careless and clumsy. Limbs were often not properly joined with bodies and the long necks and rigidity of attitudes recall the shapes of the clay idols of the period. The art of the Minoan seal cutters, like other aspects of the culture, was falling gradually into decay.

## Scribes

It is possible to see the development of Minoan civilization encapsulated in the developments of the urban centres, and the administrative control of the whole territory's economy was central to that urban development. Unfortunately, the exact location of the territorial boundaries is not known, but it is possible to make statistically based estimates of their approximate positions (Figure 23). It is reasonable to assume that the territory governed from Knossos, for instance, extended eastwards for roughly half the distance between Knossos and Mallia and southwards for roughly half the distance between Knossos and Phaistos. Problems arise when we come to consider the smaller centres, such as Arkhanes; could they have had territories which were on the same footing as those of the major temple-centres? On the whole, it seems unlikely that Knossos' territory extended only half-way to Arkhanes, only 8 kilometres to the south of Knossos. Clearly, devising a political map of Minoan Crete is fraught with problems.

The administration of each territory was finely tuned and certain aspects of it were recorded on clay tablets at the urban centres. The scribes were an important group of people: there were at least seventy of them working at Knossos in 1380 BC, to judge from the number of scribal hands identified in the clay tablets. In the heyday of the temples, the scribes used at least two linear scripts, and the evolution and interpretation of those scripts are matters of continuing controversy among scholars.

The potters of the Early Minoan period were already occasionally putting sign-like marks on certain clay vessels. From their shapes, these marks seem to have been a form of writing.

By about 2100 BC, a new kind of script had appeared. It consisted of sub-realistic images of, for instance, a fish, a leg, or a double-axe. Combinations of these hieroglyphs were carved on sealstones. Evans called it a 'pictographic' script, and its origin is still uncertain. Some of the signs resemble symbols from a Mesopotamian script pre-dating cuneiform, which suggests that the script was imported from the east. On the other hand, most of the signs are peculiar to Crete and that argues for a local origin. The overlaps between the Cretan script and other scripts, such as the hieroglyphic scripts of Cyprus and the Hittite lands of Anatolia, may suggest an alternative possibility, that they all evolved from a common ancestor, a now-lost script perhaps originating in Syria. Alternatively, it may yet emerge that the similarities simply represent marginal additions and that the Cretan script was essentially a native creation after all. Curiously, seals with these signs were still being made at the end of the Middle Minoan, around 1600 BC, and were entombed in buildings destroyed in 1470 BC, well after the appearance and general adoption of both Linear A and Linear B scripts. It may be that the old pictographic signs acquired a special magic power associated with the remote past.

Evans listed 135 hieroglyphic signs; although the total is actually rather greater than this, there are still not enough for the system to have been a purely ideographic one, with one sign for each idea. Equally, there are too many for them to have been purely phonetic or syllabic. Therefore, as Professor Alexiou has said (undated, p. 124), the system must be some sort of half-way house, with some of the signs qualifying the meanings of others. Further difficulties arise because it is by no means clear what objects the signs are intended to represent, but even if it were, decipherment would still be a very long way off.

To judge from the pottery found with it, the famous Phaistos Disc dates to about 1700 BC. It carries a double spiral statement composed of pictograms imprinted on the clay with 45 possibly wooden but more likely metal stamps. The signs at first sight seem to be completely different from those of other scripts found in Minoan Crete, and they are often for this reason said to be an import: the disc itself is sometimes explained away as a foreign curiosity. Yet there are some related inscriptions which seem to be Minoan in origin. There are inscriptions which are presented in spiral form, such as that on a gold ring from Mavro Spilio. There are comparable signs too, cut into an offering table at Mallia and engraved on a bronze axe left as a votive offering in the sacred cave of Arkalochori.

It may be that the script on the Phaistos Disc represents a chance survival of a script developed for some special, possibly religious purpose. Probably there were other scripts too, scripts of which no trace has survived. We have to remember that in many cases it was, ironically, only accidental hardening by destructive fires that preserved caches of clay tablets as samples of the Minoan scripts.

Some groups of signs on the Phaistos Disc are repeated; these may be refrains, suggesting a song or hymn, or they may simply be recurring words. It may represent a list of deities, a list of soldiers, or a discussion by a Hittite king of the building of the temple at Phaistos: all these suggestions have been put forward, though none of them has convinced even a quorum of scholars. Colin McEvedy has even proposed (1989) that the Phaistos Disc is a modern fake, a more successful Aegean equivalent of the Piltdown hoax, but this seems unlikely in view of the recurrence of some of the symbols on other Minoan artefacts. For the time being, the Phaistos Disc remains an unsolved mystery.

Between the eighteenth and fifteenth centuries BC, i.e. at the time when the Phaistos Disc was made, the Linear A script was in general use on Minoan Crete. This was, in John Chadwick's (1976) opinion, another native Minoan script. It was used for keeping accounts and also for dedicatory inscriptions. Some of the contents of the Linear A inscriptions are accessible, because some of the signs were borrowed, together with their meanings, for inclusion in the later Linear B script. Linear B is generally agreed to be an early form of Greek, but Linear A was a different language, which has so far evaded identification.

Tablets in Linear A have been found at Knossos, Mallia, Phaistos, Agia Triadha, Tylissos, Palaikastro, Arkhanes, Zakro, and what seems to be the site of the temple archive chamber at Khania. The script consists of about 70

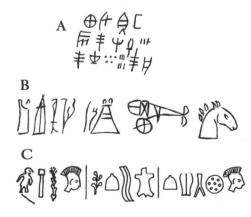

*Figure 31* Three Minoan scripts:
A: Linear A. B: Linear B. C:
Phaistos Disc script

characters. So far, too few inscriptions in Linear A have been recovered for translation to be possible. Nevertheless, by applying phonetic values known to be valid for the Linear B script, a number of interpretations have been attempted. Some say that Linear A is related to the Phoenician and Palestinian languages, and that the texts contain lists of people and quantities of produce; but it would be premature to assume this. Most probably the Linear A inscriptions are in the pre-Hellenic language of the Minoans, which may well have been related to languages spoken in south-west Anatolia, such as Luvian or Hittite. Short Linear A inscriptions are found on tables of offering and ritual vases, and the word A-sa-sa-ra, conjectured to be the name of a goddess, recurs in these ritual inscriptions at Palaikastro, Knossos, Arkhanes and Psychro (Alexiou, undated, pp. 127–9; Palmer 1961, pp. 235–6).

Relatively few Linear A inscriptions have survived, but the situation with Linear B is very different. At Knossos alone fragments of over 3000 Linear B tablets were recovered – nearly ten times the total number of Linear A inscriptions so far recorded. Tablets with the Linear B script have been found at the mainland city sites of Pylos, Mycenae, Tiryns and Thebes, as well as at Knossos, Khania (Kydonia) and elsewhere on Crete. Sinclair Hood (1971, p. 113) suggests that Linear B was developed at Knossos during the period following the '1450' disaster. Both the script and the language are the same at Cretan and mainland sites and there is general agreement that the language is an early kind of Greek. Some scholars are uneasy about this interpretation because the sign-groups give only approximations of words and can therefore be made into several different words: the sign-group 'po-lo', for example, can be made to mean as many as eight different Greek words. Another problem arises from the form of the inscriptions; most are lists of short, terse statements – objects, numbers and dedicatees – and many of the words are proper names, so it is possible to make false interpretations without the errors becoming apparent subsequently, as they would in a longer and more connected text.

It nevertheless seems likely, since increasing numbers of tablets make sense when interpreted as a form of Greek, that Michael Ventris was right. It is to be hoped that a longer, sequential text will eventually be discovered: a piece of poetry or prose would test the hypothesis conclusively.

There are tantalizing hints in the archaeological record that the Minoans may have written longer, non-bureaucratic texts on parchment. It is known that they used ink – there are clay cups with ink inscriptions inside them – and it would have been natural to use that ink for cursive writing on a material such as parchment or papyrus. In addition, some of the clay sealings have traces of vegetable matter adhering to them, implying that they were attached, possibly as signatures, to documents written on some perishable material. There is also the supportive evidence of a later Greek tradition that skins had at one time been used as writing paper. Unfortunately, as far as is known, no written parchments have survived from the Minoan civilization, and it may be that the finest Minoan thoughts were never committed to writing. It is believed that the whole of Homer may have been passed on by oral tradition for several generations before being written down in the ninth century BC. If this seems unlikely, it is recorded that, in January and February 1887, a Croatian minstrel recited from memory a series of lays amounting to twice the combined length of the *Iliad* and the *Odyssey* (Thomson 1949, p. 529).

### *Potters*

Minoan potters produced an astonishing variety of wares. One of the earliest Minoan pottery styles, dating to 2700 BC, was a type called Pirgos ware, named after a site on the coast to the north-east of Knossos. Typically, this ware had a pattern burnish on a red, grey or light brown surface, and it was applied to goblets with tall narrow stems or conical pedestal bases. Pirgos ware bears a closer relationship with late neolithic wares made on the Greek mainland and in the Cyclades than with any Cretan forerunners, and the style may have been imported (Figure 32A).

Soon to follow were pots with simple linear designs in black, brown, or red on a pale yellowish background. These Early Minoan II vessels were made around 2500 BC and are known as Agios Onoufrios ware after a site near Phaistos. At about the same time, two new styles appeared. One was a range of curious vases shaped like birds and animals, amongst which we might

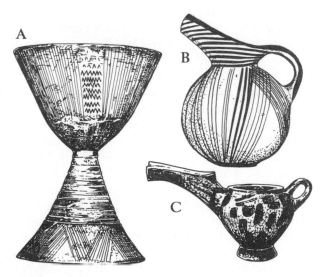

*Figure 32* Early pottery styles. A: Pirgos ware. B: Agios Onoufrios ware. C: Vasiliki ware

include the Myrtos Goddess vase. The other was Vasiliki ware; this marked the end of the pattern burnish technique and the beginning of a new finish, a reddish-brown wash deliberately applied unevenly in order to simulate the mottled texture of the stone vases that were at that time so fashionable in eastern Crete (Figure 32C). The Vasiliki ware included some peculiar long-spouted 'teapots' and jugs: the spouts have distinctive upturned sides and a curious joint or articulation before they join the main body of the vessel.

As the development of the towns continued apace in the phase immediately before the building of the first great temples, there were crucial developments in the potters' craft. They started to use the fast wheel, which enabled them to create new and far more refined shapes with thinner walls. They also began firing in built kilns rather than in open fires, which ensured a more even and consistent firing, and more predictable results (Alexiou, undated). Many of the shapes that had been developed in the Early Minoan nevertheless continued in use, especially the one-handled cup and the jar with a short spout on its shoulder, bridged by the rim. The growth of the towns meant that the urban potteries had to produce large quantities of plain ware for ordinary everyday use, such as cooking pots, storage jars of all sizes and lamps. The decorated ware was given a black lustrous surface with spiral patterns in white, purple, orange and red: some of the patterns were elaborate, clever and confidently executed, showing a sophisticated understanding of the difficulties of designing for a curved surface. This polychrome type of design seems to have been invented at Knossos, where it was fashionable for some time before it was adopted generally in the east of Crete. Perhaps the spiral designs originated in the 'Bandkeramik' of the Danube basin and arrived in Crete by way of the Cyclades, where stone pyxides were made with spiral ornaments; but Stylianos Alexiou thinks it more likely that the spiral came from the Middle East, where it was used in gold wire jewellery from an early date.

It was during the Middle Minoan II period, when the first large temples were raised, that the greatest developments in pottery took place. The gathering and concentration of craft workers into the temples seems to have stimulated technical advances of many kinds. The Kamares ware consisted of polychrome-decorated thin-walled vessels. The fine cups with their egg-shell thin fabric imitated metal originals. Beautifully made and beautifully decorated, Kamares vessels are of a quality and refinement never again to be achieved in the Aegean world. But it was a relatively short-lived style: by Middle Minoan III, beginning in 1700 BC, the potters had stopped making it. Since this was also a period of great affluence, it can only be assumed that the wealthy customers who commissioned the Kamares cups – aristocrats and priestesses among them – could now afford cups of precious metal instead.

There was also, around 1600 BC, a striking new development in pottery style, with marine reliefs added to some vases at Knossos and Phaistos, reliefs depicting shells, crabs, seaweed, rocks and dolphins. By 1500 BC another decorative style, the tortoise-shell ripple, had appeared. The potters decorated cups with closely set vertical stripes, painting them on a wet slip, deliberately causing the edges to blur. They may have intended, as with the earlier Kamares pottery, to imitate metal originals: in this case the shimmering surfaces of metal flutes.

The temples fell and were rebuilt after 1470 BC. The potters of the new temples produced yet more new styles. Now designs were recognizably drawn from nature, but stylized in such a way that they formed bold patterns. There were distinctive Floral and Marine styles and some of the vessels decorated in this way were very fine indeed (Figure 33). Even so, most of the pottery made in Crete at this time, including Knossos itself, was rather carelessly decorated. A jug from Palaikastro, for example, is bold and effective, but casually executed.

Peter Warren (1975, p. 42) has suggested that the Marine Style vases were all made at Knossos, in a single workshop. Some of the earliest examples of Floral Style vessels also came from Knossos; they are gracefully shaped vases decorated with stylized but recognizable white lilies and recalling the famous Lily Fresco from Amnisos. Perhaps the finest and technically most assured essay in the Floral Style, though, is the ewer found at Phaistos, which is completely covered with grey-green sprays of olive leaves. Vases in the Marine Style, including rhytons, bridge-spouted jugs and three-handled amphoras, are decorated with triton shells, argonauts, octopuses, starfish, rocks and seaweed – all of them treated in a free and fluid way. The most perfect example of the Marine Style is the pot from Gournia with an octopus sprawling all over its surface.

*Figure 33* Marine (left) and Floral (right) Style vases

In the Late Temple period, when Knossos dominated most of Crete, the temple potters worked in a different spirit, producing more formal, symmetrical and grandiose work. The so-called 'Palace Style' amphoras were at first made and used only at Knossos itself, which strongly suggests that they were made for the use of the ruling elite. Sinclair Hood (1971, p. 45; 1978, p. 41) sees at this time many signs of mainland influence; new forms were introduced to Crete from the Greek mainland, including stemmed goblets decorated in the Ephyrean style. In this late period, some of the traditional motifs used in Minoan pottery decoration became stiff, straight and symmetrical; the papyrus and even the octopus were organized into symmetrical shapes. Subject matter draws widely on marine motifs, as well as vegetation, helmets (Figure 7B), shields, double-axes and, for the first time, birds. The earlier vitality and sense of powerful movement disappeared from Minoan pottery. It was replaced instead by a restrained, disciplined formality that seems foreign to the Minoan spirit, but it was nevertheless hieratic, powerful and rich, and it continued into the Post-Temple Period (Late Minoan IIIA, dating to 1400–1300 BC).

At every stage in the development of the Minoan culture, the potters – and especially those working in the temple-precincts – were producing work to please their patrons. The seemingly kaleidoscopic changes of fashion in pottery shapes and decorative styles must reflect significant changes in their patrons' tastes and preoccupations. It is for this reason that the work of the potters is of such interest, in giving us an insight into shifts in taste and, possibly, shifts in the power base too. Yet all the time we have to remember the inherent, native dynamism of Minoan culture; all the way through there are changes, experiments, alternations between abstraction and naturalism; all the way through, Minoan art is freely ranging, ever searching for new forms of expression.

In the fourteenth century BC, the decorative motifs became more schematic. The octopus tentacles, sometimes reduced to six or four in number, were made disproportionately long: the papyrus flowers became degenerate. For the first time birds became a common motif. In the thirteenth century, the technical quality of the fabric was uniformly good, a well-fired reddish-brown colour, but the gradual impoverishment of the designs continued: the octopus was simplified to a wavy line encircling a vase. This was the time when the Mycenean influence over the Aegean world was at its peak. Finally, in the twelfth century BC, the Granary Style appeared – a very meagre type of decoration in horizontal bands – and the Close Style, in which the designs were hemmed in by dense fringes, bands, and multiple borders; the purely decorative aspect makes it difficult to identify the motifs. The octopus on a pot from the Diktaian Cave has twelve tentacles and is scarcely recognizable.

The style of the clay figurines of goddesses also changed, and there is a startling contrast between the tense and dramatic naturalism of the Snake

*Figure 34* Clay goddesses from the late refuge settlement of Karfi

Goddess figurine from the Temple Repositories at Knossos and the rigid and simplified idol from the Late Dove Goddess Sanctuary in the East Wing of the Labyrinth. The late idol's skirt was reduced to a simple cylinder, crudely painted with a black on white slip, and the raised hands exaggerated in size to emphasize the hieratic gesture. In the following phase, as in the very late idols from Karfi (Figure 34), the necks became grotesquely long, the faces harsh and ugly, with curious detachable feet peeping out through an opening in the cylindrical skirt; these figurines show, more than any other single artefact, the signs of decadence. In the mountain-top refuge of Karfi, a few straggling survivors tried to keep the Minoan way of life going, but it had fallen into lifeless stereotypes. It had run its course.

### Style and the urban craft worker

At the civilization's zenith, the Minoan towns gathered together craft workers with widely varying skills and enabled them to learn from one another. There are all kinds of art objects which display collaboration between different sorts of craftsmen. The ivory inlays that decorated wooden furnishings, for example, show that the ivory carvers were working in close collaboration with the joiners. Physical closeness in the temple workshops may have stimulated friendly rivalry to produce ever-finer works and thus stimulated technical and artistic development.

Enough has survived for us to be able to trace the developing skills and aspirations of some groups of craft workers, but we can be sure that there were many crafts and other activities in the city of Knossos which have left no archaeological trace. Very little, for instance, has survived of the carpenter's or joiner's craft. The stone chair in the Throne Sanctuary at Knossos seems to imitate a wooden precursor; the frescoes show folding wooden stools with cushions, such as were used in ancient Egypt; there is indirect evidence, in inlay work and bronze hinges, of storage chests, cabinets and chairs; presumably there were also low wooden beds of the same type inferred from a cast discovered at Akrotiri on Thera. The larnaxes or burial chests were apparently imitations in clay of wooden chests. A wooden lid carved with a winged griffin and a deer in a rocky landscape was found at Saqqara in Egypt; Sinclair Hood (1978, pp. 115–16) suggests that it may be the work of a Minoan wood carver working in 1450–1400 BC, perhaps as a captive in Mycenae: if so, it is a rare survival of Minoan wood carving.

The craft workers reached levels of technical skill and artistry so high that some of their works rank among the finest ever produced in Europe. The purely aesthetic value of their work is easy to appreciate. It is instantly appealing because of the Minoans' delight in grace, movement and natural forms – in short, their delight in life. Sometimes it is difficult to penetrate beyond aesthetic appreciation. The purpose of some of the objects crafted is difficult to understand because many of the finest had a religious significance. Sealstones and frescoes often depict cult scenes; stone vessels were often intended for cult use; the finest faience figurines were idols; the metal and clay figurines and miniature double-axes were intended as offerings to deities; the recurring marine motif on the pottery and in frescoes may have had a cult association with the worship of Poseidon.

But the purely secular products of the workshops were often made with comparable skill and sensitivity. During most of the long development of the civilization, there was an overt delight in the natural world and its forms. Usually there was a vitality apparently drawn from nature itself. Even this, though, can be seen as a facet of the Minoans' religious orientation. Their world-view was essentially animatistic: every living thing and every outwardly inanimate thing too was a part of the living cosmos, and therefore imbued with something of the divine spirit.

The craft workers loved complicated and attractive patterns and looked constantly for new ways of elaborating old motifs, like the papyrus, and for new sources of artistic inspiration. Often their work appears to depict the fleeting moment. The dog-handled pot-lids from Mochlos, for example, seem to show a particular dog relaxing on a particular afternoon in the hot bronze age sunshine; the crowds in the miniature frescoes seem alive with the excitement of the spectacle they are witnessing, and seem to have been caught mid-shout; the hoopoes in the Pilgrim Hostel fresco seem at first glance to have fallen from the pages of some bronze age edition of Audubon.

But this immediacy is deceptive. When we look closely at the plants and animals depicted on frescoes and vases, many of them are not really very lifelike. Often the species is elusive. The monkeys are blue and all the facial profiles in the fresco crowds are identical; the human beings depicted were, with a few very noteworthy exceptions, not shown as individuals. In this sense, much of the artwork is as abstract, generalized and impersonal as that of the ancient Egyptians. What gives it the illusion of immediacy and modernity is the sense of movement and vitality, and the spontaneity of the individual craft workers. They were, one senses, hot-blooded creators, these citizens of the Minoan towns.

Precisely how the urban system worked is still open to speculation. The fragmentary archives preserved in the temples at the time of their destruction imply minutely centralized control and a high degree of order. The traditional interpretation of the large buildings at the major urban centres as palaces argues for a simple pyramid society, with all the produce and services coming into the king's administrators' hands for redistribution. The interpretation of the large buildings as temples makes the system more complex. If large volumes of raw materials and possibly manufactured and semifinished goods were routed through the temples, what role does that leave the secular authority? In fact, once the evidence that Minos lived and ruled in the Labyrinth at Knossos has been seen as hopelessly insubstantial, it begins to look as if there might have been no king at all. Whilst that remains a possibility, it would be an extreme position to adopt, and it is still possible to visualize a full role for a dynasty of Minoan kings.

The temple was at the centre of the city of Knossos, geographically and economically, of that there seems little doubt. Agricultural produce flowed into it from the surrounding rural territory, some from estates which seem to have been owned by the temple, the rest in the form of tribute or offerings from the owners of private estates. The central administration of the temple, presumably the priesthood, redistributed the produce. In some cases the produce was earmarked for a particular deity or shrine, and therefore, by implication, the priests and servants of a particular sanctuary. In others, the dedication was more general. 'To the Daidalaion' (Knossos tablet Fp 1) would have allowed the administrators at Knossos to use the offering in any way that would benefit the Labyrinth.

Also flowing into the temple were imported raw materials such as silver, tin, copper, ivory, gold, lapis lazuli, ostrich eggs and plumes, exotic stones, and so on. Within the temple, and clustered round it, were craft workshops where the locally gathered and imported raw materials were made into manufactured goods. Some of these were to be offered as votives in the temple's sanctuaries: others entered a trading network which might take them to the farthest ends of the island or overseas. Exports included cloth, olive oil, pottery and metalwork of various kinds.

There was no money as such, so some of the produce was redistributed in the form of rations or wages. Within the temple, it is likely that some sort of allocation was made to the priests, priestesses, scribes, servants and craft workers. Whether payments were made out of the temple's revenues to sustain the king's household is not known. It is possible. It is also possible that the king held his own country estates and was, to that extent, self-supporting.

The precise nature of the temple's relationship with the town is also a matter for speculation. For instance, it may be that some craft workers, particularly those working very close to the temple, were operating under temple jurisdiction and supervision, whilst others were free to work independently. Certainly the temple depended on the town for its worshippers, for manpower in its many building and refurbishing projects, and for transport and trade.

The king, living in a residence apart from the temple, where – significantly – he is rarely, if ever, mentioned in the archives, probably had charge of the secular administration of the town and the surrounding territory as well as control over relations with other states on Crete and overseas. He also had a role to play in public ceremonial and it is likely that a carefully constructed ceremonial relationship existed between king and temple to ensure mutual support in the eyes of the people. As a secular leader, the king may have had charge of the army, although this may have been only a ceremonial role, since the tablets seem to tell us that there were generals. Much depends on our interpretation of the word 'Lawagetas', which was discussed in Chapter 2, pp. 21–9, 'Social structure'. The picture that emerges, at least as a possibility, is of something close to the idea of a constitutional monarch, a king whose power was substantially restricted by the overwhelming spiritual, political and economic power of the priesthood.

How much political and economic activity took place outside the control of the priesthood or the king is unclear. As Alexiou says, the concentration of the economy in 'royal' hands – however interpreted – leaves little margin for private enterprise. Nevertheless, the excavations at Mallia may provide evidence that Minoan society had other dimensions. To the north of the temple's West Court, an open square in the town has been interpreted as an early example of an agora, a place where citizens might gather for public meetings. A large building nearby, also to the north-west of the temple, has been interpreted as an assembly room and banquet hall for the leaders and representatives of the people, comparable to the *prytaneum* of the later Greek cities. The implication from Mallia is that free enterprise may have played some part in the Minoan economy, alongside the clearly dominant role of the temple. Systems comparable to this operated in the east, in Ugarit and the land of the Hatti, where 'guilds' of artisans were able to pursue their various callings in the town bazaars, and some development along these lines may have been possible in Minoan Crete. It may well be that future excavations at Mallia and Knossos will add substantially to the complex picture that is emerging.

# 5
# Life in the harbour towns and overseas

Fifty-two young men were chosen and made their way to the shore of the barren sea. When they had reached the ship and come down to the beach, they dragged the black vessel into deeper water, put the mast and sails on board, fixed the oars in their leather loops, all ship-shape, and hauled up the white sail. They moved her well out in the water and went to the great house of their wise king, where the galleries, courts and apartments were thronged with people.

(Homer, *Odyssey*, Book 8)

### THE PORTS OF BRONZE AGE CRETE

From the very beginning, the Minoans were in contact with people of other cultures, and the only way that contact could happen was by sea. Even in the neolithic period, a skein of east-west trade routes was established across the Aegean. Andel and Runnels (1988) have identified three early trade routes: a northern route from Anatolia to Attica by way of Samos, Ikaria, Mikonos, Tinos and Kea, a central route running from Anatolia by way of the Cyclades to Argolis, and a southern route which went by way of Crete. This southern route followed the arc-shaped line of islands which forms the outer limit of the Aegean world, an island-hopping route connecting Anatolia, Rhodes, Karpathos, Kasos, Andikithera and Lakonia, taking in the neolithic settlements of the eastern and northern coasts of Crete on the way.

It was natural that these coastal settlements would later become important trading centres in their own right, especially when Cretan influence stretched out across the whole Aegean world and beyond. It was also natural, given that Crete was on the southern edge of that world, that most, though not all, of the ports were on the north coast. In the west there was Kydonia, a port and temple-centre in its own right. Further to the east, there was a Minoan settlement at Rethymnon which may have been a port. Not far from Heraklion, at Agia Pelagia, the remains of a Minoan settlement were discovered in the 1970s on the edge of a low cliff on the west side of the bay. In the hills close by is the site of the later Greek city of Kyteon. It seems likely, therefore, that the newly discovered Minoan harbour town at Agia Pelagia was the 'Kytaiton' mentioned in the archive tablets at Knossos.

To the east were Katsamba and Amnisos, the two harbour towns serving Knossos. Katsamba harbour coincides with the eastern part of Heraklion harbour, and the ancient site is obliterated by modern port development and the unattractive suburb of Poros. Amnisos (Plate 5) appears to have had two harbours separated by a rocky promontory which was probably the heart of the town. The western harbour, now silted up, was evidently a substantial bay in Minoan times. The foundations of Minoan houses are still visible on the beach and under the water at Amnisos, showing that this section of coast has subsided since Minoan times. The 'House of the Lilies' is the most complete Minoan building to have survived there: its footings are well preserved on the eastern flank of the rocky promontory (Plate 14). On the western side, the impressive remains of the much later temple of Zeus Thanatos stand on foundation courses of large blocks of stone which look like Minoan masonry: certainly many of them have the distinctive Minoan 'mason's marks', the branch, the star and the trident, which supports this view.

Twelve kilometres to the north is the embayed island of Dia, which had its own port; with a southerly aspect, it may have been used in emergencies when persistent north winds would have prevented ships intending to dock at Amnisos, Katsamba, or Agii Theodhori from leaving port. Under these circumstances, it would have been possible for a ship sailing south from Thera to dock at Dia, unload and set sail again for destinations to the east or west. Ships docking at Amnisos could well have found themselves trapped there by a north wind, just as Odysseus claimed he was.

Further east along the coast was the port of Agii Theodhori, at the western end of Vathianos Kambos, about 1 kilometre to the west of the better-known 'villa' of Niru Khani. There is a tombolo at Agii Theodhori where the ruins of a harbour settlement can be seen on the beach and extending out under the water (Plate 15). On a small rocky islet is 'Kolymba', a rectangular cavity 40 metres long by 12 metres wide, carefully sawn out of the limestone to a depth of almost 2 metres (Plate 16). Kolymba is believed to be a Minoan dock basin, and it may be that Minoan ships were built and repaired here. The Agii Theodhori shipyard and port may have served Knossos or Mallia, or it may have had its own hinterland on the boundary of the two major territories. The size of the Agii Theodhori harbour town is unknown, but it seems unlikely to have extended all the way to the temple at Niru Khani. Modern excavations are revealing that Mallia was a substantial city, extending all the way to the shore (Figure 24). Remains of its quays have survived, as at Agii Theodhori and Mochlos (Faure 1973).

Further east still, and clustered round the Gulf of Mirabello, were the ports of Priniatiko Pyrgos, Pseira and Mochlos. Mochlos had the advantage of possessing two harbours, one facing east, one west: if strong winds put one harbour out of commission, the other could be used instead.

On the east coast itself were the ports of Palaikastro and Zakro, which were well situated for trade with Anatolia, Cyprus, the Levant and Egypt. The discovery of copper ingots from Cyprus and the tusks of Syrian elephants at Zakro confirms the reality of these eastern trading links. The south coast of Crete can boast only three proven ports: Koufonisis, on a small island off the south-east corner of Crete, and Kommos and Agia Triadha, which both served the prosperous Plain of Mesara.

### FISHING

Fishing was one of the major activities for Minoans living on the coast, but there is as yet no evidence for the way in which they organized their fishing. The rich variety of marine motifs on the frescoes and in pottery design implies that the Minoans felt a deep familiarity and empathy with marine life. A gold ornament found in the Knossos Labyrinth seems to represent the Cretan skaros or parrot wrasse, which is now quite rare in Cretan waters but still highly regarded as a dish (Figure 36c). There are gemstones which show the skaros too. One, a cornelian intaglio, shows the fish on its own among seaweed. Another, a chalcedony intaglio, shows a muscular fisherman proudly holding a skaros in one hand and an octopus in the other (Figure 35). Sealstones and a Minoan fresco at Phylakopi show flying fish, and the use of the octopus as a decorative pottery motif is well known.

The remains of fish are rare, as we would expect, although Evans' excavators found fish vertebrae in a cooking pot at Knossos. Some well-made metal fish-hooks were found at Gournia (Figure 36B), together with a lead sinker for a fishing line and some stones which could have been used for weighting nets. These finds suggest at least two methods of fishing, with line

*Figure 35* Fisherman carrying an octopus and a skaros fish

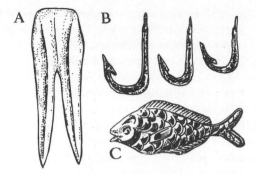

*Figure 36* Fishing. A: bronze
fish-spear found at Agios
Onoufrios. B: metal fish hooks
from the near-coastal town of
Gournia. C: small gold bead in the
form of a fish, from Knossos

and net, and there may have been others. A peculiar bronze double-headed
spear found at Agios Onoufrios near Phaistos has been interpreted as a fish
spear. This may have been used in conjunction with a net, or on its own from
an open boat.

Tuna are sometimes landed when they try to swim through holes in fishing
nets and get their teeth caught in the mesh; once trapped in this way, they
can be dragged on to the beach with the net. Ann Guest-Papamanoli (1983)
suggests that the design on a Kamares vase at Phaistos shows this fishing
method. Tuna were once caught in large numbers in spring and autumn in
the Mediterranean and it may be that the Minoans organized large-scale
tuna fishing in a similar way.

The octopus was a popular and recurring artistic motif, which suggests
that it too was fished; the chalcedony intaglio mentioned above confirms that
this was so. The octopus may have been speared by torchlight at night, just as
it is today. Sponge-fishing may also have gone on from the ports, though
there is no direct evidence of it. Certainly the sponges would have been
useful; they could have been used as a filling for cushions and mattresses,
and as a protective padding inside boots and helmets. Evans thought the
Minoans used sponges for painting, and felt he could detect that the
plastered walls of the early temple at Knossos were decorated with sponges
dipped in paint.

### SHIPS

The vessels that sailed in and out of the Minoan harbours, whether bay-
hopping round the Cretan coast or bound for far-distant ports, were
generally rather small. Usually, they had a single mast stepped amidships
and were rigged with a single square sail. Often they were equipped with
fixed oars as well. No recognizable remains of Minoan ships have yet been
identified on the sea-bed, but they are frequently represented on seals.

The earlier ships had high stems to breast the waves and low sterns: the
keel projected from the stern, apparently to make the ship run straighter,

*Plate 1* Oil or wine press at Vathypetro

*Plate 2* The Minoan village of Tylissos

*Plate 3* The Mount Juktas peak sanctuary

*Plate 4* The Skotino cave sanctuary

Plate 5 The Square of the Altars at Amnisos

Plate 6 The entrance to the Diktaian Cave

*Plate 7* Tylissos, House A, showing slots for tie-beams

*Plate 8* Minoan mudbrick wall at Mallia

*Plate 9* A stone drain at Knossos

*Plate 10* Mallia. The temple ruins in the foreground, peak sanctuary in the middle distance, and the mountains of Lasithi on the skyline

*Plate 11* Mallia. Part of the east front of the West Wing, with stairs leading into area VI (*right*) and up to the first floor (*left*)

*Plate 12* The Royal Road at Knossos, terminating in the Theatral Area (*left*) and the North Entrance and North-West Portico of the Labyrinth (*right*)

Plate 13 Tylissos. The Minoan village street passing along the west side of House C

Plate 14 The Villa of the Lilies at Amnisos

*Plate 15* Minoan buildings on the beach at Agii Theodhori

*Plate 16* Kolymba, the Minoan dock at Agii Theodhori

*Plate 17* The Diktaian Cave

*Plate 18* Pillar Crypt at the Balustrade Sanctuary (Evans' Royal Villa)

*Plate 19* Phourni. The Minoan cemetery in the foreground: the town of Arkhanes in the background

*Plate 20* The Tomb of the Lady of Arkhanes

although this feature was dispensed with later. There were other variations too: some ships had low prows and high sterns, whilst others were high at both ends. The large steersman's oar, which must always have been located at the stern, is the only clear indication of the vessel's orientation.

Many of the Minoan sailing ships were probably small enough to drag out of the water on to a beach, but some seem to have been very large. One ship is shown with a row of fifteen oars along one side. A standard vessel in the later Greek period was the *pentekonter*, the fifty-oar ship, thought by Bury (1951) to have come into use in the eighth century BC, and it may be that the seal showing a vessel with thirty oars was intended to represent the Minoan forerunner of this Greek type of warship.

Curiously, the Phaeacians, the legendary people in the *Odyssey* who sound like the Minoans in so many ways, were described as the kings of sea-craft; they were also credited with sailing galleys with *fifty* oars, in other words, larger ships than Bury credits the Homeric Greeks with possessing.

The Greek warships were designed for speed, and built longer and narrower than cargo vessels. A Pylian warship of the twelfth century BC is shown on a vase painting to have high 'castles' at each end connected by a raised gangway along the centre. Above its ram are two bowsprits and a large flag or model in the form of a fish. This sort of vessel could well have existed four centuries earlier in the Aegean. From the admittedly fairly

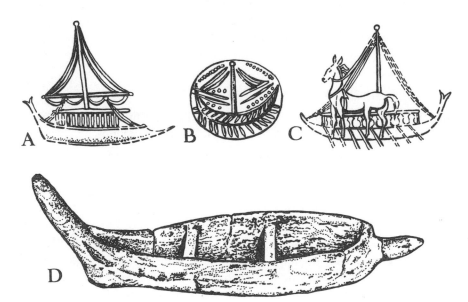

*Figure 37* Minoan ships. A: ship with raised central deck or cabin and a furled sail. B: similarly rigged ship, but with oars as well. C: ship with raised central deck or cabin and oars; the superimposed horse is hard to explain. D: clay model of a boat with a high prow, projecting keel and seats for oarsmen

simplified drawings on the Cretan seals, it looks as if the Minoans were in fact building this type of vessel by about 1600 BC. That being so, it is also likely that they were building it for the same military purpose. Thucydides credited the Minoan kings with organizing the first naval fleet, and it is possible that the Minoans did indeed have a squadron of specially designed and equipped warships that were ahead of their time.

The sleek warships contrasted with the stubbier lines of the freighters, but there were other vessels as well. A Minoan fresco from Akrotiri on Thera shows a different sort of ship again, with a lightly-built superstructure amidships covered by an awning and offering some shelter from showers and the beating sun to varying numbers of seated passengers. There was a special, elaborately canopied seat high on the stern, which we may suppose was intended for the ship's captain, and a row of twenty oarsmen on each side of the ship. These rich passenger vessels, if that is what they are, have a high prow and a relatively low stern; a carved representation of a leopard or lioness stretches and peers out over the stern. The Theran ships vary in size: the smaller ones are shown with no mast and only five oarsmen on each side, the larger ones with twenty or more oarsmen. Some were elaborately decorated, with painted designs on their hulls, garlanded canopies, 'figure-heads' in the form of leopards or lionesses and ensigns in the form of large flowers. There is no reason to suppose that these beautifully caparisoned vessels were in use only round the coast of Thera; they were probably not intended for long voyages on the open sea, but we can imagine that very similar passenger ships plied round the coasts of Crete, gliding elegantly from bay to bay.

### THE DEVELOPMENT OF A MINOAN TRADING EMPIRE

In Greece, the tradition was well established by the fifth century BC that Minos, king of Crete, had ruled the Aegean Sea and its islands.

> The earliest ruler known to have possessed a fleet was Minos. He made himself master of the Greek waters and subjugated the Cyclades by expelling the Carians and establishing his sons in control of the new settlements founded in their place; and naturally, for the safer conveyance of his revenues, he did all he could to suppress piracy.
>
> (Thucydides, I)

Archaeology seems to support the idea of widespread Minoan trading contacts and a significant number of thorough-going Minoan colonies. The distribution of the place-name 'Minoa' in the Aegean and in the eastern and central Mediterranean also seems to imply Minoan colonies. The name makes some sense as an enduring survival of bronze age Cretan influence, but we must not lose sight of the fact that it was Evans who gave the Minoan civilization its name and not the Minoans: they almost certainly called

themselves something completely different. If, however, the bronze age
Cretan king and trader-in-chief was known by the title 'minos', it is possible
that the king's colonies were named 'Minoa' after him.

There were important trading links between Crete and its neighbours in
the neolithic and early bronze age. During the First Temple Period, between
1900 and 1700 BC, the Minoans were exporting their distinctive pottery and
stone vessels to Egypt and the Near East as well as to islands in the Aegean,
but there was a massive expansion of trade after the temples were rebuilt.
The main thrust of colonial development seems to have followed in the
wake of this major rebuilding programme, in the period between 1650 and
1500 BC.

The colonial development manifested itself in three ways: the spread of
Minoan artistic and cultural influences, the diffusion of exported Minoan
products, and the establishment of Minoan settlements beyond the Cretan
shores. Naturally, there has been controversy concerning the status of these
Minoan settlements, but they are identifiable by their coastal location,
irregular street plan, Minoan style of architecture, Minoan burial customs,
Minoan shapes worked in local pottery wares (and thus not imported from
Crete), and Minoan religious ritual.

There is a short but significant list of Aegean settlements which fulfil the
requirements. Kastri on Kythera seems to have been one of the earliest, if
not the first, Minoan colony, and it was set up well before 2000 BC. There
were Triandha on Rhodes, and Iasos and Miletus on the Anatolian coast;
there was a tradition that the original colonists of Miletus came from
Milatos, a Minoan settlement just east of Mallia. Naxos and Karpathos are
thought to have had Minoan colonies too, and a very strong Minoan
influence is seen at Agia Eirene on Kea: perhaps it was an existing town that
was taken over by Minoan traders and administrators. It is probable that
Phylakopi on the island of Melos was similarly adopted, and not actually
founded, by Minoans. These changes seem to have occurred about a
hundred years after the Cretan temples were rebuilt; then, quite suddenly,
in about 1600 BC, *all* the pottery at Phylakopi was Minoan in style.

One of the most remarkable colonies was the one closest to Knossos,
Akrotiri on the island of Thera. Spyridon Marinatos emphasized the
Cycladic features of the settlement there, but many of the finds are more
typically Minoan: the house plans are not dissimilar to those at Tylissos, with
typically Minoan pier-and-door partitions, lustral areas, and Minoan pottery forms in local ware. Akrotiri was built in about 1550 BC (Late Minoan
IA) and is likely to have been a Minoan foundation. It developed its own
distinctively 'Theran' artistic spirit, which was a development from the
Minoan, while remaining in close and continual contact with Crete. The
frescoes, for example, show many elements that are borrowed from Minoan
Crete, but handled in a way that turns them into distinctively Theran
compositions.

We can speculate from the handful of known Minoan colonies that there were probably several more, possibly on the mainland of Greece itself. The status of Mycenae at this time was almost certainly politically independent of the Minoans, but culturally and artistically Mycenae was strongly influenced by them. Possibly the idea of the tholos tomb was exported to Mycenae from Crete. The Minoans were, in a very real sense, the Americans of the bronze age Aegean, exporting style and tone as much as products.

The Minoans exported lead figurines to Kambos, bronze figurines to Agia Eirene and Phylakopi, gold cups to Sparta, and swords to Mycenae. Rich gold, silver and bronze vessels and decorative ostrich eggs with faience mountings – shades of Fabergé – were exported to Mycenae and Thera. But above all the Minoans exported large quantities of decorative, painted, and distinctively shaped pottery – the finest pottery in the civilized world – all over the Aegean region. The densest concentrations of Minoan produce were found in the Aegean islands, Argolis, Messenia and the Dodecanese. It is thought that some of the grave goods found in the shaft graves at Mycenae were Minoan imports. Significant levels of trading went on outside this inner area, and scattered finds of Minoan products have been made as far west as the Lipari Islands off the coast of Italy, as far north as Troy (stone lamps), and as far east as Egypt and Syria, where Minoan vases made of precious metal have been found.

Some raw materials and perishable commodities such as food and cloth were probably exported as well. At Knossos, several different kinds of textile or garment were stored and doubtless some were exported; the tablets describe them variously as 'with wedge pattern', 'with white fringes', and 'of better quality' (Driessen and Macdonald 1984). Sinclair Hood (1971) suggests that woollen cloth and timber were sent to Egypt in exchange for linen or papyrus. The Minoans were capable of producing a large surplus of olive oil which could have been exported; some of the oil filling the store-rooms of the Knossos Labyrinth at the time of the 1380 BC fire may have been awaiting export. There were probably invisible exports too: exports of technical skill and artistry, exports of medicine and magic. The Egyptians valued magic and we know that the Cretans of the classical period had acquired a legendary reputation as seers and astrologers (Castleden 1989, p. 127).

Counterbalancing the outflow of products and services was a large range of imports. The Minoans seem to have been self-sufficient in terms of basic needs, which must have put them in a position of trading strength, but they relied on imports for supplies of exotic raw materials for the manufacture of luxury goods. There was a port called Minoa on the south-west coast of Sicily which may have been a Crete-controlled trading station. Quite what the Minoans wanted from the west is not known. Their interest may have been in Sardinian copper or Etruscan tin; the Minoans needed tin to make bronze, and the sources of their raw materials are unknown. The tin may have come from Etruria, Bohemia, Spain, or even Britain. Britain may also have been the trade-source of the small amount of amber found in Crete. A gold-mounted disc of amber found at Knossos may have come from the Wessex culture of southern England.

But the Minoans traded far more with their neighbours on the Aegean islands and coastlands close at hand. They imported via Kythera two fine ornamental stones, Spartan basalt and *rosso antico*, from Lakonia on the Greek mainland. They had contact with the Argolid cities too, although it is not clear from the archaeological evidence what, if anything, they imported from them: possibly the relationship was mainly a political or diplomatic one, or possibly – following the later Greek legends – the imports were archaeologically invisible, taking the form of slaves or tribute-children. The Minoans probably sent wine or olive oil to Mycenae; numbers of stirrup-jars made in or near Kydonia have been found at Mycenae and Tiryns, as well as Thebes, implying a regular export trade from Crete (Catling 1980). There seem to have been relatively few trading links with Attica, which is surprising, although a scatter of finds at Thorikos suggests that the Minoans may have been interested in the silver ores there; if so, the island of Kea could have been used as a trading station for their transfer to Crete.

Naxos supplied Crete with emery, which was needed for drilling and polishing the stone bowls and vases. Yiali in the Dodecanese supplied Crete with the white-speckled obsidian wanted for the fabric of the bowls; possibly the obsidian came by way of Triandha as a trading station. From Anatolia, Minoan traders brought black obsidian, possibly tin and exotic sealstones: from Cyprus, probably copper. From Syria, they brought back lapis lazuli originating ultimately in Afghanistan, as well as ivory and Babylonian sealstones. From Egypt came veined white alabaster, amethyst, carnelian, and possibly the eggs and plumes of ostriches.

It was from Egypt, too, that the Minoans imported a limited range of manufactured goods; the fact that nearly all the imports of manufactured goods were Egyptian reflects the Minoans' admiration for Egyptian culture: possibly it was the only culture they regarded as the equal of their own. Scarabs, beads, pendants, and ivories found their way to the Minoan temple sites. An ivory furniture inlay showing a sphinx at Mallia is thought to have come from Egypt, as are two ivory figurines of boys found at Palaikastro. Archaeological evidence from Egypt confirms that there were political or cultural links between Egypt, mainland Greece and Minoan Crete at the close of the Late Temple Period, 1470–1380 BC. At the base of one of the statues in the funeral temple of Amenhotep III (died 1369 BC) at Thebes, there is an inscription which includes a list of nine place-names. Four belong to the kingdom of Pylos: the important town of Pa-ki-ja-ne, and the districts of Na-pe-re-wa, Me-za-na, and Wa-e-ro. One belongs to Kythera, which lies on the trading route from Pylos to Crete. The remaining four were places in Crete: Knossos, Amnisos, Lyktos, and Dikte (Nixon 1968).

In the early days of Minoan studies, this widespread network of trading links was seen as evidence of a powerful Minoan navy, a wholesale conquest by sea and political subjugation of the tributary lands. It is clear that this was not necessarily the case. Certainly at the beginning of the New Temple Period, about 1700–1600 BC, there was a major economic and possibly demographic expansion on Crete which supplied the thrust outwards; Minoan colony settlements were set up in a band right across the southern Aegean from Kythera to Iasos. Further off, the Minoans established or developed trading relationships with communities in Messenia, Lakonia, and Argolis on the Greek mainland, as well as Cyprus and Egypt: in these areas, there is no firm evidence that they founded colonies. Then there was an outer fringe area, an area of occasional and perhaps very infrequent

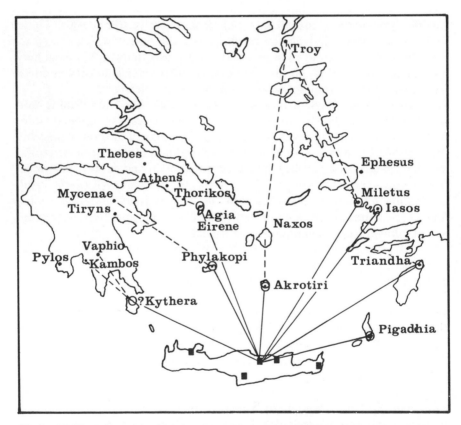

*Figure 38* The Minoan trading empire. Main urban temple centres on Crete shown as black rectangles, and known colonies or trading stations are ringed. Implied primary trading links with Crete are shown as solid lines. Probable secondary trading links, between Minoan colonies and non-Minoan towns, are shown in dashed lines. Trade routes passing outside the Aegean region are not shown

trading contacts, including Syria and possibly Palestine in the east, Miletus, Didyma, Iasos, Knidos and Troy in Anatolia, Attica and Delphi on the Greek mainland and Sicily-Lipari in the west. How much further west the Minoan merchantmen sailed remains a matter for speculation: possibly as far as southern Britain.

The development of this 'trading empire' should be seen as directly associated with the development of the Minoan civilization on Crete. The Minoans had advanced technically and artistically far beyond any of their neighbours. It was natural that their products should be in great demand. The trading empire was, in large measure, demanded by the Aegean world rather than imposed upon it. Population growth on Crete may have played its part in giving an impetus to the foundation of the colonies. Calculations of Mallia's food requirements (see Chapter 4) show a significantly large shortfall in wheat. Possibly this shortfall was met by grain production on the Lasithi Plain, but if Lasithi was not tributary to Mallia, the city would have had to look overseas for grain, 'buy' it from neighbouring territories, or go hungry. There are some indications that the population of Crete was rising significantly around 1550–1500 BC (Late Minoan IA), with new settlements appearing in previously unpopulated areas such as the Zou valley to the south of Sitia and the south coast between Arvi and Myrtos, where at least five new settlements were founded in Late Minoan I. Meanwhile, the old established centres had expanded greatly. The recent survey of the Knossos area (Hood and Smyth 1981) shows that the occupation area there had, by Late Minoan I, increased over ten times, albeit over a 1,000-year period since the Early Minoan.

The push of rising population levels and increasing economic production capacity combined with the pull of widespread demand for products are enough to explain the rapid growth of the trading empire between 1700 and 1500 BC. The only real mystery is the precise mechanism by which the inner band of Minoan colonies was established. Were the Minoan colonists welcomed and supported by the native Kytherans when they founded Kastri? Still more to the point, were they welcomed by the Melians when they took over the existing settlement at Phylakopi? Or was the colonial thrust resented and opposed? It may be that the foundation of the chain of trading posts had to be established by force, but it is probably only in this very limited sense that the Minoans imposed their will on the Aegean world outside Crete.

Sinclair Hood (1982) nevertheless gives us a salutory reminder that the Minoans lived in a world where might was right, where Egyptian rulers boasted of their subjugation of foreigners, of the cities and territories they had sacked and laid waste, and where Hittite kings boasted of holding their lands 'with a strong arm', and of capturing the idols of their enemies. The Hittite king Hattusili I, who ruled from about 1650 BC onwards, described his own march on northern Syria in these terms:

Like a lion, the Great King crossed the river Pura and overcame the city of Hassu like a lion with his paw. He heaped dust upon it and filled Hattusa (his own capital) with its possessions. Of silver and gold there was neither beginning nor end. And their gods I brought up to the Sun-goddess of Arinna.

(Lehmann 1977, p.191)

It was a ferociously aggressive world, and the Minoans lived successfully and competitively within it. There is no reason to suppose that they were very different from their neighbours in their attitude to military aggression. We nevertheless only need to postulate the forcible imposition of that inner band of Minoan trading settlements – not the whole trading empire.

We can, moreover, be fairly sure that these contacts with other communities had effects which went far beyond the Minoans' original intentions. It seems that many of the communities trading with Minoan Crete caught something of the flavour of its culture, whether material or spiritual, and developed it in their own way. Nicolas Platon (1968, p.51) suggests that it was contact with the Minoan civilization which led to the development of the Phoenician civilization in the Levant. The Philistine culture too, developing further south on the coast of Palestine, may have roots in the Minoan trading empire; Bury (1951) mentions that an ancient name for Gaza was Minoa, which implies that it too was once a Minoan trading station.

Precisely how the Minoan merchants carried on their trade is uncertain. Money did not exist in the Minoan scheme of things. It has been assumed that goods and services were traded by exchange, although relative values would have been complicated and difficult to agree. Sinclair Hood (1971, p.125) proposes that goods were paid for with an agreed weight of gold or silver. That bronze scale pans and lead weights were found as grave goods indicates that they were perhaps regarded as in some way central to life. John Chadwick (1976, p. 157) agrees that transactions would have been easier if prices were agreed in terms of a base-commodity – whether gold or silver or something else – but there seems to be no evidence of this in the archive tablets. Some tablets used the word 'o-no', thought to be 'wonos' (= price), with a commodity and then followed with an amount of some other commodity, such as olive oil or wool. This implies, if not a transaction, at least an evaluation of some produce. But there is no need to suppose that the ways of the Minoan traders were simple, straightforward, or even efficient. The tablets reveal the Minoans as lovers of minutely recorded detail; their labyrinthine architecture reveals a love of complexity and puzzles. It may be that the Minoans enjoyed the social and diplomatic aspects of long-drawn-out negotiations over the price of a cargo with Egyptian, Cypriot, or Trojan merchants. That love of haggling is still there in the Mediterranean economy, and maybe it began with the Minoan traders.

# 6
# The religious life

Single is the race, single,
Of men and gods;
From a single mother we both draw breath.
But a difference of power in everything
Keeps us apart.
(Pindar, *Nemean Odes*, VI, 1, about 450 BC)

### THE MINOAN BELIEF-SYSTEM

What ultimately gives a culture its character is its thought, and that – in a prehistoric context – is the most elusive characteristic of all. Nevertheless, the Minoans left thousands of clues to guide us. To begin with, a very large number of the objects recovered from archaeological sites had a ritual function, and many of the images carved on sealstones and painted on wall plaster and pottery show religious symbols, rituals, or mythic events. It is becoming clear now, from such studies as those of Nanno Marinatos (1984) at Akrotiri on Thera and of Mark Cameron (1987) at Knossos, that even some of the apparently purely decorative schemes on Minoan walls are actually religious in intention.

What emerges from the archaeology is a culture steeped in religion. When the largest and most ambitious building projects, the so-called 'palaces', are interpreted as temples, that preoccupation with religion is thrown into even higher relief.

The Minoan belief-system was extremely complex and we can, in the absence of detailed, first-hand, documentary evidence, only make inferences about it. What is clear is that it evolved out of the neolithic Cretan religion and that the religion of the classical Greeks at least in part grew out of it. Some of the names of pre-Hellenic deities are mentioned by Greek and Latin authors: Diktynna and Britomartis, for instance, were Minoan goddesses. It seems to have been a religion that was in transition, which may explain some startling contradictions or apparent contradictions. There are some identifiable developed deities; there are some incongruously primitive daemons too, which may look back towards an earlier period of religious feeling; there are also some images of divinities which seem to be relatively poorly assimilated foreign imports. We also have to recognize that the Minoans' view of their gods may have changed significantly during two millennia of worship and religious experience. As Nilsson (1949) says, 'gods also have their history and are subject to change'.

Some scholars have assumed that the Minoans worshipped a Great Goddess, the Mediterranean 'Magna Mater', and that they later divided her up into a series of more specialized divinities. But this, as Nilsson says, would be the reverse of religious developments observed in other cultures, where various deities are combined or where one deity is given ever-stronger and more all-inclusive attributes and thus supersedes all the other deities. John Pendlebury's (1939) view was that the Minoans always tended to combine their goddesses into a single deity. Even so, the starting-point, so far as we can find one, was polytheistic.

The 'Magna Mater' goddess is named 'Potnia', 'The Lady', in the archive tablets, and she had shrines or sanctuaries in many places. She was worshipped, in the later part of the Minoan period at least, on the mainland as well, so perhaps cult practices and deities were among the Minoans' exports. At Knossos, there are dedications of offerings to 'The Lady of the Labyrinth': 'Potnia' occurs repeatedly as the main goddess's name; later on, in the classical period, the term was used as a respectful, honorific title in addressing women of rank, but it originated as the proper name of the principal Minoan goddess.

In her aspect as a domestic goddess, guardian of households and cities, Potnia survived, transformed, in Athena, Rhea and Hera. In fact, there is even one occurrence at Knossos of the name Potnia in conjunction with the epithet 'a-ta-na'. The incomplete tablet V52+52b+8285 has been reassembled from three fragments and gives a list of dedications, including offerings to the gods Poseidon and Paiawon, who was an early forerunner of Apollo. The dedication to 'a-ta-na po-ti-ni-ja' on the same tablet unfortunately breaks off after this momentous invocation. The meaning of the epithet 'a-ta-na' is not known, but it suggests that the Minoan goddess was already being addressed, among other things, as 'Athena'. John Chadwick (1976, p. 87) comments that the word 'Athena' has a form suggesting a pre-Greek place-name, so it may be that Athena originated as the Potnia worshipped at a place called Athens or something similar. In classical times, Athena had become the warrior-queen of her city on the mainland. A millennium earlier we can assume that her personality and role were less specifically defined.

The double-axe was probably Potnia's symbol, and possibly the pillar and the snake were her symbols too. The snake, living in crevices near the hearth, made a natural symbol for the earth-dwelling Earth-mother; the 'house-snake' cult survived into modern times and the snake was sometimes known as the Master of the House or House Mother. Tablet Gg 702 from the Knossos archive refers to an offering of honey dedicated to 'da-pu-ri-to-jo po-ti-ni-ja', meaning 'Potnia of the Labyrinth'. This tells us that Potnia had a sanctuary dedicated to her in some part of the Labyrinth at Knossos, since this temple – and only this one – was referred to in antiquity as the Labyrinth, at least as far as Crete was concerned. We can be fairly sure that there were sanctuaries dedicated to Potnia in the other major temples as well, at Kydonia, Phaistos, Mallia and Zakro.

How far the other goddesses in the Minoan pantheon were separate independent deities is very hard to tell. In the first instance, it is probably simpler, and in evolutionary terms truer, to deal with them as separate. One goddess was concerned with fertility and procreation; the dove, proverbially the most amorous of birds, was her symbol. She is often shown with doves perching on her; sometimes birds are shown perched on sacral horns or on a double-axe, as if to suggest the invisible presence of the goddess. Another and possibly separate goddess was concerned with renewal and the central rites of the vegetation cycle.

Since the goddess herself was not permitted to die, the annual death and rebirth were acted out by a young male Year-spirit, a small and inferior deity who took the roles of son and consort, and represented the important principle of discontinuity in nature. In the Minoan period he remained subordinate to his goddess, but at its end, as Zeus, he became much more important; his original Minoan name, Velchanos, seems to have endured into the classical period as one of the titles attributed to Zeus on Crete. Zeus Velchanos was also known on Crete as 'Kouros', 'The Boy'. Velchanos was always subject to the goddess and always shown in attitudes of adoration. The two ivory 'Divine Boy' figurines described by Evans as probably having come from the Labyrinth, may well be representations of Velchanos before and after puberty. The older boy, leaner and more muscular, has shorter hair and a small skull-cap which may conceal a tonsure. It is known that youths grew their hair long in preparation for a ritual offering of a lock of hair to the deity. The older boy appears to have gone through this in-itiation ritual, but still stands erect with arms raised in a gesture of wor-ship and submission. Professor Stylianos Alexiou reminds us that there were other divine boys who survived from the religion of the pre-Hellenic period – Linos, Plutos, and Dionysos – so not all the young male deities we see depicted in Minoan works of art are necessarily Velchanos.

Jacquetta Hawkes (1968) suggests that perhaps there were once seashore shrines dedicated to a Sea Goddess. If so, they have been washed away by the sea. Nilsson (1949), thinking along the same lines, proposes that there was a Goddess of Navigation. A gold ring from the port of Mochlos shows a goddess sailing on a boat with a shrine apparently built on to the afterdeck

*Figure 39*  The lost Ring of Minos

behind the goddess. It may be that the goddess in this case is a priestess conveying a portable shrine from one coastal site to another.

The lost 'Ring of Minos' similarly showed a priestess steering a shrine-laden boat across a bay (Figure 39). On the rocky shore in the background, no less than three separate shrines or temples were shown, one with a presiding goddess indicating the sacral horns on her altar, and two with sacred trees growing out of them. The genuineness of the Ring of Minos has been questioned by Nilsson, but now that it is lost, allegedly buried somewhere in the garden of Nicolaos Pollakis, the priest of Fortetsa, who for a time shortly after its discovery was its owner, the question will probably never be resolved (Warren 1982). The ritual imagery of the Ring of Minos is nevertheless consistent with what we know of Minoan religious practices and it does offer some additional support for the idea of a sea-shore cult involving both fixed shrines built on the land and portable shrines ferried coastwise by priestesses. Perhaps deities were transported in ships to describe a magic circle of divine protection round the whole island. The idea of a sea-journeying goddess may be the origin of the earliest known version of the legend of Ariadne, according to which she was abducted and taken to the offshore island of Dia, where she died.

Willetts (1965, p. 136) believes that leaping into the sea was a feature of some Minoan initiation rituals. Some mythic elements seem to be trans-formations of this cult practice, for example the episode where the young goddess Britomartis leaps into the sea to escape the clutches of Minos, or the contest at Aptera between Muses and Sirens which ended in the defeat of the Sirens, who then threw themselves into the sea. Willetts detects in these later stories a reminiscence of a Minoan initiation ordeal.

The Mistress of Wild Animals or Queen of Wild Beasts was a chaste and free hunting-goddess, a forerunner of the Artemis and Diana of the classical period. Her province was terrestrial, the mountains and hillsides where wild animals needed her protection for their nurture. It may be that this goddess was worshipped at the peak sanctuaries, where it is known that pyres were lit; the later Artemis cult also involved mountain-top bonfires. This goddess survived little changed into the classical pantheon. Even her Minoan name, Britomartis, or 'Sweet Virgin', seems to have survived in a slightly spoonerized form in the later Greek name, Artemis.

Willetts suggests that the cults of the goddesses Britomartis and Diktynna were connected, and that Britomartis and Diktynna were related to each other in much the same way as the later Persephone and Demeter. Diktynna's name links her with Mount Dikte, and she was portrayed in the classical period as a mountain mother. A major centre of Diktynna-worship in the classical period was the Diktynnaion, a great temple on a peninsula to the west of Kydonia. According to some sources, the death of Apollonius of Tyana took place at the sanctuary of Diktynna. He visited the sanctuary late at night, finding it guarded by Diktynna's ferocious sacred dogs. Instead of barking and attacking him, though, the dogs greeted him as a friend. The sanctuary attendants arrested Apollonius at once as a magician and a robber, suspecting that he had tamed the dogs with the intention of stealing the sanctuary treasure. But Apollonius freed himself, shouted to the attendants so that they should witness what was about to happen, and ran to the doors of the shrine. The doors flew open to admit him and then closed behind him. From inside, the sound of a female choir could be heard announcing Apollonius' ascent to heaven (Philostratus, *Life of Apollonius*, Book 8). The Temple of Diktynna was certainly a celebrated holy place in the classical period; whether the site was a centre of her worship in the Minoan period is not known, but it seems likely.

Britomartis had a male companion, whether son, brother, or consort is unclear, and he is referred to as the Master of Animals. Both Master and Mistress of Animals are shown between pairs of attendant animals or walking accompanied by a lion or lioness. Nilsson believes that the offerings of weapons at some sanctuaries may be fetishes, representing limbs or extensions of the god. As a hunter-god and protector of animals, he was armed with spear and shield – sealstones show him so – and his weapons became religious symbols. We should therefore see shields on their own as aniconic representations of the deity; the shield motif in the frescoes at Knossos is a religious, not a military, symbol. A gem from Kydonia shows the Master of Animals grasping two lions as they apparently sit upright, just as if he was holding a pair of pups by the scruff of the neck; the image speaks

*Figure 40* The Master of Animals

clearly of the god's dominion over wild beasts. The Aegina Pendant, which probably came originally from the tomb of Chrysolakkos at Mallia, again shows the Minoan Master of Animals grasping a pair of creatures by the neck. This time he is holding water-birds against a strange background apparently consisting of snakes (Figure 1).

The Minoan Goddess of the Caves was associated with childbirth and the underworld. As a literal Earth-mother, she may have been the prototype of the Rhea of the later myths, but we also know that at least in the fourteenth century BC the Minoans knew her as Eleuthia. She was referred to in the temple archives at Knossos, although as far as we know her nearest sanctuary was the Cave of Eileithyia at Amnisos (Figure 16).

Nilsson suggests that there was a Tree Goddess. There was certainly a tree cult, and it may be that priestesses performing rituals in front of the tree were regarded as epiphanies of the tree deity. Probably different kinds of trees were regarded as sacred. Alexiou (undated, p. 89) believes that he can identify the sacred tree shown on the Agia Triadha sarcophagus (Figure 47, right) as an olive. If so, it would be easy to explain. The olive tree lives to a very great age; it appears to be indestructible, sending out shoots from a distorted, dry, and seemingly lifeless trunk, reviving annually to bring forth its fruit. Alternatively, the Minoans may have singled out particular trees as sacred by the alighting of birds on their branches, since they regarded birds as epiphanies of deities. Possibly there was a link between the tree cult and the sanctity of the pillar. In the Egyptian myth of Osiris, the dead body of a vegetation god was enclosed in a tree trunk; at the palace of Byblos in Syria, a tree trunk allegedly containing the god's corpse was used as a pillar.

Often Minoan worshippers tore branches or boughs from a sacred tree and venerated them on altars or planted them in the sockets between sacral horns. Sometimes, they built shrines round sacred trees, apparently providing access to them by means of double doors and safeguarding them by means of wooden fences or stone walls. In some ceremonies, an attendant, often male, tore a bough from the shrine-tree to the accompaniment of gestures of lamentation from the priestess and others present; this overwrought scene, shown on several rings, seems to have symbolized the death of the young god and may conceivably have been followed by the sacrifice of the male attendant who represented him. The Mochlos ring shows a sacred tree growing out of the shrine being ferried along on the priestess's ship.

The Snake Goddess was another of the Minoans' underworld deities. Snakes living in crevices are easy to understand as symbols of the life within the earth. Two figurines from Knossos show the goddess brandishing her snakes. Sometimes we are given hints that the goddesses blended with one another, adopting each other's attributes. The Dove Goddess from the Late Dove Goddess Sanctuary at Knossos, for instance, stood on a bench altar strewn with beach pebbles, which suggest dominion over the sea. The Snake Goddess figurines found in a sanctuary at Kannia had snakes wreathing their crowns; one had snakes on her arms as well and a dove on her cheek. If the Minoan deities merged as this evidence suggests, reliable identification is made much more difficult. We may eventually come to think in terms of a Minoan Universal Spirit, which manifested itself in many different trans- formations, each with a different name, character, and function, and which yet somehow was regarded as a single deity. Certainly the edges were blurred.

Nilsson suggests that there was a Cult of the Heavenly Bodies. Some of the sealstone images and rings show a moon-sickle or a rayed sun-disc: some- times both. Sometimes there is a curious line of dots curved into an arc shape, which may be taken to represent a rainbow or perhaps the Milky Way. The sun and moon frequently appear in mythic tableaux and they are clearly there in some symbolic role, as epiphanies of one or more deities. On mainland Greece in the Mycenean period the principal god was Poseidon, a name deriving from an earlier (possibly Minoan) form, 'Poteidan' or 'Potidas'. Poseidon's power was at this early time far greater than that of Velchanos: he received large-scale sacrificial offerings at Pylos, and may well have been a major deity on Minoan Crete too. There is one tablet from Knossos which lists several deities including Potnia and Enualios, a name which later was used as an alternative to Ares, the Greek war-god; it also has the first part of Poseidon's name, 'po-se-da-', but the end is broken off. Probably Poseidon was worshipped in three aspects, with roles in the heavens, on the earth and in the underworld, just as in the later Orphic literature the phases of the moon were viewed: 'When she is above the earth, she is Selene; when within it, Artemis; when below it, Persephone' (Servius ad Verg. A.4). The subterranean manifestation of Poseidon was in the form of earthquakes and tsunamis; the terrestrial aspect was seen in the form of a bull; the celestial was the sun and moon. Occasionally the last two aspects are combined. There is a bull's head rhyton from Mycenae with a gold rosette or sun-burst on its forehead. The bull's head rhyton from the Bull's Head Sanctuary at Knossos has a less conspicuous disc-shape carved into the black stone of its forehead: that too may be meant for a sun-disc.

*Figure 41* Poseidon-Poteidan commanding the sea from a coastal temple or town

The clay sealing from Kydonia (Figure 41) showing a god dominating a sea-shore temple or city may also combine two or more aspects of Poteidan. There is the human form of the god, shown as the epitome of young Minoan manhood, and there is, floating in the sky behind him, what seems to be the head of a bull. In the foreground, sea waves break at the temple- or city-gates. G. Kopcke (Tzedakis and Hallager 1987) has gone so far as to suggest that the curious high 'rock' formation in the centre of the picture may actually represent the tsunami or tidal wave generated by the great Thera eruption of 1470 BC. If so, the iconographic link with Poteidan, lord of earthquakes and tsunamis, is strengthened. The equally odd banner which the god is holding may also contain a symbolic reference to the god's domain; the large terminal shape appears to be a stylized fish.

The Bull God was the Sun God, and he was also the Earth-shaker. In the tablets he was called Poteidan, sometimes King Poseidon, Lord of the Earth. He could appear in several different forms and have several identities, and it seems that other deities had the same ability. At least one deity manifested in the form of a bird. The Agia Triadha sarcophagus shows birds perched on double-axes, indicating the presence of a deity. The clay model of a priestess in a swing, also from Agia Triadha, shows birds perched on the swing-posts, as if the act of meditative swinging itself had induced the epiphany (Figure 42). Several small terracotta birds were found with goddess idols in a shrine at Agia Triadha. The goddess figurine from the Late Dove Goddess Sanctuary at Knossos shows a bird alighting on the goddess's head; perhaps what we are being shown is the ecstatic moment in a religious ceremony when the sequence of ritual acts reached its climax, and the priestess herself was transformed into the goddess.

The birds are generally referred to as doves in the modern literature, but as Nilsson points out there is often little evidence of species. The birds on the Agia Triadha sarcophagus have been identified as eagles, black wood-peckers, ravens and even cuckoos by various scholars.

It is possible that there was a connection between the idea of bird epiphanies and the sacred tree cult; birds descending from the heavens as messengers or transformations of deities were seen to alight in trees, which conferred sanctity on the trees as the act suggested that the gods themselves had chosen the trees as their shrines. A clay tree with seven clay birds perching on it is clearly a ritual presentation of the idea. In this way, the Minoans may have seen the enshrined trees as divinely appointed trysting-places where gods and mortal men and women might meet.

The human epiphanies are rather easier for us to understand. Some religious images show a god or goddess hovering in the air: this may imply a connection with bird epiphanies. A gold ring, now in the Ashmolean Museum at Oxford, shows a priestess dancing and another woman apparently worshipping or dreaming as she reclines in a trance against some boulders.

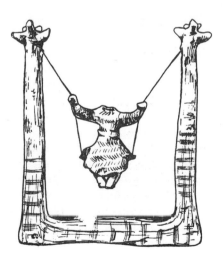

*Figure 42* Priestess in a swing

*Figure 43* A scene of sacrifice on a
gold ring

In the background is a smaller figure, a god with a bow, standing very erect, with one arm stretched high in the air as if waving or saluting. He seems to be holding a dagger. The bow suggests that he might be the Master of Animals or Enualios, the god of war. A disembodied eye and ear, perhaps symbolizing the spirit forms of an all-seeing, all-hearing, prayer-answering deity, float in the air above the worshipping woman. A curious feature of the scene is that the worshipping woman seems to be naked apart from an anklet and what may be a sacral knot tied round her neck. The nakedness itself is unusual. Is she perhaps a sacrificial victim? The god above and behind her seems poised to stab her (Figure 43).

There are many images of religious ceremonies which show epiphanies of a goddess. Often she is a small figure appearing, as if in the distance, behind or above a group of ecstatically dancing priestesses. Sometimes the goddess appears in the midst of the priestesses, manifesting as one of their number. We should visualize a common form of religious ceremony in which a group of priestesses sang, danced, chanted, and performed sacrifices and other rituals, as a preamble to a climactic event in which the leading priestess – the one Mark Cameron (1987) called the 'goddess-impersonator' – actually became the goddess.

The Minoans also regarded certain inanimate objects as incarnations of a deity. Evans was among the first to recognize that single pillars were treated as idols. There are several images, which are clearly icons, showing isolated pillars with a pair of attendant heraldic beasts. At Mycenae, the pillar is shown attended by griffins, which in Minoan Crete at least were the customary attendants of the goddess Potnia. At Mycenae, too, is the famous Lion Gate, which shows the pillar mounted upon a Minoan-style altar and flanked by protecting lions. In Minoan Crete, Potnia is shown with attendant lions or griffins. It is a short deductive step to equate the pillar with the goddess Potnia or the Mistress of Animals. The same line of reasoning confirms the sun-disc as a manifestation of a deity. There is a gem in the Heraklion Museum showing two rampant lions with their forepaws perched up on an altar: at the centre, in place of a pillar or some other representation of the deity, is an unmistakable rayed sun which, as we have already seen, is one of the manifestations of Poteidan (Figure 44).

The architectural design of the Tripartite Shrine takes on new layers of meaning once the column is seen as an idol or as an actual incarnation of a deity. The shrine's form, a raised central cella with two flanking cellae a metre or so lower, symbolizes the three realms of the cosmos. The colouring of the cella back walls as shown on the Grandstand Fresco from Knossos indicates that the three cellae represented the underworld (red), earth (yellow ochre), and heavens (blue). Each cella had a corniced roof supported by one or two centrally placed columns, symbolizing the deity's presence in and dominion over that realm. Whether the Tripartite Shrine was dedicated to a particular deity or was sacred to all the deities of the Minoan pantheon is hard to tell. The fresco fragments at Knossos which seem to show the Tripartite Shrine at the centre of the Knossos Labyrinth have rows of sacral horns along the cornices and two pairs of sacral horns inside each cella. If the Bull God was Poteidan, and the sacral horns are bull horns, there is a *prima facie* case for believing that the shrine was dedicated to Poteidan. Yet, like the Christian cross, the sacral horns were used in a general symbolic way, and it may be that the Labyrinth was, as a whole, dedicated to Poteidan even though individual sanctuaries and shrines within it were dedicated to other deities, in much the same way that within a cathedral there may be chapels dedicated to a variety of Christian saints.

The sacral horns appear in a great many images of religious significance. They are found painted on larnakes (clay coffins), engraved on bronze tablets, painted on frescoes, depicted on rings and gemstones. They are frequently mounted on altars or on shrine cornices in a way which strongly implies that they were a central, universal religious symbol. But they were also used architecturally, to add interest to the horizontal line of a cornice. Nilsson quotes the carved steatite vessel found at Knossos, showing the stepped balustrade of a ceremonial staircase; the staircase was obviously not itself a shrine, yet the balustrade's cornice is decorated with sacral horns

*Figure 44* Two lions attendant on a sun-disc

(Figure 52). In the foreground of the picture, though, is a procession of worshippers carrying offering bowls stretched out in front of them. They are clearly approaching a shrine or altar of some kind, or they would not be behaving in this way; in addition, our new view of the whole of the Knossos Labyrinth as a temple allows us to argue that even a staircase, as part of a temple-complex, might well be in a general sense dedicated to a presiding deity. The many fragments of clay and stone sacral horns found on the site suggest that the Labyrinth at Knossos bristled with sacral horns. Certainly they were decorative and they must have added a barbaric vibrancy to the temple's complex roof-line, but they also indicate a general dedication of the building to Poteidan.

Fragments found in the southern sector and in the north-west corner of the Knossos Labyrinth belonged to pairs of sacral horns that may originally have been a metre or more high. Horns at Niru Khani were mounted on a stepped base, evidently an altar, at the southern edge of the temple's large East Court.

Evans was right to assume that the sacral horns represented bull's horns. A vase from Salamis on Cyprus shows a double-axe alternately between sacral horns of a purely Minoan type and the horns of a realistically rendered bull's head. Nevertheless, other origins for the sacral horns have been proposed: the raised hands and arms of the goddess, or the sun-disc rising between two mountains, a symbol which in Egypt stood for Elysium. It is likely that the Minoan sacral horns acquired these and possibly additional symbolic meanings, becoming a layered symbol, in much the same way that the Cross of Christ has been transformed in religious art to take on all sorts of new overtones.

The so-called 'sheep bells' found at Knossos, Poros, Tylissos and Vorou illustrate this point. These curious drum-shaped clay objects characteristically have two perforations on one side and two or three stalks rising from the top. The two side stalks may be taken to represent bull's horns, the drum as the bull's head, the perforations as its eyes. Yet it is also possible to see the form as a stylized if rather primitive representation of the female deity. The central stalk is her head, the longer side stalks are her upraised arms, the drum her body and dress, the perforations in her chest the nipples. In this way, the stylized clay objects may be seen as early forerunners of the more recognizable goddess-idols of the Late Minoan period. They were certainly not bells of any kind. Nevertheless, the situation is made more complicated by variations in the design: several of the objects have *four* eyes or nipples instead of the expected two, so there is probably some additional layer of symbolic meaning that has yet to be penetrated.

Perhaps the religious symbol most strongly associated with the Minoan culture is the double-axe. The double-axe was an everyday implement, and yet the great majority of those that survive were intended for ritual use; some were made of very thin sheet bronze, some were very large, some were very small, some were made of lead or of soft stone. Sometimes the blades were elaborately ornamented. Sometimes the edges were doubled, to turn the emblem into a quadruple-axe, either for artistic emphasis or to symbolize some kind of union or symbiosis. Their earliest known appearance was at Mochlos, around 2500 BC (Early Minoan II), and large numbers of them have been found at later Minoan sites. It may be thought odd that no large bronze double-axes were found at Knossos or Phaistos, but this is probably because the sites were ransacked in antiquity and plundered of their usable and precious metal objects. Any large bronze objects will have been taken and melted down long ago, probably in the fourteenth century BC. Even so, pyramid-shaped stone bases for medium-sized double-axes survive in the Labyrinth, proving that double-axes were scattered about the building, like crucifixes in a church.

From the evidence of a fresco found in the north-west corner of the Knossos Labyrinth, small votive double-axes were stuck into the flanks of wooden columns. Evans argues that this practice was paralleled by that of sticking double-axes into crevices in the stalactite pillars in the lower cave at Psychro (Plate 17). The implications are interesting. The frescoes and furnishings of the Throne Sanctuary were intended to simulate the environment of the peak sanctuary at Juktas; perhaps the treatment of the many pillars supporting the ceilings was intended to symbolize the stalactites of the cave sanctuary at Skotino (Plate 18). The overall intention of the Minoan priestesses seems to have been to house the whole pantheon in the Labyrinth, luring deities from their various shrines and sanctuaries in outlying areas.

The meaning of the double-axe is not known. Possibly it was the weapon used for sacrificing the bulls. On Minoan pottery, the double-axe is sometimes painted over a bull's head. Later, in the classical period, heifers sacrificed to Dionysos at Tenedos were slaughtered with a double-axe. Alternatively or additionally, the axe may have symbolized the Sky-god or Thunder-god. In Caria in later times there was a Zeus Labrandeus, who was a god wielding a double-axe. Contemporary with the Minoan deities was the

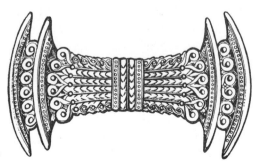

*Figure 45*  An elaborate ritual
double-axe from the Zakro temple

*Figure 46* Head of a priestess, showing
facial make-up and sacral knot

Hittite Weather-god Teshub, who carried a double-axe in one hand and a
thunderbolt in the other. There may have been some generic connection
between the Anatolian deity and the Minoan deity whose symbol was also
the double-axe. Teshub was a Hurrite god whom the Hittites adopted and
developed. Zeus Labrandeus, also worshipped in Anatolia, but at a later
date, may have been a further development of the Hurrite-Hittite god. Gods
also have their histories.

Perhaps the double-axe was, like the sacral horns, an epiphany or symbol
of Poteidan, but on the other hand there are many images of a priestess-
goddess wielding a double-axe. Although the Greeks were later to picture
both Zeus and Poseidon wielding a double-axe representing a thunderbolt,
the weapon was earlier held only by Rhea. According to Robert Graves
(1960), in the Minoan and Mycenean cultures the double-axe was forbidden
to males, which is certainly consistent with the Minoan iconography. A
mould from the Minoan town of Palaikastro shows a priestess or goddess
holding a double-axe aloft in each hand. The implication of images such as
these is that the double-axe was the symbol of a powerful female deity,
probably Potnia.

Another important religious symbol was the sacral knot. This consisted of
a strip of patterned cloth with a fringe at each end, a knotted loop in the
middle and the two ends hanging down like a modern neck-tie. It appears as
a motif in pottery decoration and models of it in ivory or faience were found
at Knossos, Zakro and Mycenae. A sacral knot appears in a fresco at the
temple of Niru Khani, and also on the so-called 'Parisienne' fresco fragment
from Knossos (Figure 46). The priestess in question wears the knot at the
back of her neck, and it is likely that she is one of the celebrants in a rite of
sacred communion: other fragments of this fresco show alternate standing
and sitting celebrants, mostly women, some offering, some (the seated ones)
accepting the communion chalice.

Mark Cameron (1987) felt that the knot symbolized possession by a man, a token of the collective sacred marriage which all young people had to go through as the culmination of their initiation sequence. Although this is possible, the fresco iconography does not really supply enough evidence to support it. It seems more likely that the knot symbolized the bond between the communicant and the deity, or that it was an attempt to bind the deity by magic, which is much the same thing.

Shields and helmets, depicted in certain contexts, were also religious symbols. Deities are sometimes shown with sword, spear, or shield; sometimes the objects appear alone, as if standing in for an absent deity. Large figure-of-eight shields were depicted on the walls of the East Wing of the Labyrinth, possibly to indicate that the building was under divine protection; the dappled hides of which the shields were made presumably came from the bull, the sacred beast, and this may have given them additional prophylactic value. Some ritual vessels have shields painted on them. A symbol of lesser importance was the cross and its variants such as the star, wheel and swastika. One of the most startling finds at Knossos was a marble Greek cross found in the Temple Repositories. Probably the cross stood for the sun. A stone mould from Sitia combining the cross, the wheel and the flaring sun-disc all in one symbol tends to confirm this (title illustration, Chapter 1).

The Minoans worshipped many gods and goddesses in a wide variety of forms, both animate and inanimate; they regarded the whole cosmos as animated by deities and spirits. In the religious paraphernalia and artwork of their culture, we see a religion half formed, with elusive nature spirits appearing and disappearing in all kinds of manifestations, now taking on the status of a fully-fledged deity, now evaporating into an atavistic mist. The Minoans gave their gods, goddesses and spirits names, areas of responsibility and probably personalities and personal histories, and yet – to judge from the iconography – the deities were capable of endless overlapping transformations. This should not surprise us, if we remember that, even after another millennium of evolution Zeus was still credited with the ability to transform himself into an infinite number of forms: a bull, a swan, thunder and lightning, and a shower of gold.

### SACRED ENCLOSURES

No less diverse were the places where the Minoans worshipped. We saw earlier, in Chapter 3, that widespread and elaborate cult practices centred on the peak and cave sanctuaries. The Minoans also had rural sanctuaries in open sites that were unconnected with peaks or caves. The archaeological evidence for these sacred enclosures is slight, but Bogdan Rutkowski (1986) argues that the images carved on sealstones and rings are sufficient proof that they existed. The images show vegetation in the foreground and background, and sometimes rocks too, but there is little evidence of a more precise location. Occasionally we may be able to identify a palm, fig, or olive tree, but even this is not enough to limit the location to a particular ecological zone; oak trees, for instance, can be found from 680 metres down to sea-level.

The minor sacred sites may have been fairly informal in layout, precincts hallowed by some long past and barely remembered appearance of a deity, but not separated off from the rest of the landscape in any visible way. Sometimes, we may imagine, boundary stones or small cairns were used to mark the edge of the precinct, or a rough, low drystone wall. The more important sacred precincts were probably bounded by more substantial walls: the Gypsades Rhyton seems to show one of these. The sacred tree cult mentioned earlier led to the building of enclosure walls round individual trees or groups of trees thought to have been visited by deities. Several seal impressions and rings show a high wall with a double cornice surmounted by sacral horns, or a high fence surrounding a tree.

Within the enclosure, which may have been quite small, there were sometimes cult buildings, sometimes not. A clay model from Arkhanes, and dating from the very end of the Minoan civilization, shows the sort of modest shrine that may have been erected in a sacred enclosure: an oval hut with a conical roof, entrance doors and a cult idol inside. These were lightly built and have not survived well in the archaeological record; nevertheless, the remains of cult houses measuring about 4 metres across have been found at Gazi, Kefala (in the Pediados district), Plai tou Kastrou near Kavousi, and at Pachlitsani Agriada. Some of the sacred enclosures may have had much more elaborate structures like the tripartite shrines at Juktas and in the Knossos Labyrinth.

As well as cult buildings, the sacred enclosure may have contained altars of various shapes, as shown on the Gypsades Rhyton, and decorated with plaster and paint, as shown on the Agia Triadha sarcophagus. There were probably also sacrificial tables and statues of deities, like the clay goddess found at the sacred enclosure of Sachturia.

Here, as in the temples, priestesses danced. The iconography necessarily shows rather small numbers of dancers; generally the seals and rings only allow space for three or four figures, but we should assume that we are being shown only the nucleus of a larger religious ceremony. The dancers appear to whirl energetically about with their hands on their hips, flung wildly out into the air, or waving high above their heads. A gold ring from Kalyvia shows a naked woman pulling down a bough of the sacred tree and another worshipping at a boulder. Another image shows a priestess beside an altar, summoning a deity by blowing a triton shell (title illustration, Chapter 2). Each image shows just one key event in what was evidently a complex series of rituals. We are never shown a complete ceremony. The frescoes allow more scope, but even they show little more than one event at a time. What the Sacred Grove and Dance Fresco does show us, though, is that large numbers of dancers and spectators were involved in the ceremonies.

Occasionally we are shown men dancing. The Gypsades Rhyton seems to show two men involved in a line dance of some kind, whereas the clay model from Kamilari shows four naked men in a ring dance within a circle of sacral horns: the rim of the model appears to represent the boundary of the sacred enclosure.

### SACRAL ROBES

Occasionally, as in the Kamilari model just mentioned and the two women on the Kalyvia ring, the celebrants are naked, but this seems to have been exceptional. More often, religious ceremonies required special clothes.

The Agia Triadha sarcophagus shows men and women involved in a funerary rite; some of them have an animal skin wrapped round as a skirt. It falls straight from the waist and the hem is rounded, but with what looks like a short tail at the back. The men and women who wear this garment are naked above the waist. The untreated, untrimmed, unadorned sheepskin was probably the first human garment and may therefore have been associated in the Minoan mind with the distant and primeval past. Interestingly, the draped xoanon representing the deity on the Agia Triadha sarcophagus is apparently wearing a full-length sheepskin robe; this may be to emphasize his antiquity or his rustic origins (Figure 47).

Other figures participating in the same religious ceremony wear a cloth robe covering both upper and lower parts of the body and falling straight down without folds or flounces to the ankles. This robe has a triple-striped band on the shoulder and a similar band running down the side under each arm: another band decorated the hem. The robe could be in various colours – blue, orange, white – and might be held at the waist by a belt or cord.

Another and very peculiar sacral garment was the cuirass. This is the dress

*Figure 47* Two images of sacred trees on the Agia Triadha sarcophagus. Left: a tree beside a xoanon of a deity and a shrine. Right: a tree in a walled sacred enclosure

worn by the priest on the Harvesters' Vase. It covers the upper part of the body and consists of bands of semicircular scales all pointing upwards, ending at the lower edge in a belt from which hangs a broad piece of pleated cloth. The garment is so peculiar that we might dismiss it as a quirk of the rhyton carver's imagination, but for the fact that it features again on a seal impression from Agia Triadha, where the rhyton also originated. It is by no means certain what this garment is. The only way the scale effect could have been achieved is with layers of shaped leather or metal: either would have made the garment extremely heavy and unwieldy. It also seems un-connected with any military use. The scales suggest the scales of a fish rather than armour; was the priest perhaps a priest of Poteidan? The lower half of the Harvesters' Vase priest is broken off, so we have no way of knowing how his lower half was clothed, but the seal impression shows that underneath the pleated skirt the man was wearing the sacral hide garment. The overall effect is visually complicated and inelegant, and could only be explained by recourse to arcane ritual references, which at this distance of time we have little hope of tracing.

The priestesses wore a double garment. It consisted of the straight robe mentioned above, with an elaborate flounced and layered over-skirt tied on at the waist. The detailed structure is detectable from the Theran frescoes (Marinatos 1984). The bodice of the robe has a deep cleavage plunging to the navel. The belt tying the skirt on drew the bodice edges in round the breasts (if they were to be exposed) and presumably lent them some support from the sides and from below. The striped and layered skirt was open at the front to reveal the braid-decorated robe beneath. The overall effect, with head-dress, necklaces, bracelets, rings and so on, must have been barbarically opulent. When numbers of priestesses dressed in this way and danced themselves to a pitch of religious ecstasy, the sight must have inspired awe among the beholders. It is easy to identify with the excited crowd of onlookers in the miniature frescoes.

It was the priestesses who dominated religious ceremonies. In the iconography, they far outnumber the priests and male attendants, and it may be significant that on Side A of the Agia Triadha larnax the lyre player is a male dressed in a priestess's robe. This suggests that there was a subordinate caste of priests who were transvestite, who became nominal priestesses in the service of the deity: they were probably eunuchs. Perhaps as a result of Syrian influence, companies of eunuch priests may have inhabited the Minoan temples; in a later period, it is known that eunuch priests served Cybele and Attis in Anatolia. In the Minoan temples, it was usually the priestesses who conducted the ceremonies, performed the sacred dances and occupied the most important spectator seats for major rituals. In both the Sacred Dance and the Grandstand Frescoes, the priestesses are shown seated in places of honour, centrally, prominently and with a clear view of the ceremonies being conducted before them.

Among other functions, priestesses probably chanted prayers and invocations to the deities. In open-air ceremonies, they apparently used a triton shell to amplify and distort their voices. There is a seal from the Idaian Cave showing a priestess holding a triton shell to her lips as she stands on a step in front of an altar decked with sacral horns and sacred boughs (title illustration, Chapter 2). The triton shell was used right through into modern times in Crete by rural postmen and shepherds, both as a megaphone and as a horn. Probably it served the same functions in the hands of the Minoan priestesses. Triton shells are frequently found in shrines, and with the narrow end cut away to make a mouthpiece.

Votive offerings include elaborately decorated model robes representing the sacred vestments worn by priestesses when they conjured up the goddesses they served. By putting on special clothes and performing certain rituals, a priestess might be transformed into an epiphany of the goddess. It is probable that Minoan citizens offered real robes to the temple for this purpose: some may have been woven in the temple itself, given that loom-weights were found in the cellars of the East Wing of the Labyrinth. Probably the finest of these garments were used to adorn wooden cult images of the goddess. There were many ways of inducing the deities to reside in the shrines and temples. A recently proposed reconstruction of the Procession Fresco from the Knossos Labyrinth (Hägg and Marinatos 1987) shows one of the leaders of the procession presenting a fringed garment, presumably the ritual overskirt, to the priestess who is about to become the goddess. This clever and inventive suggestion makes sense of the otherwise inexplicable presence of a fringe hanging in the air between the two figures.

Above all, the Minoans wanted to see their gods. Somehow, the deities had to be made to appear before the worshippers, and this appearance might take many different forms. Gods and goddesses could appear in the form of boulders, trees, birds, snakes, or pillars, but we can be sure that an appearance in human form had the greatest emotional impact. The later Artemis of Ephesus was confidently expected to show herself in specially designed windows of appearance placed high in the temple's pediment. Probably a priestess took on the role of Artemis and became the epiphany of the goddess. This type of ritual was already a very ancient custom by the time the famous Temple of Artemis was built, around 600 BC; it had been a common practice in Anatolia, Syria, Mesopotamia and Egypt (Trell 1988). Nanno Marinatos (1984) has argued persuasively that windows of appearance were used in Minoan rites at Akrotiri on Thera, so it is very likely indeed that they were used in Crete itself. The architects who designed the Temple of Artemis at Ephesus were, moreover, Knossians; Khersifron and his son Metagenis grew up within sight of the Knossos Labyrinth's crumbling walls. It is likely that there were windows of appearance located on the first floors of the Minoan temples, overlooking both West and Central Courts.

### DANCING AND DAEMONS

Dancing, as we have already seen, formed an integral part of the ceremonies that led up to an epiphany. The priestesses' complete abandonment to the dance, as depicted in some of the ring images, shows that they were using dance, just as the dervishes were to use it much later, to induce a state of religious ecstasy. It is known that Dionysos was worshipped at Pylos shortly after the Minoan period on Crete and it is possible that his orgiastic cult was preceded by a Minoan proto-Dionysian cult.

Beer or wine may have been used to help produce the euphoric state. Drugs may have played a part too. Poppy-growing started early in Anatolia and certainly spread to Crete during the Minoan period. There is a Minoan seal showing a goddess holding three poppy seed-heads. The famous late figurine of a goddess found in a small rural shrine at Gazi wears a diadem embellished with three carefully depicted poppy seed-heads, and they have been cut as if for the extraction of opium. This figurine, aptly nicknamed 'The Poppy Goddess', dates from about 1350 BC and makes a clear connection between the manifestation of the deity and the taking of opium. Whilst the orgiastic dancers may have been stimulated by alcohol, it is likely that

*Figure 48* The Poppy Goddess

opium was used to heighten the states of meditation during long vigils and bouts of prayer, the curious seclusions which the ancients called 'incubation'. These opium-induced trances may have produced states of awareness and revelation which explain some of the fantastic imagery of Minoan religious art, and which may even go some way towards explaining the extraordinary architectural achievements of the temple-builders.

Thomas de Quincey paid a very revealing tribute to the power of opium in his *Confessions of an English Opium Eater* (1821). First he was at pains to deny opium's power to intoxicate, asserting that the drug produced a static, 'chronic pleasure' lasting perhaps ten hours. Then he invoked opium directly, leaving no doubt as to the limitless power which the drug-user feels he has been given:

> Thou buildest upon the bosom of darkness, out of the fantastic imagery of the brain, cities and temples, beyond the art of Phidias and Praxiteles – beyond the splendour of Babylon and Hekatompylos [Egyptian Thebes, one of the sources of opium]: and from the anarchy of dreaming sleep, callest into sunny light the faces of long-buried beauties.

But the opium-taking habit led de Quincey on to far less pleasant and exhilarating experiences, and we are justified in assuming that the Minoans too suffered the adverse effects of opium. This is, at least, one way of explaining an otherwise very peculiar aspect of Minoan religion – the daemons. Some of these daemons are shown as followers, guardians and attendants of deities and sacred objects; others are fantastic composite monsters which seem to be spontaneous creations of the unconscious mind.

There is a dog-headed creature that recurs in several images. Evans sees it as an adaptation of the Egyptian dog-ape, possibly developing from the monkey frescoes in the Knossos Labyrinth; the monkey was not native to Crete and the animal may have been taken for a monster and so given an impulse to the creation of other monsters. A tablet from Phaistos shows an orderly but sinister procession of four daemons, each with its left arm hanging down and its right arm raised, holding a staff (Figure 49). One has a dog's head, another a boar's head, a third a bull's head and the fourth a bird's head. Possibly they are priests or temple attendants wearing animal masks: the Minoan religion had certainly not developed so far that such things were incongruous. Nilsson (1949) points out that the Phaistos daemons are similar to daemons shown on Babylonian and Assyrian amulets, believing that the Minoan daemons were simply copies of these foreign monsters.

There are nevertheless many images which seem to be spontaneous Minoan creations – strange and haunting images like the one on a sealstone depicting a daemon carrying two animal carcases on a pole. Is he a deity bearing off animals that have been sacrificed to him? Another shows a large and lordly daemon with a wasp-tail, standing between two human

*Figure 49* Procession of
animal-headed daemons

attendants. Another shows the converse, a humanoid god standing between two daemons: he is mastering them by grasping their tongues.

The daemons are closely linked with religious cult activity. It seems that
they are not gods exactly, but made of the same stuff as gods. Sometimes
they stand in for a deity, haunting the sacred places and occupying a position
midway between gods and men. Perhaps the Minoans regarded them as
fearful intermediaries – essential but frightening go-betweens. In this sense,
they may have occupied the same position in the Minoan religious system as
angels and demons in the Christian belief-system in medieval Europe.

The Minoan religion was itself in transition, and we can see the humanoid
deities as more evolved than the daemons, who were older nature-spirits.
The daemons roamed the forests and mountain sides, lurked in the caves and
rock crevices, fostering nature under the supervision and ordinance of the
evolved gods and goddesses.

We should not treat the daemons as foreign implants, yet they do
nevertheless have what Nilsson describes as an 'antithetic' quality compared
with the rest of the Minoan pantheon. The opium-taking may well be all that
is needed to explain this. De Quincey wrote that habitual opium-taking
reawakened the childhood capacity that we all recognize and remember, for
conjuring up monsters in the dark. It was 'a power of painting, as it were,
upon the darkness, all sorts of phantoms. . . . At night when I lay awake in
bed, vast processions passed along in mournful pomp; friezes of never-
ending stories . . .' This nightmare of processing phantoms reminds us of the
procession of daemons from Phaistos, which could have been seen in the sort
of opium trance de Quincey described. De Quincey reported that these
endless processions produced in him feelings of deep melancholy and
gloom. He was not merely frightened: he became profoundly and suicidally
despondent. It may be this kind of experience that led some Minoans to
submit willingly to sacrifice.

A belief in daemons or evil spirits led on naturally to a need for exorcists;
exorcism, it is reasonable to assume, became one of the priestly functions.
The Minoan priests and priestesses became so expert in this art that they
became famous for it throughout the Aegean world. An exorcism relating to

a disease, and allegedly written in the tongue of the Keftiu, survives in an Egyptian papyrus of the fourteenth century BC (Alexiou, undated, p. 108). No doubt there were formulae for getting rid of evil spirits, and it may be that the mysterious painted symbols written inside two cups from Knossos are spells of this kind.

The activities of Early Minoan priestesses were focused on the peak and cave sanctuaries and the sacred enclosures, but after 2000 BC they focused increasingly on the temples. Relatively little is known of the first great temples, which were built between 2000 and 1900 BC and destroyed by earthquakes in 1700 BC, except that they stood on the same sites as the later temples. The foundations of the later temples largely obscure the plans of their predecessors but, from the patchy remains that have been investigated, the older temples seem to have been similar in style, scale and layout to the later temples, although they were perhaps slightly less complicated.

The ruins seen today are essentially those of the 'second' or 'new' temples, built in 1700 BC and destroyed in the Thera eruption of 1470 BC. Only one of them, the Labyrinth at Knossos, was restored and repaired so that it could continue to use after 1470, and it was more or less completely abandoned some ninety years later after a major fire. After that, the Minoans appear either to have lost interest in temple-worship, or to have restructured their economy in such a way that it could no longer sustain – or no longer needed – large temple-complexes.

The Labyrinth at Knossos is generally recognized to have been one of the greatest architectural achievements of the ancient world. Had its fabric endured with its frescoes undamaged for just a few centuries longer, it might well have been ranked as one of the world's Seven Wonders. Its outline plan, as recovered by Sir Arthur Evans' excavations, is a ragged square roughly 150 metres across, covering an area of about 20,000 square metres. The footings and parts of the walls of around 300 chambers have survived on the ground floor; the presence of several staircases implies the existence of upper storeys and, taking into account the destroyed upper floors as well, the original temple may have had a thousand chambers altogether. The Knossos Labyrinth was exceptional in its size and complexity, but there was a strong family likeness among the Minoan temples. The large buildings at Zakro, Mallia and Phaistos possess plans that have many features in common, though with significant variations; their designs may have been based loosely on that of Knossos or they may have evolved independently from a common set of functions. They are really not similar enough, either to each other or to Knossos, for us to assume that they were copied from the Knossos Labyrinth as a model.

The temples' most distinctive common feature was the large rectangular

Central Court oriented roughly, but not exactly, north-south and measuring about 45 by 23 metres. In *The Knossos Labyrinth* (Castleden 1989), the evidence is summarized for believing that it was in the Central Court that the bull-leaping ritual took place, a ceremony that was itself central to the Minoan belief-system. From the significant number of representations of bull-leaping on frescoes and sealstones, it is possible to reconstruct with some confidence the events that took place in the Bull Courts.

To begin with, it is important to recognize that the various images represent different stages of more than one acrobatic feat, and that in some instances there is an element of idealization. Teams of bull dancers were evidently involved and they rehearsed a repertoire of spectacular and dangerous-looking feats for the benefit of a host of onlookers: there is little doubt that the crowd of spectators shown in the Grandstand Fresco is watching a display of bull-leaping, and the Tripartite Shrine fixes the location as the Central Court of the temple. Some members of the team distracted the bull by turning somersaults on the paved court: while the beast's attention was diverted, an acrobat might leap crosswise over its back. Other team members, the bull-grapplers, hurled themselves on to the bull's horns to pad them with their own bodies and make the beast lower its head (Figure 50). While the bull's head was low, the bull-leaper might dive between the horns to land, head and hands first, on the bull's back: momentum carried him on over the bull's tail, to land on his feet behind the bull. In a variation on this feat, the bull-leaper performed the 'Diving Leap' from a vantage point; the large, stepped stone block in the north-west corner of the Bull Court at Phaistos was probably used for this purpose, and there may have been similar free-standing vaulting blocks at Knossos and Mallia.

Some images, like the bronze statuette thought to have come from Rethymnon, show a bull-leaper landing upright on his feet on the bull's back. To have reached this position, he must have somersaulted over the

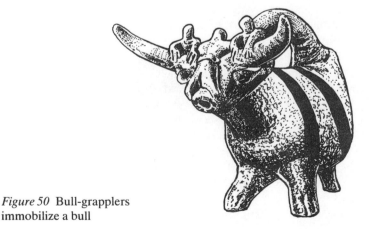

*Figure 50* Bull-grapplers
immobilize a bull

bull's head. Gaining enough height and momentum for the somersault would have required the energy of a team of acrobats to propel him up and over the horns.

Acrobats are shown, independently of bull-leaping, on a number of Minoan artworks. A sealstone shows two acrobats performing handstands. A gold sword hilt from the temple at Mallia shows an acrobat performing a back somersault (Figure 29); perhaps, as Professor Alexiou suggests (undated, p. 49), in reality this feat was performed over the self-same sword planted in the ground, point upwards. Feats of this sort were probably performed as a preamble and as an accompaniment to the bull games. Whether the boxing and wrestling matches shown on the carved rhyton from Agia Triadha, a miniature fresco from Tylissos and certain sealings were part of the same or a different festival is not known: the way they are depicted suggests that they too had the quality of ritual struggle.

Controversy has always surrounded the Minoans' bull-leaping exploits, and there are many who are sceptical that they ever took place. But the surviving works of art can be interpreted in such a way that credible acrobatic feats may be reconstructed. Certainly it is hard to believe that bull-leapers grasped the horns, and relied on the tossing movement to get them safely over the bull's head. Although at first sight the Bull-Leaping Fresco found in the cellars of the Labyrinth's East Wing seems in its present reconstruction to show, on the left, a bull-leaper waiting to be hoisted into the air, the figure is in fact a bull-grappler and represents a group of two, three or four grapplers whose job it was to pad the horns, keep the bull's head low and the rest of its body still during the leap. It is the second figure, in the centre, who is the bull-leaper, the star performer. The third figure, on the right, represents another group of helpers waiting behind the bull to catch the leaper after the successful vault. If a single leaper had grasped the horns and hoped to be thrown neatly over the bull's head, the chances of achieving a successful vault would have been very low. Bulls usually shake their heads erratically, lowering them vertically and twisting them sideways as they jerk them up to inflict the maximum injury. In this situation, Minoan bull-leapers could never have cleared the horns. The whole manoeuvre would have been far safer if the leaper did not touch the horns at all, by using either the 'Diving Leap' or the 'Somersault Leap' described above.

Feats as daring as those shown on the frescoes and sealstones are certainly possible and they probably were really performed, but it seems likely that they were carefully choreographed and presented to make them seem as dangerous as possible. The skill of the teams of acrobats, performing all manner of diversionary handstands and somersaults on the ground between the bull and the spectators, must have convinced those watching that they were seeing something infinitely more perilous and spectacular. No doubt the bull-leapers and their teams used the power of suggestion as well as enormous skill and daring to excite their audiences.

*Figure 51* A man captures
a wild bull

Parallels between Minoan bull-leaping and Spanish bull-fighting, for instance, should not deceive us into seeing bull-leaping as mere 'theatre of cruelty' entertainment. It was not a game, but a serious and central ritual in the Minoan belief-system. The bull was a manifestation of Poteidan, and dancing with the most powerful god in the Minoan pantheon was no light matter. Probably the bull dance expressed the interweaving of human and divine destinies; there were elements of collusion and elements of struggle with the deity. Probably the rite was an ordeal, one of many rites of passage that young Minoans, girls as well as boys, had to undergo in order to achieve higher status.

Many colonnades, staircases, doorways and corridors open on to the Central Courts and, if the bull dance really did take place there, they must have been protected in some way from the rampaging bulls. At Phaistos, there is evidence that doors closed off some of the openings. On the east side of the Bull Court at Mallia, there is evidence of a series of rails supported on stout wooden posts, and a door closing off the northern end of the colonnade. The Bull Court at Knossos is not well preserved, but it is possible that a fence of some kind ran round its edge; a fragment of fresco found in the Labyrinth shows a strongly made three-rail wooden fence with a priestess or attendant leaning on it, watching the spectacle.

Ranged along the western sides of the Bull Courts were suites of important cult chambers built in stone and mudbrick, and framed with horizontal and vertical timbering. The interiors were plastered and decorated with frescoes which developed a complex cycle of religious ideas. Mark Cameron (1987) came to believe, after studying these frescoes intensively, that the

West Wing of the Knossos Labyrinth in particular was given over to a whole programme of initiation rites and ordeals.

There was usually at least one chamber in the New Temples with a gypsum bench along its walls. At Knossos, the two main chambers of the Throne Sanctuary and the principal chamber of the Snake Goddess Sanctuary had bench-altars; at Phaistos, there were two chambers with benches opening from the Central Court. There were also pillar crypts in the West Wing. Although the sacred character of the pillar crypts has been questioned, there is plenty of evidence that they too were cult structures. In a pillar crypt belonging to a building on the Gypsades Hill at Knossos, 200 small conical offering cups were found, still containing remains of vegetable matter. Under the floor of the pillar crypts in the West Wing at Knossos were deposited the ashes of animal sacrifices: the pillars above were incised repeatedly with the sacred double-axe symbol. The crypts were small, too small to have needed a central pillar to support the ceiling, so we can only presume that the pillar had a symbolic significance to the Minoans (Plate 18). Ferguson (1989, p. 5) mentions the idea that the pillar might have been a representation or reduction of a sacred tree. Certainly, instances of stone worship are not unknown in antiquity, and they may preserve a vestige of the even earlier belief-system of the megalith-builders. The Old Testament speaks of a stone raised by Jacob on the spot where he experienced a mystic vision; Jacob worshipped the stone and anointed it with oil. Similarly, liquid libations were offered to the pillars in the pillar crypts by the Minoans, to judge from the rectangular depressions in the floor beside many of them.

On the east side of the Central Court at Knossos and Phaistos, there were suites of chambers separated from each other by pier-and-door partitions. At Mallia, a similarly designed suite was located in the north-west corner of the temple.

At intervals round each temple there were adyta, sunken and secluded rectangular areas which are thought to have been used for important ceremonies (Marinatos 1984). Suites of store-rooms occupied a large area of the temple. They were used to store the very large volume of offerings and tribute that came in from the townspeople and from the people living in the surrounding countryside; administrating the inflow and redistribution of this temple tribute was a major function of the Minoan temple.

There were small sacristies and strongrooms for storing precious cult equipment; there were vestries where the priestesses put on their ceremonial dress in readiness for ritual, and refectories for the priests, priestesses, initiands and temple servants; there were service areas and kitchens. A detailed study of the Knossos Labyrinth (Castleden 1989) shows that its design resolves into a number of distinct functional areas; using this kind of analysis, it is possible to identify several separate sanctuary suites within the temple. It may be possible to analyse the plans of the other ancient Cretan temples in the same way.

*Figure 52* Procession at a temple

It seems that neither temple nor town was fortified, so it was possible for the temples to grow outwards from the nucleus of the Central Court virtually without restraint. The only restrictions to growth were the topography of the site and the West Façade. Fronting the West Court, which was an important ceremonial area in its own right, the elaborately indented West Façade was a fixed backcloth for ritual. In front of it, large-scale and public religious festivals took place, bringing temple and town together. As Nanno Marinatos has perceptively argued (1987), the common architectural features of the West Courts at Knossos, Phaistos and Mallia imply a use for harvest festivals. In each West Court there were large cylindrical granaries, and the curious pattern of paved causeways suggests that the granaries, as well as the temple entrances, were focal points.

A notable feature of the temple was the unobtrusiveness of its entrances. Knossos had seven or eight entrances, all different in design, all more or less inconspicuous. The entrances led into passageways that followed more or less devious routes towards the Central Court; it may be that the twists and turns of these passages had some magico-religious significance.

To the casual eye, there is little sense of planning. All appears chaotic, yet comparisons among the temples reveals that, although complicated, their plans are ordered and carefully thought through. The Minoan architects clearly intended to produce an effect that was bewildering, impressive and disorienting. Their intention was to create a narrative experience for the pilgrim or initiand, an experience full of unsettling incident and surprise. It was one of the temple's functions to produce these effects and they are part and parcel of the Minoan religious experience; the temple itself was in a very real sense an extreme expression of that experience. De Quincey's opium dreams were full of daemonic pomp and circumstance: they also included architectural nightmares which paralleled Piranesi's neurotic and obsessive drawings of complex, claustrophobic interiors. De Quincey frequently dreamt of a fantastically elaborate and labyrinthine building. The Minoans, under the influence of exactly the same drug, may well have had visions of a fantastic, maze-like building, and based the design for the Labyrinth on their visions. De Quincey's dream was, on his own account, of a building vision described by Wordsworth in *The Excursion*, Book II:

> The appearance, instantaneously disclosed,
> Was of a mighty city – boldly say
> A wilderness of building, sinking far
> And self-withdrawn into a wondrous depth,
> Far sinking into splendour – without end!
> Fabric it seem'd of diamond, and of gold,
> With alabaster domes, and silver spires,
> And blazing terrace upon terrace, high
> Uplifted; here serene pavilions bright
> In avenues disposed; there towers begirt
> With battlements that on their restless fronts
> Bore stars.

Some such vision, provoked by religious ecstasy and zeal, stimulated by opium, may have lain behind the elaborate and dizzying designs of the Minoan temples.

As the temples increasingly absorbed the Minoans' religious vitality, so the cults of the peak sanctuaries declined. They were still visited; sacrifice was still made; the deities were still honoured; but the real seat of religious power now lay in the temples. It was a natural enough development. Secular, economic power gravitated towards the lowlands and to the urban centres in particular. It was inevitable that spiritual power should devolve on the urban temples. Probably the priestesses systematically brought the peak sanctuaries and other rural shrines under their control, just as Solomon was to do a thousand years afterwards, building an urban temple and then extending his power over the high places.

When the temples were rebuilt in 1700 BC, the pottery style reflected a change of philosophy of some kind. The Marine Style, with its fish, seaweed, shell and octopus motifs, shows a concern for the abundance of life in the dark waters of the Mediterranean; implicitly, it invokes the god Poteidan or

Poseidon, to whom the Knossos Labyrinth was dedicated (Castleden 1989, pp. 112–13, 138–9). The twilit subterranean chambers carried undertones of the cave sanctuaries. The Throne Sanctuary at Knossos was specifically designed to simulate the peak sanctuary environment. Gods and goddesses were lured to the towns. It was as if a diffuse religious power permeating the whole island was gathered and transferred from the mountains and hillsides to the temples and then, after the destructions of 1470 BC, to just one temple, at Knossos. After the virtual abandonment of the Knossos Labyrinth in 1380 BC, that power retreated underground, to the cave sanctuaries. It was in this late period, between 1380 and 1200 BC, that the cave cult really came into its own, acting as a night-safe for the whole fund of Minoan religious beliefs. From this cave cult sprang the peculiar, complicated, mixed-origin myth of the birth of Zeus Cretagenes, 'Cretan-born Zeus', as it was told by the Greeks in the fifth century BC.

### BURIAL CUSTOMS

The care which bereaved Minoans sometimes lavished on their dead suggests a belief in the afterlife, and the idea of an Elysium, a pleasant Heaven awaiting people at the end of their earthly lives, is thought to have been a Minoan creation. It is not known whether the Minoans had any concept of reward or retribution in the afterlife, though they seem to have believed that the human soul survived death. The butterfly, a common motif in Minoan art, is thought to symbolize the soul (Alexiou, undated, p. 121). The fact that the butterfly is engraved on circular gold weights from a tomb at Mycenae may indicate that, at least in the Mycenean period, there was a belief in the weighing of souls to determine their fate after death. Bronze scale-pans have been found in Late Minoan tombs in Crete itself.

Since most burials have been robbed, archaeology rarely gives us the sort of fine detail about the Minoans that we would like to have. The Agia Triadha sarcophagus is invaluable in showing us the funeral ceremonies that were offered for some important person around 1400 BC. They consisted of an elaborate sequence of libations poured into a large vessel on an altar between two double-axes mounted on painted pyramidal bases; grave-goods were dedicated to the sheepskin-draped statue of a god in front of another altar; offerings of food and drink were dedicated at a third altar set up in front of a sacred tree shrine; music was played and an ox and two goats were sacrificed.

The Early Minoan burials were mainly in collective tombs, each one a family grave that continued in use over several generations. A small settlement might have just one tomb: Knossos was ringed by such tombs. Nearly all the burials were inhumation burials. The isolated cremations found in the Ailias cemetery on the eastern fringes of Knossos and dating to around 1600 BC may be the graves of foreigners from Anatolia, where cremation burials were the norm. More usually, the body was bound up in a folded position, with the knees under the chin. Then it was simply laid on the floor of the tomb, or forced into a large storage jar which was laid on its side in the tomb; a third alternative, which became more popular with time, was to place the trussed corpse in a clay box or larnax.

The earlier collective tombs were cut, like artificial caves, out of the soft limestone. They had no particular design, often had several connecting chambers, and continued in use right through to the Late Minoan period. A large rock-cut tomb dating to 1600–1500 BC has been excavated at Katsamba; its grave-goods included pottery cups, engraved seals (one imported from Syria), and inlaid gold rings.

In some parts of Crete the rock was too hard to carve in this way, so caves or built tombs were used instead. At Mochlos, there were some rectangular tombs which belonged to wealthy families. In the Mesara Plain the built tombs were usually circular. A classic example of these is the Kamilari tomb near Phaistos, which was built around 2000 BC and was in use for several hundred years. Its massive cyclopean ring of masonry still stands to a height of 3 metres. Perhaps it was never roofed: if so, it must have had a very high corbelled vault, either in stone or in mudbrick. On the whole, the evidence points to these Mesara round tombs having been roofed; the surviving wall stumps are very thick and have faces that slope inwards, and there are sometimes fallen wall blocks in the interior, suggesting a collapsed beehive vault. Vaults with a ground-level diameter of 9 metres or so, such as the one at Platanos (Figure 53C), were certainly technically feasible; they must have been imposing structures in their original state.

The Mesara tombs often had annexes as overspill ossuaries and cult rooms built onto them. The Apesokari tomb (Figure 53B) had burials in the corbelled circular chamber and in some of the outer chambers: it also had a rectangular cult room. In the vestibule was a niche with a small bench-altar to support a piece of stalactite as an idol. Outside the tomb entrance was a larger, rectangular altar which may have been used for sacrificial offerings. The vaulted tombs at Lebena, or Lendas, on the south coast have a similar layout to those in the Mesara Plain, with a round main chamber and rectangular cult rooms adjoining.

There has always been a tendency to build houses for the dead to resemble houses for the living. The curious thing about the Minoans is that they were, in Mesara at least, building round tombs and rectangular houses: the rooms were rectangular even in the neolithic period. It may be that the round tombs are a reference back to a very ancient and primitive type of house, long-since abandoned except for tomb architecture, or they may be an exotic, a design imported from a foreign land where both tombs and houses were round. In favour of the latter explanation is the sudden appearance of the Cretan round tomb in about 3000 BC: they are not known in Crete before that time. It may be, then, that the idea of the circular tombs was brought in by the

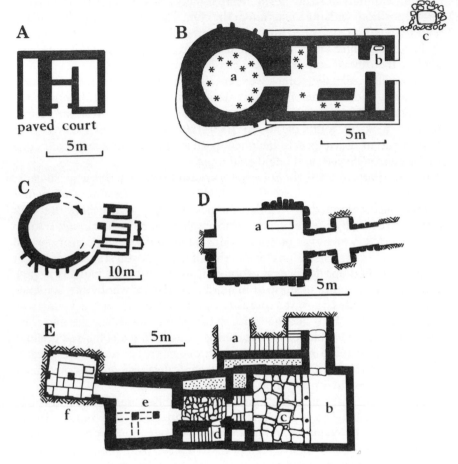

*Figure 53* Minoan tomb plans. A: a built tomb at Mochlos. B: a built tomb at Apesokari. a = burials, b = altar in niche, c = altar outside. C: large circular tomb with rectangular cult rooms adjoining, at Platanos in the Mesara Plain. D: the Royal Tomb at Isopata. a = grave pit. E: the Temple Tomb at Knossos. a = winding rock-cut entrance passage, b = portico, c = open, paved courtyard, d = covered lobby and staircase up to shrine on first floor, e = built pillar crypt later subdivided with walls to make an ossuary, f = rock-cut tomb chamber, lined with gypsum slabs, with late grave-pit in north-east corner

immigrants who arrived in Crete from Anatolia at the beginning of the bronze age.

At the beautiful ridge-top site of Phourni, above the Minoan town of Arkhanes, there is an extraordinary Minoan mortuary-complex which seems to have been in use continuously from 2500 to 1250 BC (Plate 19). It is still not fully excavated, but it has already emerged as one of the richest and most extensive prehistoric cemeteries in the Aegean. It has several circular tholos tombs, of which one, 'E', dates to the Pre-Temple Period, 2500–2000 BC.

But of all the tombs so far uncovered at Phourni, Tholos 'A', which is located well to the north of the two main mortuary houses, is the most spectacular. It dates from about 1390 BC, just a few years before the fall of the Labyrinth on the plain below. It consists of an 8-metre-diameter beehive tomb, with a large square capstone still in place, and a 20-metre-long entrance passage on the east side; it is like a simpler, trial-run version of the great tholos tombs at Mycenae, and it may well be that the Mycenean tholos tombs originated as a Minoan idea (Plate 20).

Phourni's Tholos 'A' had its main chamber robbed in antiquity, but in 1965 the side chamber yielded the first untouched high-status burial of Minoan Crete. Among the grave goods were 140 pieces of gold jewellery, which had originally adorned the corpse of an important woman, who may have been a queen or a high priestess. With the great lady's body were the remains of a sacrificed bull and horse. Near this tomb are several large rectangular mortuary-complexes, consisting of many small rectangular chambers, and these seem to have evolved as family tombs for the Minoan township of Arkhanes, whose distant successor Phourni still overlooks (Plate 19).

The Temple Tomb on the southern edge of Minoan Knossos is a tomb like no other in Crete (Figure 53E). The tomb chamber is a relatively small square chamber cut out of the living rock of the Gypsades hillside. Its walls and floor were sheathed in gypsum slabs, whilst its ceiling was painted blue and supported by a gypsum pillar. The original burials, placed there around 1550 BC, were unfortunately robbed in antiquity. All that was found in the tomb chamber when it was excavated was the apparently hasty, late burial in a pit under the floor of an old man and a child. Was the man the last Minoan king or the last Minoan high-priest of Knossos? The date of this burial, around 1380 BC, may be very significant, for it was then that the Labyrinth was virtually abandoned and the development of Minoan culture took a new direction. Sinclair Hood (1971, pp. 144–5) writes of the Temple Tomb as the only certain example of a Minoan royal tomb, but its status is so peculiar that we cannot be sure who was buried there, either at the beginning or at the close of its period of use.

The building attached to the front of the tomb chamber included another pillar crypt (later partitioned and turned into an ossuary), some cult rooms, a walled courtyard and a portico. The Temple Tomb was evidently a very special tomb, but its precise original function seems to be impossible to ascertain. It may, at the time when it was built, have been intended as a final resting-place for the priestesses of the Knossos Labyrinth, rather than, as is often assumed, for the Knossian kings.

Another allegedly 'royal' tomb is the Great Tomb at Chrysolakkos, which

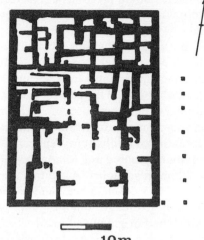

*Figure 54* Plan of the Chrysolakkos tomb                    **10 m**

stands at the northern edge of the Minoan town of Mallia, a little inland from the cliffed headland, and it is thought to have served as a family vault for Mallia's royal family in the New Temple Period (for instance, by Hood 1971, p. 145). This was a large rectangular building in the same tradition as the mortuary houses at Phourni, with a rabbit warren of small chambers inside and a colonnade along the east front; it differs from the Phourni mortuary houses in having been built all at once. The surviving lower courses of the outer wall are of smooth, beautifully cut and polished blocks of dense grey stone.

It is obviously significant that many of the Minoan tomb entrances open towards the east; the Temple Tomb and the Tomb of the Lady of Arkhanes both face east, the direction from which the rising sun's resuscitating rays shine. The east-facing Chrysolakkos colonnade probably had the same ritual significance. Unfortunately, the burials were thoroughly plundered for their precious grave-goods in antiquity, and we must be thankful that at least the Wasp or Bee Pendant survived the looting (Figure 28). The local name of the place, the Gold Pit, implies that a good deal of gold was robbed from the site before the French archaeologists started excavating it in the 1920s, and there is good reason to suppose that the so-called Aegina Treasure, which is now in the British Museum, originated here.

The 'Royal Tomb' at Isopata was a later rich tomb, post-dating the Thera eruption. The Isopata Tomb, dating to 1450–1400 BC, was an impressive chamber tomb with a large, corbelled, rectangular chamber and a high stone vault. It had a long entrance passage sloping down from the east. The Isopata Tomb was wrecked in 1941–2, during the Battle of Crete, by being turned into a gun emplacement by German soldiers, so drawing British shellfire upon it.

The collective burials continued, but the size of the tombs gradually diminished. By the time of the Thera eruption in 1470 BC, most of the burials were in small tombs holding at most four members of a family. Usually the burials were accompanied by some personal grave-goods, such as a seal-stone or a metal signet ring, but they were also usually robbed soon afterwards. In the Late Minoan period new styles of burial came in, the larnax burials. The larnax was a clay sarcophagus, often with panelled sides and gabled lids, and elaborately decorated all over with painted images. From their shapes, they were apparently copied from wooden originals, and it seems likely that the clay coffins are really copies in clay of wooden clothes-chests. Just occasionally, wooden chests were used as coffins, but only for very wealthy people. The Agia Triadha Sarcophagus is a superb example of a larnax, though made of stone coated in plaster. It is beautifully painted with scenes of the dead person's funeral along the sides, and scenes of Elysium, or the way to Elysium, on the ends; smiling goddesses in plumed head-dresses ride along in a chariot drawn by a griffin on one end, and by a goat on the other, presumably ready to convey the human soul to Elysium, to live ever after with the gods. The Agia Triadha sarcophagus is a marvellous work of Minoan art; but it is also a positive and glowing affirmation of the Minoans' beliefs concerning human mortality and the life after death.

# 7

# The Minoan personality

My spear and my sword and that fine shield, which guards my skin,
are my great wealth. For I plough with this, I reap with this, I tread
the sweet wine from the vine with this, I am called master of the serfs
with this. But those who dare not hold the spear and sword and that
fine shield, to guard their skin, all fall and kiss my knee, calling me
master and great lord.

> ('The Song of Hybrias', about 500 BC: one of
> the earliest surviving Cretan lyric poems)

Corporate personalities are often attributed to ancient civilizations, in much
the same way that they are to modern nations. We see the ancient Egyptians
as strong, conservative, shrewd, and at the same time devout believers in the
immortality of the human soul. We see the classical Greeks as articulate,
candid, precise, and beset by a rather cold and pessimistic philosophy that
nothing will come right of itself; that in turn is redeemed by their underlying
faith in language, 'the spirit of thought', and in the human race itself. In his
*Antigone*, Sophocles spoke for the Greeks in general when he wrote,

> Many marvels walk through the world,
> Terrible, wonderful,
> But none more than man.

Yet, side by side with their prevailing rationality, there were contradictory
traits in the Greek personality. They were prickly, passionately quarrel-
some, and warlike. They were believers in democracy, and yet they kept
slaves. The more we find out about a culture, the more internal contradictions and variations we are likely to find, and the more difficult it becomes to
define its personality. Indeed, it may only be possible to see a corporate
personality when our knowledge is superficial and only a handful of characteristics is perceived. This is apparent in the average modern European's

idea of the Americans or the Chinese, which tends to be a simplified image assembled from impressions of a small sample of American or Chinese people actually seen and a larger number of fictional and sub-fictional characters encountered in books, magazines and television programmes. The way in which this process produces a dangerously cartoon-like image is all too familiar: it can turn the imagined people into contemptible grotesques, figures of fun, butts for jokes, aliens beneath consideration, or even imagined enemies. The risk is no less great when we try to form a mental image of a long-dead people; cultural or temporal chauvinism may cause us to err in making them too barbaric on the one hand, or dissatisfaction with our present civilization may cause us to see them as a noble ideal irretrievably lost on the other. Either of these tendencies is likely to cause us to misrepresent the ancient Egyptians or the ancient Greeks – or the Minoans.

There is nevertheless the possibility that adherence to a particular ideology will give a particular flavour and direction to a culture. A set of ideas, strongly held by a significant proportion of a population can produce a distinctive style of group behaviour, a distinctive way of responding to situations, and a distinctive culture. In this way, we are justified in seeking to identify distinctive qualities in the Minoan culture. The ideology which held the Minoans in its grasp may have been responsible for releasing an archetype, in the way described by Jung in his essays 'Wotan' and 'After the catastrophe' (1964, pp. 179–93, 194–217). Jung's view was that in the 1930s and 1940s the German people were possessed by the North European god of storm and war, Wotan, a fundamental attribute of the German collective psyche unleashed by Hitler. Jung had difficulty in deciding whether it was Wotan or Dionysos who had taken control of the German people, but was in no doubt that a communal psychological infection, a *furor teutonicus*, had thrown the entire German nation into a state of frenzy.

Jung's Wotan was the rain-water of an ephemeral desert storm, which can find its old river bed at any time, after however long an absence. Jung wrote as a Swiss, and in the midst and the aftermath of the Nazi horror, and he did not write dispassionately or objectively; nevertheless, his interpretation has the ring of truth.

> From the east comes Hrym with shield held high;
> In giant-wrath does the serpent writhe;
> O'er the waves he twists, and the tawny eagle
> Gnaws corpses, screaming 'Naglfar is loose!'
>
> (*Nibelungenlied*)

Were the Minoans perhaps also possessed by one of their deities, the powerful archetypes that normally reside, unexpressed, in the unconscious mind? If they were taken over by some *euphoria minoica*, it could explain the particular and rather discomforting sense of elation which much of the Minoans' artwork communicates.

It is nevertheless very difficult to reach back into the thought world of the Minoans. There are powerful and suggestive forms and images, but the documentary evidence is elusive. The Homeric sagas contain some of the oldest thoughts and ideas about Crete and the Aegean world in general, yet they were written down about 600 years after the Knossos Labyrinth was abandoned, which is a long enough lapse of time for large-scale changes to have come about. John Chadwick (1976, p. 185) reminds us that there are some very specific ways in which the Mycenean world differed from the Homeric. The titles of officials on the Linear B tablets (*hequetas*, *telestas*, *lawagetas*) are altogether missing from Homer; Homer uses two words for king, whereas the closely related words *wanax* and *guasileus* of the tablets signify two distinctly different roles – king and chief. In addition, the Minoans wrote in at least four different scripts – Hieroglyphic, Linear A, Linear B, and the pictograms of the Phaistos Disc – three of which remain undeciphered: the fourth, Linear B, seems to have been used exclusively for accounting, inventories and religious dedications. In spite of the existence of the four scripts, there seems, tantalizingly, to have been no Minoan literature: none, at any rate, that has survived.

### THE TRADITIONAL VIEW

The idea of a Minoan personality is nonetheless strongly rooted. The artwork is so vivid, so immediate in its appeal that we may feel an instant affinity with the Minoans as people. As Maitland Edey (1975, p. 57) has said, we sense that if we could get one step closer we could get to know them. Our view of them is nevertheless largely the result of Sir Arthur Evans' skilfully presented publicity for peace-, flower- and leisure-loving Minoan aesthetes. Although a great deal of new archaeological evidence has come to light since Evans' time, and alternative visions have been proposed, for example by Hans Wunderlich (1975), it is to a very great extent Evans' presentation of the Minoans that has prevailed, right down to the present day.

This firmly established twentieth-century tradition has it that the Minoans were talented, subtle, luxury-loving, worldly, sophisticated. They were sensitive, elegant and graceful; they loved refined and sumptuous decor, beautiful art objects and jewellery. They loved peace and the rule of law, detesting tyranny and warfare. They had no personal ambition, a trait inferred from the complete anonymity of artists, sculptors, rulers and military leaders: there were no boastful lists of great achievements or conquests, and no monumental portrait-statues of kings of the type found in Egypt. In fact, no individuals emerge at all. There is no Solomon, no Pericles, no Akhenaton, no Imhotep. From this it is argued that the Minoan culture was an anonymous one, where function within the hierarchy was all-important, personal identity nothing.

Henry Miller, voicing the conventional view in *The Colossus of Maroussi*

(1980, pp. 123–4), saw the Minoans as splendidly sane, rich, peaceful and powerful, a clean, salubrious and joyful people: 'the prevailing note is one of joy'.

Above all, the Minoans have been seen as nature-lovers. They responded to all the various aspects of the natural world: plants, flowers and animals, birds, fish and landscape, sea, shells, rocks and seaweed. The princes and great ladies of the Minoan courts wandered languorously amid flowers, birds and butterflies in their royal gardens.

The Minoans were great admirers of the human body, as the classical Greeks were to be later, but the Minoans had their own distinctive ideals of physical beauty. They liked to see long, slender, graceful but muscular limbs, narrow waists and dark hair falling in long flowing ringlets – on both men and women. They liked to see broad shoulders and deep chests on men, and firm full breasts and full hips on women. Minoan women were elegant, graceful, poised, well-mannered and sexually alluring, with their breasts displayed and their lips and eyes accentuated by make-up. The men too were elegant and dressed in a way that was sexually provocative; the torso and thighs were exposed and the narrow waist and prominent codpiece were obvious focal points. Both men and women, as depicted in works of art, were consciously and self-confidently graceful, attractive and fashionable, in a way that looks startlingly modern.

Minoan art, in harmony with these characteristics, focuses on themes from nature – crocuses, sailing nautiluses, dolphins, octopuses, swallows, ibexes among them – rather than themes from contemporary events. There is no sense of history, of political events, of even the possibility of war in the frescoes, with the one exception of the miniature fresco fragments showing a

*Figure 55* The leader of the people?

band of men saluting their leader (Figure 55) by brandishing their spears –
and even this may be a ceremonial rather than a military gesture. One of
their most outstanding traits, the tradition has it, was their love of peace, the
*pax minoica* spreading effortlessly as a result of pure and massive cultural
superiority across the Aegean Sea. The Minoans' strength at sea was so great
that they had no need to fortify their Cretan cities at all: none of them had
defensive walls.

Jacquetta Hawkes (1968) has drawn attention to the essentially feminine
quality of Minoan culture. Women did not necessarily dominate men
socially and politically, nor were men effeminate; it is merely that feminine
qualities – that is to say, qualities that, however irrationally and preju-
dicially, in the contemporary western world we would be more likely to
associate with women than with men – were to the fore. We could cite as
examples love of art and nature: love of miniatures, models and toys: love
of jewellery, ornament and detailed decoration: love of peace: lack of
interest in politics, self-aggrandisement and war. Jacquetta Hawkes de-
velops her theme to the point where she argues that the personality of
classical Greece was produced as a result of the fertilization of the feminine
Cretan culture by the masculine Achaean, or Mycenean, culture of the
Greek mainland. The marriage of the two mythologies produced the
goddess Athena who, in her own person, combined the masculine qualities
of a warlike goddess of victories and a goddess of intellectual strength and
wisdom with the feminine qualities of the Minoan goddess, associated with
weaving, wearing a long flowing gown, and acting as a dependable protec-
tress and mother figure for the whole community.

### TESTING THE TRADITION

This traditional view of the Minoans has prevailed throughout the twentieth
century. Nevertheless, we should examine the different elements within that
orthodox view, to see how far the archaeological evidence supports them.
Some may turn out to be well founded, others mere wish-fulfilment. First, let
us look at the oft-repeated assertion that the Minoans were peaceable. It is
one of their most attractive characteristics, and the more so because they
were surrounded by warlike and very assertive neighbours – the Myceneans,
Egyptians and Hittites that we know of, and there were probably many
more besides.

The assumption that the Minoans were total pacifists is based mainly on
the apparent lack of solid, built fortifications. Nevertheless, Lucia Nixon
(1983) quotes Alexiou's very significant list of Pre-Temple sites on Crete
whose location seems to show an interest in defence: Pyrgos, Fournou
Korifi, Vasiliki, Khamaizi, Kastri near Palaikastro, and Debla. Then, in the
Old Temple Period, and dating to around 2000–1800 BC (Middle Minoan
I–II), came Agia Photiou. This hilltop site overlooking the north coast of

Crete was first developed as an open settlement, consisting of a rectangular building 18 by 27 metres and comprising 36 rooms. Almost at once it was destroyed – whether by the inhabitants themselves or by invaders is impossible to tell – and replaced by a circular building 7.5 metres in diameter. The hilltop was surrounded by a substantial circular wall which the excavator interprets as defensive in intention (Tsipopolou 1988). The similar minifortress settlement of Khamaizi lay to the west of Agia Photiou and would just have been visible from it. We may, in these two sites, be glimpsing part of a chain of coastal military bases which once ringed Minoan Crete and kept it secure.

In the Old and New Temple Periods, we could add Phaistos to the list of fortress sites, with its precipitous slopes defending it from sudden attack on three sides. Although the temples may not have been surrounded by fortress walls, there is every reason to suppose that they were secure. If we interpret the 'palaces' as temples, and therefore not necessarily the headquarters of the King or the Lawagetas, there is no reason to suppose that the buildings would have been regarded as a military target. Nevertheless, the temples were richly equipped with great ceremonial bronze double-axes, with cult objects in gold, lapis lazuli, and other precious materials, so they would have been well worth looting. Ransacking an enemy's temple and stealing his cult idols was also an easy way of humiliating and demoralizing him. We know, for example, that the Hittite kings indulged in this tactic (Lehmann 1977, p. 191). For these reasons it would be surprising if the temples were left completely undefended. In fact, there are indications that the Knossos Labyrinth was made secure. There is clear evidence, in the form of pivot-holes in the floor at the West Porch at Knossos, that both the entrances into the Procession Corridor were equipped with substantial double doors. Tablets found in the West Wing of the Labyrinth record quantities of weapons; perhaps the entrances and various other strategic points round the temple were guarded by an armed security force.

There may alternatively, or additionally, have been psychological defences. Possibly the power of the temple priestesses was such that they could exact awe-inspiring retribution from anyone committing sacrilege. Possibly there was an agreement, stated or tacit, that neighbouring Cretan states would not attack one another. Since warfare is clearly irrational, it may have occurred to the Minoans to make war taboo, at least among themselves. Taking this idea a step further, to the state of affairs that seems to have existed between 1470 and 1380 BC, an almost island-wide network of religious controls and economic interdependence centring on Knossos may have made any attack by a Cretan unlikely.

Nevertheless, there were some security measures at Knossos. Evans' reconstruction of a section of the eastern façade of the Knossos Labyrinth as a high, windowless curtain wall is probably right. The West Court was bounded on its western side by a curving wall which may have been no more than a retaining wall to stabilize the tell material beneath the West Court terrace, but there are indications that the wall rose above the level of the West Court; there were clearly entrance gaps where roads passed through it, and those entrances may have had gates. The Labyrinth wall on the eastern side of the West Court, the West Façade, had no windows on its ground floor, and this feature too would have made the building secure against attack.

There may be something in the traditional idea that the Minoans did not need to defend their cities on land because they were defending them at sea. We infer that there were war-galleys in the Minoan-Mycenean world (see Chapter 5), and we know that hundreds of rowers were called up to defend Pylos during the military crisis that led to its fall. No doubt there were coastguards stationed all along the Cretan shoreline, just as there were at Pylos, and seaborne enemies were dealt with before they ever reached the coast.

It is possible that Khamaizi, a small rounded structure on a north coast hilltop between Mochlos and Sitia, was one of these coastguard look-out stations. Other small, isolated, near-coastal buildings which are otherwise difficult to account for could have functioned in the same way, without necessarily being massively constructed or in any other conspicuous way defensive.

Nor were the Minoans weaponless. They deposited weapons as ritual offerings in cave sanctuaries and graves, and there is no reason to suppose that the weapons were not used for warfare. Men are often depicted, in figurines, for example, with daggers hanging from their belts, although this is likely to have been a simple precaution against robbery or personal attack. Other weapons were used in hunting; the Lion Hunt Dagger shows bows, spears and shields in a non-military context. Swords too could have been carried for self-defence or for hunting. Nevertheless, the whole panoply of weapons and military equipment was available to the Minoans – including body-armour and chariots – and it could have been used for warfare.

The threat from overseas must have been ever-present, given Crete's situation. The threat at home, from neighbouring city-states, probably varied significantly through time: during the long Minoan period there must have been times of peace, times of tension and unrest, and times of war. Lucia Nixon (1983) suggests that Crete may have been torn by war during the Pre-Temple Period, but the building of the temples as power centres brought the phase of unrest to an end. Perhaps the establishment of well-defined urban centres, with firm control over their hinterlands and developing networks of trading and diplomatic relationships, led to a more harmonized political regime from 2000 BC onwards. Even so, as we saw in Chapter 2, the possibility that a subject territory or even a confederation of dissatisfied subject territories rose up against Knossos in 1380 BC is very real.

The various sporadic burnings and destructions of the temples and other, lesser Minoan centres are very difficult to evaluate. How can we tell, three-and-a-half thousand years on, whether a fire was started accidentally or deliberately? How can we tell, after that lapse of time, whether a fire, if deliberately started, was an isolated act of arson by a discontented slave, or part of an armed insurrection, or an onslaught by an invading Mycenean army? It is difficult to define an invasion in purely archaeological terms: hence our many difficulties in interpreting the later stages of the Minoan period on Crete. It is equally difficult to point to hard evidence of Minoan militarism, especially in the face of a well-established, or at any rate long-established, view that Minoans were non-aggressive. One feature of the culture which is impossible to overlook is the double-axe. Whatever it may have come to symbolize as a full-blown mystic symbol in temple iconography, the double-axe has the look of a weapon, a battle-axe.

It may be that a good deal of latent aggression was sublimated and controlled by religious rituals. A major distinguishing feature of the Nuba people of the Sudan is their lack of aggression. Their fighting is channelled into ritual wrestling matches which are the focus of their belief-system. The Minoans developed bull-leaping into a major, focal cult activity, and there were other violent, agonistic rites too, such as boxing and wrestling. Performing or watching blood sacrifices will also have released some of the aggression.

Identifying the Minoans as nature-lovers seems at first far less tendentious, far less controversial, yet, if it is an inaccurate reading of the evidence, it may seriously mislead us. Lucia Nixon (1983) argues that the use of nature motifs on frescoes and painted pottery is not really enough to justify characterizing a whole people as flower-lovers. It is a valid argument, and by substituting nineteenth-century Britons for bronze age Cretans we can see how misleading a line of thought Evans' might be; the roses on their teacups and the ivy-covered trellises printed on their wallpaper would not blind us to the Victorians' capacity to exploit child labour and commit acts of ruthless military aggression in India and Africa.

But the more important point is that the nature motifs in Minoan art are for the most part not merely decorative, as they are in nineteenth-century European art. The Minoans used nature motifs to conjure up the habitats of deities. This can be clearly seen in the décor of the Throne Sanctuary at Knossos, where a symbolic peak, the stone throne itself, was set in a wild landscape of fresco mountains; the griffin on the west wall was regularly depicted as the goddess's heraldic attendant. The representation of plants and animals may often indicate a religious dedication or thought. The representations are, moreover, not very true to nature. The freedom with which many of the images are painted or carved is deceptive; the artist was not capturing the fleeting moment in the manner of a French impressionist, but rather conveying life and vitality to an idea of the thing depicted. It is an otherworld that we are being shown on the Minoan murals, with species of plants and animals that, in many cases, we have never seen in the everyday world. The dream-like, poeticized effect may be deliberate, part of the exotic thought-world which the Minoans inhabited.

The carefree image sometimes applied to Minoans may also be wide of the mark. The faces in the frescoes are often smiling; sometimes the heads are thrown up as if convulsed with laughter or song; yet the ecstasy of a major religious experience might have produced the same effect. Similarly, the scenes of dancing are unlikely to be scenes of secular recreation: from the contexts, they are much more likely to be ritual dances designed to produce an epiphany of a deity. In other words, in spite of the apparent diversity of the material, we are actually looking at one particular side of the Minoans' lives, their experience of religious ecstasy. There was a darker side too, the shadowy initiation rites and ordeals; we can infer these (e.g. Marinatos 1984) even though we are rarely shown them.

That the Minoans were admirers of physical beauty in both men and women seems self-evident from their works of art. Often the figures pose in attitudes of exaggerated pride and nobility, such as the attendant bearing a rhyton in the Cupbearer Fresco at Knossos (Figure 57), the young Minoans and the so-called Priest-King from the Procession Fresco, the prince or older initiate on the Chieftain Cup (Figure 56), and the faience Snake Goddesses. The Minoans are often portrayed giving vent to extreme emotion, whether dancing ecstatically to greet a goddess as she approaches, or swelling with pride as they present offerings in the temple, or prostrated with grief over the god's departure.

*Figure 56* Two figures from the Chieftain Cup

It is impossible to tell from the evidence whether there was scope for individual ambition in Minoan Crete. It may be, as the traditional view has it, that personal ambition was unknown: certainly no evidence of it has survived. On the other hand, ambition and the pursuit of power may have existed, but simply went unrecorded. For the time being it remains an open question, yet it is surely significant that there are no portrait-frescoes or portrait-statues of any of the Minoan rulers, and no inscriptions boasting of power and conquest.

With the Minoans' creativity and originality we are on surer ground. The wide range of distinctive artefacts which only the Minoans could have designed and made indicates an intensely dynamic and original culture. Some of the ideas may have been borrowed – the hieratic poses of the Procession Corridor, possibly from Egypt, the sacral bull horns, possibly from Anatolia – but the Minoans developed them in a way that was always recognizably Minoan. The sacral horns became stylized to the point where they could stand singly and function as a focus on an altar, or stand in rows to make an ornamental pinnacled parapet for a temple roof cornice. The 'Egyptian' poses of the figures were developed in a way that was less monumental, more animated and vital than the original, so that the figures seem to be about to come to life. It is, above all, this vigorous vitality and immediacy that gives Minoan works of art their distinctively Minoan flavour.

In the New Temple Period, Cretan artists achieved a mastery of equilibrium; the images of people, for instance, appear to be completely natural and yet those images are careful compromises between the objective reality and the concepts imposed upon it. There is an equilibrium here which verges on the classical, and yet conveys very different effects – of delicacy, suppleness and muscular tension, of energy, movement and youthfulness.

Sometimes we tend to be swept along by the free treatment which the artists gave to their subjects and, as a result, we overlook the beautifully fine detail which is also a characteristic of much of their work. Obviously the sealstones and signet rings by their very nature contain a great deal of fine detail, but it exists in large-scale designs too. Close inspection of the Procession Corridor and Cupbearer Frescoes reveals that the various different textile patterns of the young men's kilts have been painted with great precision (Figures 6 and 57). Similarly, the geometrical, stepped outlines of the painted garden wall in the Villa of the Lilies at Amnisos contain detail that is not at all evident on first viewing: the main impression is of white lilies growing against a low, stepped, buff wall, with an exhilarating red background beyond. The wall's cornice is indicated by no less than seven separate zones of ochre; some of them are, moreover, textured with a subtle and very carefully drawn criss-cross pattern that suggests a textile or basket-weave pattern. This eye for precise minute detail is what gives Minoan art its particular and uncanny sharpness.

## THE NEW MINOANS

How far does the traditional picture of the Minoans stand, and to what extent do we need to revise our view of them? Certainly some revision is necessary, since Evans' milk-and-water Minoans could never have survived in the tough world of the bronze age Aegean, let alone produced a flourishing civilization that lasted over a thousand years.

There must have been a sterner, stronger side. We should recognize that a society may possess a dark side that it does not express in its art and which does not leave any archaeological trace. In some ways, societies function like individuals, who may go to great lengths to project a particular public persona and conceal certain aspects of personality; even an experienced biographer may fail to unearth the shadow-personality. We should certainly not take the laughter, the dancing and the apparent *joie de vivre* at face value. The Minoans, we can assume, had a dark side even if it was not expressed in art or archive.

The bull sacrifice was probably a regular occurrence at the temples, yet it is very rarely depicted: the scene with the trussed bull on its sacrificial table shown on the Agia Triadha sarcophagus is a rarity. Equally, war and conquest may have been important activities, as important to the Minoans as to the Hittites or Egyptians, even though they left them unexpressed in their art. In fact, the nearest approach to a record of battle is to be found in the Minoan colony of Akrotiri on Thera, where the North Wall Frieze in Room 5 of the West House unequivocally shows a naval engagement: there have been some fatalities, to judge from the naked bodies shown in the water, while in the background a fragmentary line of at least five soldiers advances, armed with boar's tooth helmets, long spears and large rectangular cow-hide shields. The large South Wall Frieze, which may at first sight be taken to show another naval engagement, nevertheless seems to depict a major religious festival: no arms are involved on land or sea and the ships seem to be dressed overall with garlands and bunting.

In fact, as with the personal ambition issue, it is possible from the evidence so far reviewed to argue either for peace-loving Minoans or for aggressive, assertive, warlike Minoans whose exploits were in the main unrecorded. The problem is encountered again in the debate concerning the nature of the 'Minoan sea-empire'. In Chapter 5, we reviewed the evidence that indicates the existence of Minoan trading-stations and colony-towns in the southern Aegean. Evans argued that the Minoans held dominion over Mycenae but others disagreed from the start, on the grounds that the Myceneans were obviously a warlike people and well able to hold their own territory. This view nevertheless falls into the trap of seeing the Myceneans as they apparently saw themselves – all-conquering warriors – and not as they may actually have been. The Myceneans may not, in spite of their Homeric and modern publicity, have been particularly good warriors. Equally, the

Minoans were certainly not as soft, feminine and peace-loving as their press.

The Minoans were a sacrificial people. The famous, but fragmentary, Procession Fresco in the Knossos Labyrinth shows a procession of worshippers coming to offer oblation to the deity or deities of the temple: at one point we seem to see the feet of the goddess they are honouring, but the rest of the figure is lost. The Cupbearer, probably best interpreted as part of the self-same decorative scheme and part of the same procession, proudly carries a rhyton, a ritual libation vessel. The Minoans were always making offerings to their deities: it was an integral part of their belief-system. In the Late Dove Goddess Shrine at Knossos there was a typical clay offering table, a round tray with three legs, cemented down to the floor, a permanent begging bowl for the goddess.

Some offering tables were equipped with pits or hollows in their surface. The best-known of these *kernoi* is the round stone *kernos* in the temple at Mallia, which was evidently used for the *panspermia* offerings, a presentation to the deity of tiny quantities of all kinds of grain and other farm produce. In classical times a similar practice prevailed: small amounts of wheat, barley, oats, lentils, beans, oil, milk, wine, honey, opium poppy-seeds and sheep's wool were offered in little cups. A sweetmeat made from various fruits was probably placed in the central hollow of the Mallia *kernos*. In some of the old Cretan monasteries, an object similar in conception to a Minoan *kernos*, a combination of candlesticks and vials to hold wheat, wine, and oil, can still be seen: some Minoan practices have survived until modern times, although it should be emphasized that the use of the *kernos* was already an ancient practice when the Minoans adopted it, since they inherited it from their neolithic forebears.

The libation vessels are recognizable from their impractical shapes, with round or pointed bottoms, and with holes in their bases for the outflow. They are also recognizable from the inventiveness of their decoration. Early vessels, from before 2000 BC, were in the form of the Magna Mater, with holes in the breasts for pouring: these may have been used for offerings of milk. Later rhytons, in the form of a bull's head, would seem the appropriate choice of vessel for a libation of blood from a sacrificed bull. And it is blood – and the preoccupation with the shedding of blood – which is the most disturbing feature of the Minoan personality.

The altars in Minoan sanctuaries were stained with the blood of many sacrifices. A fresco at Akrotiri on Thera shows an altar surmounted by sacral horns: both horns and altar run with the blood of recent sacrifices. That evidence and the evidence of the Agia Triadha sarcophagus are enough to show a more violent aspect of the Minoans, and we should perhaps have been prepared for the discovery in 1979 of the first conclusive evidence of human sacrifices in a Minoan sanctuary.

The small temple of Anemospilia stood on the north slope of Mount

*Figure 57* The Cupbearer, from a
fresco in the Knossos Labyrinth

Juktas, on the prow of the ridge overlooking the lowlands that focus on
Knossos. Its three oblong shrines ranged along the uphill side of a 10-metre-
long hall which served as an area where sacrifices were prepared; there were
auxiliary altars in the hall. A life-sized wooden cult statue stood in the
central shrine on a low bench altar. At its feet, a low knob of living rock
projected through the floor; this is thought to have been a holy rock on to
which blood libations were poured. In the northern shrine there was a
free-standing altar block which clearly functioned as a sacrificial table. The
remains of a seventeen-year-old youth with his legs drawn up were found
on the table. Analysis of the bones showed that the blood had drained from
the upper half of his body. He had probably had his throat cut with the long
bronze dagger engraved with a boar's head that lay beside him (and now
displayed in Heraklion Museum).

The skeletons of three people involved in the boy's ritual murder were found nearby. One had apparently been carrying a vessel with a yellow spotted bull painted on its side; the remains of the (male or female) skeleton were found in the hall, outside the doorway to the central shrine where the idol presided over the sacred stone. It seems possible that this temple servant was carrying a vessel full of blood freshly drained from the boy's still warm body to make a blood libation in the central shrine, at the very moment when the building collapsed, entombing the victim and his killers alike. A second figure, a strongly built man perhaps in his thirties, lay on his back on the floor beside the boy. This man, evidently of high rank, to judge from his ring made of iron and silver, and probably a priest, had apparently sacrificed the youth just minutes before the building fell down on them. Nearby was the body of an anaemic woman, probably a priestess.

The inference made by the excavators, Yannis and Efi Sakellarakis (1981), was inevitable: an impending catastrophe caused the priests and priestesses at the Sanctuary of Anemospilia to offer a human sacrifice. They were attempting to propitiate the deities of the underworld – very likely Poteidan himself – just moments before a great earthquake brought the roof of the sanctuary down. From its date, about 1700 BC, it was almost certainly the same earthquake that caused the destruction of the Old Temple at Knossos. The criminologist Dr Koutselinis feels that a *prima facie* case could be made for the priest as the murderer; after cutting the boy's carotid artery, the priest laid the dagger on the body and began to collect the blood in jars. It is interesting that the assumption is automatically made that it was the *man* who murdered the boy, when the priestess, whose body lay almost as close to the victim's, could as easily have wielded the knife; from what we are learning of Minoan gender roles, a priestess would have been quite capable of such an act.

The victim's legs were tightly folded up, feet to buttocks, and must have been tied there. How the boy went to his death is not known. He may, as the ethnologist Dr Konstantinos Romaios suggests, have been the priest's (or priestess's) son, and he may have met his fate as a matter of unquestioning filial obedience. Alternatively, he may have been a religious fanatic who willingly volunteered; or he may have been drugged or physically over-powered and sacrificed by force. We shall probably never know.

The idea that the beautiful, graceful, flower-loving Minoans were capable of committing such brutal acts is difficult for many of us to accept, but the archaeological evidence is not susceptible of any other interpretation. The consternation caused by the Sakellarakis discovery is partly a tribute to the success of Evans' propaganda for the Minoans as languid flower- and peace-lovers. It is also partly due to a wrong-headed tendency to associate a love of flowers with other specific qualities or tendencies – qualities such as passivity, pleasantness, softness, agreeableness, harmlessness, ineffectual-ity. Yet there is no inherent logic in these associations. However harmless most modern flower-lovers may be, there is no reason why we should expect to project the association – even if it were a valid one now – back three thousand years into an alien culture. There is no reason why an obsessive delight in the natural world should preclude a taste for bloodshed and violence, or any other taste or predilection for that matter. Lord Kitchener was a flower arranger.

Although the discovery at Anemospilia is so far the only unequivocal archaeological evidence of human sacrifice, there is no reason why we should regard it as anything other than an integral, if infrequent, part of Minoan religious ritual. There are even some temple archives which may record people offered as human sacrifices. One, on Knossos tablet Gg 713, includes a dedication to a god followed by a human offering: 'for Marineus, one female servant'. Another entry gives a list of men's names and then goes on to the dedication, 'to the House (= sanctuary) of Marineus, ten men'. Possibly wealthy slave-owners offered tribute to the temples in the form of temple servants, but they may equally have been offering people for sacrifice on altar-tables like the one at Anemospilia.

Close on the heels of the Sakellarakis find, actually in the same season, came Peter Warren's discovery at Knossos of evidence of child sacrifice and cannibalism. In the western part of the Minoan town of Knossos, 100 metres from the Bull's Head Sanctuary (Evans' Little Palace), Warren found a mass of children's bones in an ordinary Minoan house. It seemed that a sheep had been sacrificed at the same time the children had died. Warren reluctantly interpreted the remains as those of a mass child-sacrifice. Worse still, the bones had many knife-cuts on them, showing that the flesh had been deliberately and carefully carved off. The only interpretation seemed to be that the children had been murdered and then eaten in an act of ritual cannibalism (Warren 1980–1).

'The House of the Sacrificed Children' gave an altogether new and distasteful dimension to the picture of Minoan religious and social customs, yet – given the sinister reputation of the Knossos Labyrinth in classical folklore and the memory of King Minos as a violent, implacable and bloodthirsty tyrant – we perhaps ought to have been prepared for something of the kind. Both the Anemospilia human sacrifice and the Knossos canni- balism are represented as unique events, aberrations from the norm, but this is not perhaps the soundest archaeological interpretation. Archaeology yields only a fraction of what actually once was, records only a fraction of what actually once happened; we can be fairly sure that, whatever happened at Anemospilia and the 'House of the Sacrificed Children', it happened many more times than the once or twice that these chance archaeological survivals may at first suggest.

Donald Tumasonis (1983) has commented that the Anemospilia finds may have triggered a line of thought which led directly to the cannibal-sacrifice claim for the Knossos finds. Without the Anemospilia discovery, possibly the Knossos finds might have been interpreted differently. Are they susceptible of another interpretation? In fact, the cache of children's bones could be interpreted as a second interment. In some cultures, a preliminary phase of burial or exposure to rid the skeleton of its flesh (and presumably spirit, too) was followed by a second and final burial rite, in which the clean, dry bones were secreted in an ossuary or grave. The second rite might be preceded by the removal of any bits of flesh still adhering to the bones, which needed to be completely clean before being finally buried. Something of this practice seems to have survived into recent times within the Greek world. Only a hundred years ago, in the village of Leonidi in the Peloponnese, baskets of human bones were seen being stripped with knives by men and scrubbed with soap and soda in wash-tubs by women; the job took two days to complete, after which the bones were white, clean and ready for burial. It has been a common practice in modern Greece to leave a body in the ground for 3–7 years, until the flesh has gone. After this time, the bones have been ritually cleaned and then re-interred, often in a family ossuary. If the flesh has not fallen away, the use of knives might be a last resort (Lawson 1910).

It is obviously not possible to decide definitely what happened to the children whose remains Peter Warren found at Knossos, but it would at least seem wise to leave the door open to interpretations other than cannibalism. The sacrifice of a sheep at the time of the final burial does not in itself prove that the children too were sacrificed, only that their re-burial was accompanied by some form of religious ritual, as we would expect. This softer explanation is preferable, not because it leaves the harmless, flower-loving image of the Minoans untarnished, but because it is more in accord with what we know of the later burial practices of the region – and of prehistoric burial practices too.

So, provisionally and cautiously, cannibalism can be set aside. This still leaves the hard evidence for animal and human sacrifice unshaken. The Minoans' militarism remains an open question, although there is much to commend Sinclair Hood's (1982) argument that there is no reason to suppose that the bronze age Cretans were any less aggressive than their neighbours. There is also the thought, mentioned earlier, that the Minoan culture, with its very distinctive and independent character, simply could not have survived as a separate entity in the bronze age Aegean without being fiercely assertive. We can be fairly sure that the Minoans had to defend themselves in armed combat against predatory neighbours, and repeatedly at that.

There is a clear dichotomy between the traditional Minoans and the darker, more aggressive Minoans who are now emerging. How can the problem of the apparent contradiction be resolved? The Greek legends of an implacable Minos and his sinister Labyrinth housing a ravenous, child-devouring monster exist as a reminder that the classical Greeks were themselves aware that the Minoans possessed a shadow side. It was not the

*Figure 58* Young god with sacral horns
attended by daemons

classical Greeks who fostered the idea of the Minoans as urbane and
super-civilized aesthetes: they evidently knew – or chose to remember – the
darker side better. That darker side was temporarily forgotten in the
excitement of the Minoan discoveries early in the twentieth century AD, and
in particular Evans' discoveries at Knossos, which revealed a civilization
that was all lightness, sophistication and vivacity. Yet we have been misled
to a great extent by both the discoveries and the way in which they have been
interpreted. The frescoes, for instance, show us how the Minoans liked to
see themselves, so they are in a real sense a partial and subjective view. In
addition, much of the artwork is of a religious nature. A very large
proportion of the images we have of the Minoans comes from the temple at
Knossos and other cult centres, and we should not expect that temple-art will
give us a well-rounded picture of a people. The Minoans have, in other
words, not deceived us deliberately by misrepresenting themselves; it is
simply that we have drawn largely from their religious art in reconstructing
their general attitudes and behaviour.

There are many pitfalls in any search for the Minoan personality. It is
nevertheless unfortunate that, because of these problems, many modern
research accounts are rather tight-lipped and circumspect, often focusing on
one narrow aspect of the culture. This reaction to Evans' broad, sweeping,
synthetic approach is understandable, but it is unfortunate in that there is a
need to re-integrate all the fragments and threads of the culture into the
living whole that it must once have been. We may be able to see only
contradictions in appearance, attitude and behaviour, but we can be sure
that, between three and four thousand years ago in Crete, those would have
been seen as apparent only – an iridescent surface shimmer – and that all
would have been subsumed in an organic cultural unity.

Sometimes despairing voices are raised, bemoaning the fact that all we
have left of the culture is its artefacts, but this is to ignore what some of the
artefacts can tell us. The signet rings, for instance, show us one cult scene
after another with various permutations of religious symbols, gestures and

rituals. Attitude, emotion, commitment and thought-world are all engraved there. The frescoes too, carefully and imaginatively interpreted, as they have been by researchers such as Mark Cameron and Nanno Marinatos, can be made to yield encoded thought-systems and elaborate patterns of ritual behaviour. On the simplest level, these works of art give us images – very powerful images – of the way the Minoans liked to see themselves.

Because of the lack of documentation, the legal and social position of women is hard to judge. The culture was significantly altered by the mainland Achaeans (or Myceneans) and Dorians before the documented period began, and evidence offered from later times may not be applicable. Jacquetta Hawkes (1968) argues that it may be significant that inheritance in ancient Anatolia was matrilineal until the fourth century BC, and that in the Anatolian province nearest to Crete, Lycia, children were customarily named after their mothers, not their fathers. From this, all we can say is that a concept of matrilineal descent was available in the area; we cannot argue that the Minoan society was a matrilineal society.

There is, on the other hand, good evidence from bronze age Cretan sites that priestesses were more important figures than priests. The miniature frescoes from Knossos show groups of priestesses as the elite of large-scale ceremonial functions. It is relatively rare for men to be shown in commanding positions. There are exceptions; there is the Chieftain Cup, where either a platoon of soldiers is reporting to a prince or senior officer or a group of boy-initiands is reporting to an older youth who has already been initiated; there is a sealstone showing a male holding two lions by the scruff of the neck, though he represents a deity, the Master of Animals; there is the so-called 'Priest-King' Fresco, which actually shows a temple attendant, a servant of the goddess; there is the commanding figure of a prince, officer or lawagetas in a miniature fresco fragment, taking the salute from a host of spear-brandishing warriors (Figure 55). Poseidon-Poteidan apart, the goddesses seem to have been more important than the gods, although this point must not be overstated, since several gods are mentioned by name on the Linear B tablets. Even so, the prevailing social structure, at least in the religious sphere, is summed up by the Procession Fresco from the Knossos Labyrinth, where a priestess, or a priestess epiphany of the goddess, is shown receiving tribute, adulation and worship from two approaching lines of men.

Since Minoans of both sexes were accustomed to seeing such images, images of suppliant, subordinate males worshipping dominant females, it is reasonable to assume that the images reflect a more general social attitude. But whether women were dominant outside the religious sphere is impossible to say. On the one hand, religion was obviously of prime importance in the Minoan thought-world and pre-eminence in the religious sphere might be argued to lead directly to pre-eminence in the temporal world. In addition, the easy, relaxed, self-confident manner of the women shown in the frescoes implies that such women would be likely to be outgoing, participating in a wide range of social activity. On the other hand, there is no evidence at all from the tablets, which record some aspects of Minoan administration, that women were attaining positions of major importance, so the positive documentary evidence is lacking.

It has frequently been said that Homer's description of the Phaeacians may have drawn heavily on the world of the Minoans (e.g. Thomson 1949): many of the scenes described could have been taken from the Knossos frescoes. Nausikaa, the Phaeacian princess, gives Odysseus careful instructions how to approach her royal parents:

> When you enter the palace, walk straight across to my mother. You will find her by the fire, spinning sea-purple wool, with her chair against the pillar and her serving-women at her side. My father will be sitting there too, sipping his wine like an immortal, but pass him by and clasp my mother's knees – then, however far away, you may be sure of a safer journey home.
>
> (*Odyssey*, Book 6, 303–15)

In the streets, Odysseus meets a girl with a pitcher who tells him more about the queen:

> Not only he [King Alcinous] but her children and the whole people honour her. They look on her as a goddess when they salute her as she passes through the streets. . . . If you win her heart, you will have good hope of returning to your own country and setting eyes once more on your kith and kin.
>
> (*Odyssey*, Book 7, 66–77)

In the event, the supplication to Queen Arete turns out to have a ritual value only; Oysseus is raised up by Alcinous and led to the chair next to his own: but the symbolic deference to the queen had to be made first. We should perhaps also bear in mind that the Greeks were later to remember, for example in Plutarch's 'Life of Theseus', that it had been the custom in Minoan Crete for women to appear in public to watch the games. That folk-memory should be taken seriously, because it harmonizes with the fresco evidence from Knossos and is at variance with later Greek practice.

Given the background, queenship is possible, no less than kingship, in Minoan Crete. Around the time of the abandonment of the Labyrinth in 1380 BC, Queen Hatshepsut reigned in Egypt, although custom required – significantly – that she be called 'king'. Jacquetta Hawkes (1968) has proposed that the Minoans may have been ruled by a Priestess-Queen rather than a Priest-King. It is possible, but there is no evidence of it. On the whole (see Chapter 2), a king with limited power is more likely, with the real power residing in the hands of the Lawagetas and the priestesses.

The Palanquin Fresco, of which only fragments survive, shows a dignified female clothed in a white robe being conveyed through a crowd at some public festival. The fresco came from the Labyrinth, and the existence of a terracotta model of a palanquin with a seated female in a ritual context in another part of the Labyrinth supports the general idea that high-status women were publicly paraded as part of a religious festival. In Egypt, a wooden idol representing a deity was carried round from temple to temple to signify that the gods were visiting one another, re-consecrating the shrines. The circulation of the idol had the additional purpose of describing a magic path of protection round the settlement. At Knossos, and the other Minoan centres, the priestesses sometimes functioned as manifestations of deities, so it is possible that *they* were conveyed round the temples, courtyards and roads of the Minoan townships, bonding temple and town, goddess and people, and conferring divine protection to whole towns. The so-called 'Royal Road' connecting the Bull's Head Sanctuary with the main temple-complex at Knossos comes to mind as a natural route for a palanquin procession of this type; we can visualize the goddess returning on her litter to the Labyrinth, to be formally greeted and welcomed home in the Theatral Area.

Whatever the specifics of the situation, Jacquetta Hawkes is right in seeing the Minoan civilization as gaining much of its distinctive colour from qualities that we often think of as feminine. Attempts to explain this are fraught with difficulties. It could be argued that it happened because the original colonizers of Crete managed to settle there without fighting for it and without having to defend it subsequently, it being a large and isolated island remote from the mainland. But facile explanations that hinge on environmental determinism cannot seriously be entertained any longer; cultures somehow generate their own energies and characteristics, and often the links with external situations, factors and events are unclear. It is quite possible, as we have already seen, that the Minoans were aesthetes who were also capable of military aggression and violence.

After only a century of research, we still know far too little about the culture to be able to explain all its characteristics. Perhaps, in the end, it will prove more fruitful to return to the Jungian idea of a nation awakening to an archetype residing in the collective unconscious of its people. Under the right conditions, whatever they might be, the kraken wakes, and the whole nation may be swept along in the grip of the unleashed archetype. Perhaps we should see the Minoan civilization as a whole symbolized in the Isopata Ring: a group of opulently dressed and bejewelled priestesses dancing ecstatically to produce an epiphany, willing themselves to be possessed by the goddess who hovers in the air among them.

The Minoans were above all creative and original people, fiercely life-affirming and devoted to the worship of their many goddesses and gods. From the evidence so far gathered, their attention was finely divided between economic production, trade, bureaucratic regulation and the preservation of their material well-being on the one hand, and devotion to a complex and demanding religious creed requiring festivals, sacrifices and the building of temples and shrines on the other. There are great gaps in our knowledge of the Minoans, and we have to be ready to modify our view of them in the light of new archaeological discoveries. Minoan archaeology is still excitingly young and we can be sure that many new and unexpected things remain to be learned about this remarkable civilization.

Its most disappointing feature is the absence of literature. Tantalizingly, in spite of the several scripts which evolved during the bronze age in Crete, not one of them, on the available evidence, seems to have been utilized to record thought. There are lists of places, of people, of amounts of commodities, of deities even, yet no *comment* on any of them. But perhaps some tablets will one day be found that will tell us of some event, an account of a military expedition perhaps, or an invocation to Potnia, or a fragment of bardic poetry. It may be that the Minoans never used their scripts for such purposes, but we should keep an open mind. We have, after all, come very close indeed to losing the literature in classical Greek; only six epics have survived to us out of what may originally have been scores – only forty-five plays out of thousands. Let us hope that somewhere in Crete, perhaps buried among the rubbled foundations of some yet undiscovered and unplundered temple, there is a cache of Minoan poetry, history, or liturgy waiting for us.

The fourth-century BC Athenian orator Isocrates wrote a panegyric on what it meant to be Greek (*Panegyricus*, 47). It would perhaps be asking too much to hope for a Linear B tablet telling us what it meant to be Minoan – which is what we most want to know. But we are nearer to knowing. The conclusive evidence of boy-sacrifice from the Temple of Anemospilia gives some depth to the picture, some of the shadow side that was previously missing. The circumstantial evidence of opium-taking explains the vividness of the Minoans' religious experiences, their ecstatic and bizarre visions, their daemons, and may go a long way towards explaining the extraordinary architecture of their huge temples. The Minoans were sensual aesthetes and visionaries with bloodstained hands, and possessed of a much fiercer, darker, grimmer and more exotic beauty than we hitherto imagined.

# Appendix A:
# List of cave sanctuaries

Agiasmati, near Kapsodasos, not far from Sphakia. Neo, LMIII, Classical.

Agia Phaneromeni, near Avdou. Earliest finds LMI.

Agia Sophia, near Topolia. Neo, LMI–III and later.

Amnisos, Cave of Eileithyia. Continuous use, Neo-Roman.

Aphendis Christou, near Kastelli, Pediados. MMIII onwards.

Arkalochori, Profitis Elias grotto. EM, but mainly MMIII–LMI.

Arkoudia on Akrotiri, Kydonia. LMIII and later.

Chosto Nero, near summit of Juktas. MMIII, LMI and later.

Garephallou Spilios at Liliana, Pediados. LMIII.

Ida, Spiliara tis Voskopoulas cave. MM, LMI, LMIII and later.

Kamares, Mavri Spiliara grotto. Neo, EM, mostly MMII.

Kato Sarakina, near Khania. Neo onwards, but sacred function uncertain.

Kera Spiliotissa, near Vrysse, not far from Khania. Neo, EM, LMI–III.

Klisidi, near Myrtos, Ierapetra. Stone bench and cult stalagmite.

Korakia Trypa, near Georioupolis. Bronze age pottery. Sacred function uncertain.

Koumaro, Kydonia. MM and LM pottery.

Kouroupas. LMIII and later.

Leras grotto, near Choraphia, Kydonia. Neo and LMI mainly.

Mamelouka Trypa, Charodia Gorge near Perivolia. EM–LMIII: cult use MMII–LMI.

Mavro Spilio, Knossos. LM.

Melidoni, Gerospilios Cave. LMIII. Sacred function uncertain.

Patsos, Amariou. LMI–LMIII.

Platyvola or Skotini Spilia near Kato Pigadi. Neo–LMIII.

Psychro. MMI–LMIII and later.

Skales, Sitias. Bronze age pottery.

Skordolakkia, near Asphendou. Palaeolithic? Minoan? Iron age? Undatable!

Skotino, Pediados. LMI.

Spilios, near Milatos. LM.

Stravomyti, near Karnari Metochi. MM–LM and later.

Trapeza, near Tylissos. MMIII–LMI.

Tsoutsouras. LMIII.

Vernofeto. Paintings attributed to LMIII (by Paul Faure).

Vigla, near Keratokambos, Viannou. Bronze age.

Vitsiles, near Kanli Kastelli, Temenos. MMII. Sacred function uncertain.

EM = Early Minoan; MM = Middle Minoan; LM = Late Minoan. Dates indicate dates of finds from the caves. Whether these in turn indicate the period of cult use is another matter.

# Appendix B:
# List of peak sanctuaries

Ai Lias, near Vorrou. MMIII–LMI.
Ambelos, Sitias. Figurines.
Ankouseliana, A. Vasiliou. MM.
Agia Triadha. Figurines on hill slopes probably came from a sanctuary at top.
Choudesti, near Vathypetro. MM.
Demati, near Skinias. MMI.
Drapanos, Drapanokephala. MMIII–LMI.
Etia, Sitias. MM.
Gonies, Philiovimos, Maleviziou. MM.
Juktas. MMI–LMIII and later.
Kalamaki, Kephala, near Vai.
Karfi, Lasitiou. MM.
Kato Zakro, Gorge of the Dead. MMI.
Keria, near Gonies, Maleviziou. MM.
Kophinas, Monophatsiou. MM and later.
Korphi tou Mare, near Ziros, Sitias.
Koumasa, Monophatsiou, summit of Korakies Hill. MMII–LMIII.
Krasi, Entichti, Pediados. MMI.
Lastros, Sitias. MMII.
Linaron Selli, Monophatsiou. MM.
Maza, on summit of Korphi, near Kalo Chorio, Pediados. MM.
Modi, near Palaikastro, Sitias.
Perivolakia, Sitias.
Petsophas, Sitias. EMII–LMI and later.
Plagia, Sitias. Now destroyed.
Pobia, Kainourgiou, Vigla. MM.
Prophitis Elias, Mallia. MMI.
Pyrgos, Maleviziou. MM.
Sklokas, Akrotiri Peninsula. MMI–II.
Thylakas, Goulas, near Mesa Kakkonika, Merabellou.
Traostalos, Sitias.
Vigla, near Epano Zakro, Sitias. MM.
Vrysinas, near Rousospiti.
Xykephalo, Sitias.
Zou, on Prinias, between Zou and Katsidonia.

EM = Early Minoan; MM = Middle Minoan; LM = Late Minoan.

# Appendix C:
# List of sacred enclosures

Arkokephalo, Viannou. Remains of building.

Aski, near Kastelli, Pediados. Sanctuary walls.

Epano Zakro. Clay figurines.

Kalo Chorio, Pediados. Clay idol.

Kamilari. Two clay figurines.

Kato Symi, Viannou. Temenos beside a spring, chambers of MMIII sanctuary.

Katsaba, Temenos. Offerings MMII–LMI.

Kephala, near Episkopi. Remains of LMIII sacred enclosure.

Keramoutsi Kavrochoriou. Clay figurine.

Kostili, near Miksorouma. Clay figure and lamp.

Kremasma, near Kato Sisi, Merabellou. MM figurines.

Pachlitsani Agriadi, near Kavousi, Ierapetra. Remains of sanctuary, votives.

Pankalochori, Tethymnon. Clay idol.

Phyties, Arkhanes. Remains of sacred enclosure.

Piskokephalo, Sitias. Remains of building and MM clay votives.

Poros, near Katsambas. Objects MMIII–LMI.

Sachtouria, Agia Vasiliou. Clay figurine.

Skinias, Monophatsiou. Objects from sacred enclosure.

Skopi, Sitias. Remains of oval building, MM figurines and pottery.

Sphakia, near Zou. Sanctuary, MMIII.

Stous Athropolitous, near Epano Zakro. Remains of building.

Vaveloi, near Nea Praisos. MM clay figurines.

EM = Early Minoan; MM = Middle Minoan; LM = Late Minoan.

# Appendix D: Chronology

| Date BC | Pottery period | Cultural phase | Selected events |
|---|---|---|---|
| 3200 | Neolithic | Neolithic | Well-established settlement pattern; village on site of Knossos Labyrinth. |
| 3000 | | | |
| 2800 | EMI | Pre-Temple or Early | Pirgos ware made. |
| 2600 | | Shrine Period | Vasiliki built; first occupation period at Fournou Korifi. |
| 2400 | EMII | | Agios Onoufrios and Vasiliki ware made. Minoans trading with Syria; second occupation period at Fournou Korifi. |
| | EMIII | | |
| 2200 | | | Fournou Korifi destroyed by fire. Appearance of 'pictographic' script; earliest peak sanctuaries. |
| 2000 | MMI | | Knossos Labyrinth and other early temples built. |
| | | Old Temple | Kamares ware made. |
| 1800 | MMII | Period | |
| | | | Major earthquake destroys old temples; |
| 1600 | MMIII | New Temple | Zakro temple built; Phaistos and Knossos Labyrinth rebuilt; appearance of Linear A. |
| | | Period | |
| | LMI | | |
| | | | Major Thera eruption* destroys temples |
| 1400 | LMII | Late Temple Period | and towns; Knossos Labyrinth repaired; Linear B appears; 1380 Labyrinth abandoned; Myceneans now in control?? |
| 1200 | LMIII | Post-Temple Period | Trojan War? Mycenean domination of Aegean world. Many Minoan sites burnt; arrival of refugees from mainland Greece; Minoan refuge settlement at Karfi until about 1000 BC. |

| Date BC | Pottery period | Cultural phase | Selected events |
|---------|----------------|----------------|-----------------|
| 1100    | —————— | – – – – – – – – – | |
|         |                |                | Fall of Mycenean centres on Greek mainland, destroyed by invaders; fall of Hattusa, the Hittite capital. |
|         | Subminoan      |                | |
| 1000    | —————— | Postminoan     | |

EM = Early Minoan; MM = Middle Minoan; LM = Late Minoan.

*The debate over the precise date of the catastrophic bronze age Thera eruption continues. The chronology in this book, at least as far as the Thera eruption sequence is concerned, accords with the chronology proposed by J. V. Luce in *The End of Atlantis* (London: Thames & Hudson, 1969): a series of premonitory earthquakes and eruptions beginning in about 1500 BC and culminating in a caldera eruption of exceptional ferocity in about 1470 BC.

In the summer of 1989, the Third International Congress on Thera and the Aegean World, held on Thera itself, brought forward new evidence that the catastrophic eruption occurred 160 years earlier, in about 1630 BC. A study of tree rings shows low-growth for the year 1628 BC in California, England, Ireland and Germany, arguably caused by a dust-veil thrown up by the Thera eruption. A Greenland ice-core shows a high acidity level in the year 1645 BC, give or take 20 years; the sulphur fall-out from a massive volcanic eruption could have produced this peak of acidity.

Nevertheless, at the time of writing, the case has not been made convincingly enough to justify altering the dates of Minoan – and Egyptian – chronology. Archaeologists remain unconvinced by the very indirect nature of the evidence, which may not relate to Thera at all. For the time being, the later dates for the Thera eruption sequence should be retained – not least because they leave undisturbed the well-established and trusted chronologies from ancient Egypt.

# Notes on the illustrations

it is also possible that water was ducted from the roof by way of enclosed shafts instead. In the background is the continuous wall separating the Great Goddess Sanctuary from the Double-Axe Sanctuary beyond.

10  The photograph is taken from the courtyard known as the Court of the Keep, looking southwards. In the foreground are the ruins of the doorway into area V, sometimes called 'the Keep', in accordance with Evans' name for the corresponding area at Knossos, immediately to the north-west of the Central Court. The summit of the dark hill in the centre is the site of Mallia's peak sanctuary, now occupied by a small church, which shows on the picture as a white speck. A sanctuary here, at 125 metres, would have been readily accessible to the people of Mallia – much more so than the Middle Minoan sanctuary at Karfi (off the picture, top left) at a height of 1,100 metres.

11  Although different in detail, the general concept at Mallia is similar to that at Knossos. In the north-west corner of the Bull Court at Mallia, there are four steps up into a self-contained suite of a dozen or so chambers; at Knossos, in the corresponding location, there are five steps leading down into a similar suite. At both temples, there is a porticoed staircase up to the first floor immediately to the south of this suite. The grooved structure separating the two is a moulded plinth to which two cylindrical wooden columns were attached; they would in effect have been pilasters, an architectural idea taken up again in the classical period.

12  The photograph is taken from the point where the Royal Road, one of the streets of the Minoan town of Knossos, splits into two. The right-hand branch passes up a gentle ramp towards the North-West Portico, the North Entrance and the northern end of the West Court. The left-hand branch terminates in the Theatral Area, a place apparently designed for ceremonial greeting and leave-taking. The restored road surface shows the causewayed central lane and the lower side wings. Possibly the central lanes, being higher, drier, and therefore more secure under foot, were the paths used by palanquin-bearers.

13  The structure of this typical Minoan roadway can be seen, as can two 'sleeping policemen', one in the foreground and one in the middle distance. Their function is discussed in the text. The ruins are of House C (left foreground and background) and House A (right background).

14  View towards the south-east of the north-western corner of the villa, which has been tentatively identified (on insufficient evidence) as the residence of the Minoan port commander. Inside, a pier-and-door partition can be seen and, to the left, an area of the distinctive green schist paving which is found at many Minoan sites. The large block in the centre has been pulled over in antiquity. Spyridon Marinatos attributed its movement to the sucking, dragging effect of a withdrawing tsunami produced by the Thera eruption. Finds of pumice-stone among the foundations reinforced this view. He was probably right.

15  Subsidence along the northern and eastern coasts of Crete has taken several important Minoan sites down to, or below, sea-level. At Agii Theodhori, there are visible remains of several Minoan walls, including this one. The tumbled blocks to the right have been displaced from upper courses of the wall. Reconstruction and consolidation would seem desirable here.

16  To left of centre is the large rectangular dock, probably created for shipbuilding and ship repair. To the right is a level platform, also artificial, which was presumably created as a working area. The steel posts cemented into it are the remains of fittings added during the Second World War.

17  This was the subterranean setting of many Minoan religious ceremonies.

Architectural references to several of its components (stone, darkness, pillars, pools of liquid in the floor, winding descents) were incorporated into the designs of the urban temples (see Plate 18).

18 Pillar crypts were designed for the appeasement and worship of chthonic deities. Libations were poured into the carved rectangular libation pits in the floor. This one is unusually well preserved; situated half-way down the hillside, it was buried under later debris from the town of Knossos on the crest of the hill.

19 Phourni exhibits a range of different burial monuments – shaft graves, ossuaries, rectangular mortuary buildings, and tholos tombs – built over a period of at least 1,250 years. It is not fully excavated, yet it is already established as the largest and richest bronze age cemetery in the Aegean. Arkhanes, the modern town below, is like Tylissos in that it has somehow clung on to its bronze age name.

20 This fine tholos tomb dating to about 1400 BC may have been a predecessor and model for the larger and grander tholos tombs on the Greek mainland, which date to around 1250 BC or later.

### FIGURES

1 Gold pendant or pectoral 6 centimetres high, part of the Aigina Treasure, which was probably stolen in antiquity from the Chrysolakkos mortuary-complex at Mallia. The style and quality of the craftsmanship are unmistakably Minoan, even though an Egyptian influence is apparent. The nature-god, the Master of Animals, is shown grasping a water-bird in each hand (compare Figure 40). Below him are three birds in flight, perhaps bearing him aloft on a magic carpet. Controversy surrounds the three curving structures, but they appear to be snakes, serpents, or giant worms. The god wears a typical Minoan kilt with beaded tassel, and large ear-rings. The unusual head-dress looks as if it is a two-tiered crown of feathers.

2 A bronze votive offering of unknown provenance, made 1550–1500 BC. It is unusually finely detailed and well finished, compared with most other votives.

3 Clay model from the Kophinas peak sanctuary, made in about 1900 BC. It shows an elaborately tiered head-dress with a frill round the upturned brim.

4 Clay heads from female figurines, probably of votive worshippers. Found at the Piskokefalo sanctuary, and made around 1700–1600 BC.

5 The existence of a range of cosmetic implements reinforces the idea gained from the frescoes and figurines, that the Minoans were very concerned about grooming and self-presentation.

6 There is no reason to doubt that the fresco painters accurately depicted contemporary textile designs. Some of the simpler designs could have been woven: others were probably embellished with embroidery and appliqué work. The designs are often surprisingly intricate.

7 Finds of helmets (C and D) at Knossos go a long way towards establishing the Minoans as a 'normal' bronze age people, prepared to do battle when their interests were threatened.

8 Dagger A was found in a shaft grave at Mycenae, but seems to be a Cretan product, probably made between 1600 and 1500 BC. It would originally have had a rounded pommel, probably a polished stone. Dagger B was found in the 'Chieftain's Tomb' at Knossos and was made in about 1400 BC; the gold is delicately engraved with lions hunting in a mountain landscape.

9 Fresco fragments (A) were associated with the Palanquin Fresco fragments,

although they may not have been part of the same ceremonial scene. The
rounded shapes at the top are the lower edges of figure-of-eight shields. The
tunic, not seen on other Minoan figures, may be part of the charioteer's military
uniform. The Pylian chariot has semi-circular rear wings, like the Knossian
chariot: these were probably added to protect the charioteer's legs from arrows
shot from the rear quarters. The four-spoked wheels seem to have been
universal (see title illustration, Chapter 1). The curving structure at the front of
the Pylian chariot may be a strengthening brace. The chariot symbol clearly
shows the light (wooden?) structure of the chariot, and the harness for two
horses.

10 Bronze dagger blade 24 centimetres long, found in a shaft grave at Mycenae but
made by a Minoan craftsman. The design is executed in gold (flesh and lions),
silver (shields and shorts) and niello (background). Two other similarly decorated dagger blades were found in the shaft graves and another, complete with
gold hilt, was found at Pylos. These weapons were among the most attractive
products manufactured by the Minoans for the Greek mainland market.

11 The Minoan area of influence is shown at its minimum extent; it may be that their
influence extended further afield, for instance in contacts with the Sicilians and
Libyans. The areas of influence of Hatti, Mitanni, and Egypt overlapped in Syria,
making Ugarit and Byblos focal trading towns.

12 Vathypetro had some of the features of the large urban temples, but on a small,
informal scale only. There was a rectangular Inner Court, a Tripartite Shrine, a
West Terrace and store-rooms. The walled alley running away to the south-east
led to a cluster of Minoan houses. This plan is based partly on published plans and
partly on additional ancient wall footings evident at the site itself. The 'porch
platform' is a low foundation wall forming three sides of a square; it may
represent the base of a roofed, verandah-style main entrance.

13 The three principal surviving houses have significantly different plans, implying
that each may have functioned slightly differently from the others. Houses A and
C are very well preserved (see Plate 2).

14 Terracotta bull. A votive offering from the 'palace' site at Agia Triadha, dated to
about 1300 BC. The original, in Heraklion Museum, is badly broken, but the
cracks have been omitted here in order to focus attention on the original design.

15 Fragments of a carved steatite rhyton found on the Gypsades Hill at Knossos.
The steep rocky slopes of the mountain setting are shown below and to the left of
a typical peak sanctuary. The sanctuary has a tripartite form, with raised central
cella, although the columns are not visible. The sanctuary is embellished with
horizontal cornices topped with sacral horns, and two masts.

16 The low, G-shaped wall represents a small shrine within the cave, and shows
conclusively that the stalactites were the focus of the Minoans' attention, at least
in this cave. This accords well with the whole complex of cult practices focusing
on pillars (see Plates 17 and 18).

17 The interpretation of the site follows Todd Whitelaw's 1983 interpretation. The
Period I buildings have been omitted for the sake of clarity; they stood in the open
space between houses 3 and 6.

18 The site was excavated at the beginning of the twentieth century, and has lain
exposed since then, yet it remains in a remarkably good state of preservation.
Much evidence of the daily lives of the ordinary Minoan people was found in the
ruins of the houses. The summit area is poorly preserved, so the reconstruction of
the temple area is necessarily tentative and incomplete. Gournia's temple seems

to have been designed differently from other temples; e.g. the large principal chamber with a central 'avenue' of columns and piers, the stone sacrificial table at the southern end, on a terrace above the Bull Court. Even so, features found at other temples are retained; e.g. the indented West Façade, a West Terrace, a rectangular Bull Court and a Theatral Area composed of two flights of steps arranged at right angles.

19 The reconstruction is based on the stumps of the masonry plinths and column sockets surviving on the western edge of the Bull Court, which supply the plan, and the representation of a very similar shrine on fragments of the Grandstand Fresco. The shrine was the centrepiece of the Bull Court's west side. In the central cella, there was a red column against a blue background. In the left cella there were black or blue columns against a red background. In the right cella there were black or blue columns against a yellow ochre background. The sacral horns were white. The check pattern was black and white, and the 'castle' motifs were black on a yellow ochre background. The half-rosettes at the centre were painted white, red, and black.

20 These diagrams of just one small part of the plumbing system at Knossos illustrate the complexity of the engineering design. The sewers were flushed mainly by rain-water ducted into the system from light-wells or from pipes leading down from the roof. The sewage from these lavatories was discharged through the east curtain wall and down an open duct which is still very well preserved.

21 The doors, gypsum floor, wooden seat, and the upper parts of the walls have gone, but this faithful reconstruction gives an idea of the sophistication of everyday life at Minoan Knossos.

22 The map shows the location of selected sites. The uneven distribution is very apparent. It is not clear yet whether there really were very few Minoan sites in the western third of Crete; possibly important sites await discovery there.

23 The Thiessen polygons make no allowance for the size or 'pull' of each centre, nor do they allow for variations in relief, soil fertility and food production. The real locations of the boundaries are not known, but it is likely that conspicuous physical barriers were utilized. The boundary between the Knossos and Phaistos territories, for instance, probably followed the crest of the ridge separating the Mesara Plain from the lowlands draining towards the north coast.

24 Contours are at 10-metre intervals. The coastline has been reconstructed to give two small harbours, one facing north-east, one facing west. The headland between the two is split by a rocky cleft which may have had some cult significance: the Chrysolakkos tomb is nearby.

25 This reconstruction is taken from Castleden (1989) and is based on several sources: the ruins themselves, the published plan of the present state of the ruins by Sinclair Hood and W. Taylor (*The Bronze Age Palace at Knossos: Plan and Sections*, Athens and London: British School of Archaeology at Athens and Thames & Hudson, 1981), and Theodore Fyfe's manuscript plans of the wall footings as originally excavated. The excellent manuscript plans in Mackenzie's Daybooks have also been used. There are significant departures from Evans' map and reconstructions; this reconstruction attempts a rational compromise between the Mackenzie and Fyfe plans on the one hand and the present state of what seem to be the original wall footings. Existing published plans (except my own) usually show the western limb of the Procession Corridor giving way to the cellarage below the South Terrace; in this plan, the building is reconstructed to the common floor level of the Procession Corridor, West Court and Bull Court,

which I believe makes the connections significantly clearer and more logical. The many different floor levels in the East Wing make it very difficult to give a simple ground-floor plan. I have attempted a plan which makes the interconnection or (equally important) non-interconnection of chambers as clear as possible.

26 A fine two-handled jar, 40 centimetres high, carved out of white, brown and grey-green marble, found in the temple of Zakro. Although the shaping of the stone is a technical and artistic *tour de force*, the form (particularly of the high curving handles) is frankly not really appropriate to the material. Possibly the shape was borrowed from a metal original. Made 1500–1470 BC.

27 The bronze artefacts found in the Tomb of the Tripod Hearth are dated to about 1400 BC.

28 This famous gold pendant came from the Chrysolakkos burial-complex at Mallia. It measures 4.6 centimetres across and was probably made between 1800 and 1600 BC. Overlooked by treasure-seekers, it probably represents a tiny fraction of the rich grave-goods once deposited at Chrysolakkos. Much of the Aigina Treasure is thought to have come from the same site.

29 The decorative gold sheet covering helped to preserve the wooden disc handle of this sword, which may have been purely ornamental or ceremonial in function. Diameter 6 centimetres. Made 1550–1500 BC.

30 This is the typical attitude of the Minoan worshipper, standing to attention with one fist planted on the forehead in a gesture of adoration.

31 The Linear A sample is part of an inscription on a clay tablet found at Agia Triadha. The Linear B sample is an inscription on one of the chariot tablets (tablet Sc 230) found in the Knossos Labyrinth. The inscription tells of a chariot, a pair of horses and a tunic belonging to a charioteer named Opilimnios.

32 A: A pedestal bowl or goblet 22 centimetres high with a dark, blue-grey burnish, found at Pirgos (the type site) near Knossos. Made in Early Minoan I, or around 2700 BC. B: A jug 20 centimetres high from Agios Onoufrios (the type site). Made in Early Minoan I–II, around 2500 BC. C: A teapot-shaped jar or jug 18 centimetres high from Vasiliki (the type site). Made in about 2500 BC.

33 The Marine Style clay vase from Gournia carries what must surely be the most successful octopus design ever attempted: the tentacles sprawl round the entire surface in a series of free arabesques, with wisps of seaweed filling the spaces. Made in about 1450 BC. The Floral Style clay vase from Mallia was also made in about 1450 BC. The dark-on-light designs draw on leaves, flowers and rocks; the treatment is similar to that of the Marine Style.

34 The goddess on the left is 90 centimetres high. Both idols have non-supporting, detachable clay feet, just like the much earlier and larger wooden idol at Anemospilia, dating to about 1700 BC (see Castleden 1989, pp. 120–1). The Karfi idols were made in about 1050 BC, right at the end of the Minoan civilization.

35 Mottled chalcedony intaglio from Knossos. The curious drapery round the fisherman's thighs may represent the same flounced or layered shorts seen on the huntsmen of the Lion Hunt Dagger, but wetted and clinging to the man's flesh. The fisherman may be offering the octopus and fish to the gods, like the boy with the fish in the Akrotiri fresco.

37 A: a broken and incomplete seal impression from Knossos. B: a Minoan seal impression, unknown provenance. C: a broken and incomplete Minoan seal impression. D: clay model 20 centimetres long from an Early Minoan tomb at Palaikastro. The shape is characteristic of early boats and ships of Crete and the Cyclades. Some models have high stems and high sterns, which makes them look

very like horns of consecration, and there may be a conscious symbolic reference to the ship in the form of the sacral horns.

38 The map has been devised to show as clearly as possible the geographical structure of the Minoan trading system in the Aegean, as it developed in the sixteenth century BC. The array of trading stations across the southern Aegean acted as a springboard for further trading links with places further afield, in mainland Greece and the interior of Anatolia.

39 Extraordinary for the large number of separate shrines and ritual incidents shown on it, this large gold ring has been dismissed by some scholars as a fake. In the text, the case is argued for its authenticity. Found by chance by a boy on the spot where the Temple Tomb was later discovered, and then bought by the priest of Fortetsa. It is to be hoped that it will one day be rediscovered, whether in America or in Nicolaos Pollakis' garden in Fortetsa.

40 A gem found at Kydonia (Khania). It shows a male deity grasping two helpless lions by their manes. The significance of the three parallel lines behind the figures is obscure; perhaps they are steps.

41 Clay sealing found in fire debris from the Minoan city of Kydonia, and dating to Late Minoan IB (1500–1450 BC); the right-hand half is blackened and broken up by fire. This reconstruction is based on a photograph of the single, damaged original and the excellent pencil drawing in Tzedakis and Hallager (1987). The metal ring bezel forming the imprint was 2.7 by 2 centimetres and the image was worked in unusually high relief. The commanding male figure standing on the parapet of a building may be intended for a Minoan king or leader, although his gigantic stature – he is shown over three storeys tall – suggests that a deity is intended. He holds out his staff in the same dramatic way as the famous image of the Mountain Mother Goddess. The symbol to the left looks like a fish, and should perhaps be seen in conjunction with the two pellets above it. Rows of pellets are sometimes used to represent continuous features like tresses of hair; here the fish and pellets together may represent a pennant of some kind attached to the staff. The god is in effect holding a standard. To the right is what seems to be a stylized bull's head, perhaps symbolizing Poteidan. The building shown 1–3 storeys high and surmounted by many sets of sacral horns lining parapets at many different levels, could be a temple or a city; a temple seems more likely. Interestingly, the whole structure seems to be enclosed by a wall with vertical slits in it and two large, monumental gateways. The gates are made of vertical tree trunks; over them are decorative or symbolic panels with half-rosettes, just like those on each side of the throne in the Knossos Throne Sanctuary. In the foreground, the sea is depicted with the conventional 'net' pattern and the waves breaking on the shore with the conventional 'coral' pattern. The large rock in the centre has been adventurously interpreted by G. Kopke (in Tzedakis and Hallager 1987) as 'a record of the eruption of Thera', presumably showing the moment when colossal tsunamis crashed over the walls of a coastal city or temple. Whilst this is possible – and it would fit in very well with an interpretation of the figure as Poteidan – it does seem to be overstretching the evidence; the feature looks more like a rock than a towering wave. The site, if a real site is represented at all, may be that of Kydonia itself or of some other coastal temple-city, such as Zakro. Or perhaps an otherworldly city is intended, a Minoan Asgard across the sea. If that is the case, this is a vision of heaven, with the chief of the Minoan gods making salutation from his tower.

42 Clay model from Agia Triadha. Yellow ochre with painted red stripes. A bird

perches on top of each swing-post, indicating that a deity has alighted. Although at first sight a toy, this was probably a model with a religious intention. Swinging may have been used as an aid to meditation, which in turn was a way of approaching the gods.

43 Gold Minoan ring in the Ashmolean Museum, Oxford. Original provenance unknown. A naked woman prays or submits at a group of boulders; she wears a sacral knot at the nape of her neck. A priestess in a flounced dress stands to the left, apparently touching her own sacral knot. A dramatic epiphany of an armed god appears in the air between them, holding a bow and what seems to be a dagger; the dagger seems poised to strike the naked woman. This may be a rare depiction of a human sacrifice (see also title illustration, Chapter 7).

44 Gem of unknown provenance in Heraklion Museum. Two lions stand with their forepaws resting on a low, three-pillared altar (= shorthand for tripartite shrine?). The arrangement is reminiscent of the Lion Gate at Mycenae, where a single Minoan pillar stands on the altar between the two lions. Here, instead of the single pillar, is a sun-disc, which is taken to represent Poteidan-Poseidon.

45 Large, finely detailed double-axe made of a single thin sheet of bronze in about 1470 BC. Its blades are doubled, which emphasizes its ritual use. The whole surface is covered with engraved stylized lilies, implying a dedication to Potnia. The axe was probably originally raised on a wooden pole, like the axes shown on the Agia Triadha sarcophagus.

46 The fresco fragment known as 'La Parisienne' was originally part of a sacred communion fresco of the same type as the one Evans called the Camp Stool Fresco. Some participants sit on cushioned folding chairs, receiving the sacrament from standing officiants. The fragment is of interest for several reasons. It clearly shows a hair-style that was common among both men and women, with a few curls drawn forward over the forehead and a cascade of long, waving ringlets falling down the back. It shows the eyes and eyebrows exaggerated with black eye-liner and the lips emphasized with rouge. The drawing of the sacral knot and the dress is hasty, crude and rather unsatisfactory on the original mural.

47 The two trees are rendered very differently and may be intended as different species. The armless and apparently legless figure has been the subject of a long and unresolved controversy. The most natural interpretation is that it represents a statue of a god wearing a sheepskin robe. The shrine behind the xoanon is elaborately decorated, probably with painted plaster, as is the wall of the sacred enclosure which surrounds the olive tree.

48 Clay statue of a goddess 79 centimetres high, from a small shrine at Gazi, west of Knossos, dating from Late Minoan III, the Post-Temple Period. On her crown are three large and carefully modelled poppy-heads, confirming a link between the worship of the goddess and opium-taking.

49 Figures on a rectangular plaque 8 centimetres long, made of carved shell in 1480–1470 BC. Found in the Phaistos temple. The holes in the corners of the plaque (not shown here) suggest that it was originally fixed to a wooden box. Some of the details have been picked out with paint. This procession of robed animal-headed daemons with long staffs is an early example of a ritual scene that was taken up later by the mainland Myceneans.

50 Clay jug or rhyton in the form of a bull-grappling scene. Made in the Pre-Temple Period. Two members of a bull-grappling team hang on to the bull's horns, while a third, facing the other way, lies across the bull's face. This would have had the

effect of immobilizing the bull while the bull-leaper (not part of the model) dived over the bull's head.

51 Detail from one of the two gold cups found at Vaphio on the Greek mainland, and made by a Minoan craftsman in 1550–1470 BC. The quality of craftsmanship in this very naturalistic piece is unsurpassed. It is, as Peter Warren has said, 'perhaps the finest surviving picture of a Minoan male'. The depiction of the bull and the olive tree is also very fine.

52 Development of a scene on a fragment of a carved steatite vessel from the Gypsades Hill at Knossos. Two men are processing with bowls in their outstretched hands. This offertory procession is probably closely connected with the function of the rhyton on which it was carved. The architectural background shows a balustraded staircase, with sacral horns and masts or banners mounted on the balustrade. It may represent part of the Knossos Labyrinth, possibly the Stepped Portico at the south-west corner of the complex.

54 Some pillar bases of the east colonnade survive. The exterior wall is of very fine masonry and the structure as a whole seems to have been for high-status burials. It was built during the Old Temple Period. Looting and excavating in the interior have left it virtually wrecked.

55 Detail from a miniature fresco fragment found in the Knossos Labyrinth. The figure is about 8 centimetres high. Most of the head and the raised right arm are missing, here reconstructed. The hair, which is worn thigh-length, is painted black, the skin Indian red, the loincloth white, the spear or staff yellow ochre, and the background a dusky blue. The leader is acknowledging the enthusiastic salute, with raised spears, of at least twenty warriors, who are depicted on other fragments of the same fresco. The illustration was sketched freehand from the fresco fragment in Heraklion Museum. Interestingly, the figure carries no recognizable marks of office at all.

56 Detail from carved steatite libation vessel, 12 centimetres high, from Agia Triadha, made between 1650 and 1500 BC. The figure with the staff stands in front of a wall, holding his staff out commandingly in front of him. He wears wristlets, armlets and an elaborate necklace, implying high rank. He is approached by a smaller male who carries a sword and what may be a fly-whisk or a shepherd's crook; he heads a procession of males who are almost completely concealed under animal skins. The scene may be interpreted as a group of soldiers led by a junior officer reporting to a senior officer or a prince with hunting trophies. An alternative view is that a group of boys who have just completed one of their initiation ordeals is reporting to an older youth who has already been initiated: a kind of prefect, he is supervising the initiation ceremonies of the younger boys. Certainly the youthful appearance of the figures fits in with this second interpretation. Many of the images in Minoan art are images of the young. This illustration has been developed from two photographs, one centred on each figure. As a result, the figure of the prefect or prince is correctly proportioned, and not foreshortened as usually shown: he is sturdier and more thick-set than in most published representations.

57 The almost complete upper part of one of a series of life-size tribute-bearers painted on the walls of the Cupbearer Sanctuary in the Knossos Labyrinth. A youth carries a conical rhyton. In the original, the rhyton is painted blue (black in my drawing) and red. The youth's hair is dark brown, his skin a deep Indian red. The areas of the nipple, the locks of hair on the shoulder, and the rim of the rhyton have been reconstructed. This is another highly idealized picture of the

young Minoan male; when the grainy, mottled texture of the decayed fresco is omitted, as in this drawing, the image is startlingly youthful.

58 A carved gemstone from Kydonia shows a young, short-haired god apparently standing on or hovering above a pair of sacral horns. To his right is a rampant winged goat. To his left is a typical Minoan daemon bearing a ewer. The daemon is animal-headed, bipedal, and wearing a characteristic wasp-tail robe.

### CHAPTER TITLE ILLUSTRATIONS

1 A stone mould from Sitia. A decorative symbol incorporating a cross, rays, a wheel, and flames: it represents a flaming sun-disc. The Minoan chariot wheel had four spokes (see Figure 9), so the symbolic reference to a sun-wheel is probably not accidental.

2 A gem from the Idaian Cave. The priestess may be blowing the shell horn or using it as a megaphone to summon a deity. She stands on some steps in front of an altar decked with sacral horns and three sacred boughs.

3 A gold ring from Mochlos. To the right is a masonry structure very similar to those on rings from Mycenae and Knossos; it has a high, narrow aperture (a doorway?) with a cornice. In the centre is a stretch of water and a boat floating on it. A goddess or priestess is conveying a sacred tree along the coast in an elaborately tiered shrine which is placed on the after end of the boat.

4 A clay sealing from Zakro. The priestesses may be involved in a public procession, or simply on their way from one part of a temple to another. The large double-axe seems to be hovering in the air in front of one of the priestesses, or standing in the background. The priestess on the right is apparently carrying the robe over her arm; its detail is indistinct, but it seems to have a quilted or scaled texture above and a pleated texture below, in which case it is a cuirass.

5 A Minoan seal showing a ship with two large fish, which may be tuna, and a substantial quadrident (or four-pronged trident). The implication is that ship, fish and quadrident are connected.

6 A Minoan ring, said to have come from eastern Crete, now in the National Museum of Copenhagen. The image is carved in green jasper. It shows a goddess appearing in the centre, slightly above the level of the worshippers. To the right are two women greeting her with upstretched arms. To the left are two men, also greeting her with upstretched arms; they have cast aside their shields to worship. Significantly, the men have knelt before the goddess, whereas the women have not. This may be another indication of the superior status of women in Minoan society. To the right of the goddess, in the sky, are two rows of dots, which may signify a rainbow.

7 A sealstone found at Khania and dating to about 1450 BC. The seated female with unusually exaggerated breasts is probably a goddess. The sword poised above the girl on the left strongly suggests that she is about to be sacrificed; beneath the girl is a suggestion of the sacrificial table. The goddess sits on a complicated structure reminiscent of the tripartite shrine. The form behind her may be a sacred tree, with its fruit or foliage bending symbolically over her shoulder.

# References

## 1 INTRODUCTION

Alexiou, S. (undated) *Minoan Civilization*, Heraklion: Spyros Alexiou.
Bury, J. B. (1951) *A History of Greece to the Death of Alexander the Great*, London: Macmillan.
Castleden, R. (1989) *The Knossos Labyrinth: A New View of the 'Palace of Minos' at Knossos*, London and New York: Routledge.
Evans, A. (1921–36) *The Palace of Minos at Knossos*, 4 vols, London: Macmillan.
Higgins, R. (1981) *Minoan and Mycenaean Art*, London: Thames & Hudson.
Nilsson, M. P. (1949) *The Minoan-Mycenaean Religion and its Survival in Greek Religion*, Lund: Gleerup.
Spanakis, S. (undated) *Crete: a Guide*, Heraklion: Sfakianakis.
Thomson, G. (1949) *Studies in Ancient Greek Society: the Prehistoric Aegean*, London: Lawrence & Wishart.

## 2 THE PEOPLE

Alexiou, S. (undated) *Minoan Civilization*, Heraklion: Spyros Alexiou.
Baumbach, L. (1983) 'An examination of the personal names in the Knossos tablets', in O. Krzyszkowska and L. Nixon (eds), *Minoan Society: Proceedings of the Cambridge Colloquium, 1981*, Bristol: Bristol Classical Press.
Cameron, M. (1987) 'The "palatial" thematic system in the Knossos murals: last notes on the Knossos frescoes', in R. Hägg and N. Marinatos (eds), *The Function of the Minoan Palaces: Proceedings of the Fourth International Symposium of the Swedish Institute in Athens, 1984*.
Castleden, R. (1989) *The Knossos Labyrinth: A New View of the 'Palace oj Minos' at Knossos*, London and New York: Routledge.
Chadwick, J. (1976) *The Mycenaean World*, Cambridge: Cambridge University Press.
Faure, P. (1973) *La Vie quotidienne en Crète au temps de Minos*, Paris: Hachette.
Hood, S. (1971) *The Minoans*, London: Thames & Hudson.
—— (1978) *The Arts in Prehistoric Greece*, Harmondsworth: Penguin Books.
Hooker, J. T. (1987) 'Minoan religion in the Late Palace Period', in O. Krzyszkowska and L. Nixon (eds), *Minoan Society: Proceedings of the Cambridge Colloquium, 1981*, Bristol: Bristol Classical Press.
Immerwahr, S. A. (1983) 'The people in the frescoes', in O. Krzyszkowska and L. Nixon (eds), *Minoan Society: Proceedings of the Cambridge Colloquium, 1981*, Bristol: Bristol Classical Press.
Lang, M. L. (1969) *The Palace of Nestor, Vol. 2: The Frescoes*, Princeton: Princeton University Press.
Lehmann, J. (1977) *The Hittites: People of a Thousand Gods*, London: Collins.
Luce, J. V. (1969) *The End of Atlantis*, London: Thames & Hudson.

Marinatos, N. (1984) *Art and Religion in Thera: Reconstructing a Bronze Age Society*, Athens: Mathioulakis.

Nixon, I. G. (1968) *The Rise of the Dorians*, Puckeridge: Chancery Press.

Palmer, L. R. (1961) *Mycenaeans and Minoans*, London: Faber & Faber.

Platon, N. (1968) *Crete*, Paris/Geneva/New York: Nagel.

—— (1971) *Zakros: the Discovery of a Lost Palace of Ancient Crete*, New York: Scribners.

Säflund, G. (1987) 'The Agoge of the Minoan youth as reflected by palatial iconography', in R. Hägg and N. Marinatos (eds), *The Function of the Minoan Palaces: Proceedings of the Fourth International Symposium at the Swedish Institute at Athens, 1984*.

Warren, P. (1975) *The Aegean Civilizations*, Oxford: Elsevier-Phaidon.

Willetts, R. F. (1969) *Everyday Life in Ancient Crete*, London: Batsford.

3 LIFE IN THE COUNTRYSIDE

Bintliff, J. L. (1977) 'Natural Environment and Human Settlement in Prehistoric Greece based on Original Fieldwork', *British Archaeological Reports Supplementary Series*, 28.

Branigan, K. (1975) Review of *Myrtos* by Peter Warren, *Classical Review*, 25: 116–18.

Burn, A. R. and Burn, M. (1980) *The Living Past of Greece*, Harmondsworth; Penguin Books.

Chadwick, J. (1976) *The Mycenaean World*, Cambridge: Cambridge University Press.

Effenterre, H. van (1983) 'The economic pattern of a Minoan district: the case of Mallia', in O. Krzyszkowska and L. Nixon (eds), *Minoan Society: Proceedings of the Cambridge Colloquium, 1981*, Bristol: Bristol Classical Press.

Evans, A. (1921–36) *The Palace of Minos at Knossos*, 4 vols, London: Macmillan.

Faure, P. (1973) *La Vie quotidienne en Crète au temps de Minos*, Paris: Hachette.

Graham, J. W. (1987) *The Palaces of Crete*, Princeton: Princeton University Press.

Hood, S. (1971) *The Minoans*, London: Thames & Hudson.

—— (1983) 'The "country house" and Minoan society', in O. Krzyszkowska and L. Nixon (eds), *Minoan Society: Proceedings of the Cambridge Colloquium, 1981*, Bristol: Bristol Classical Press.

Newey, J. (1989) Personal communication on derivation of 'Kydonia'.

Pashley, R. (1837) *Travels in Crete*, London: John Murray.

Platon, N. (1968) *Crete*, Paris/Geneva/New York: Nagel.

Rutkowski, B. (1986) *The Cult Places of the Aegean*, New Haven and London: Yale University Press.

Seymour, J. and Girardet, H. (1986) *Far from Paradise: The Story of Human Impact on the Environment*, Basingstoke: Green Print.

Spanakis, S. (undated) *Crete: a Guide*, Heraklion: Sfakianakis.

Warren, P. (1972) *Myrtos: an Early Bronze Age Settlement in Crete*, London: Thames & Hudson.

—— (1975) *The Aegean Civilizations*, Oxford: Elsevier-Phaidon.

—— (1982) 'The place of Crete in the thalassocracy of Minos', in R. Hägg and N. Marinatos (eds), *The Minoan Thalassocracy: Myth and Reality; Proceedings of the Third International Symposium at the Swedish Institute in Athens, 1982*.

—— (1984) 'Circular platforms at Minoan Knossos', *Annual of the British School at Athens*, 79: 307–23.

Whitelaw, T. (1983) 'The settlement at Fournou Korifi, Myrtos', in O. Krzyszkowska and L. Nixon (eds), *Minoan Society: Proceedings of the Cambridge Colloquium, 1981*, Bristol: Bristol Classical Press.

Wunderlich, H. G. (1975) *The Secret of Crete*, London: Souvenir Press.

#### 4 LIFE IN THE TOWNS

Alexiou, S. (undated) *Minoan Civilization*, Heraklion: Spyros Alexiou.

Branigan, K. (1983) 'Craft specialization in Minoan Crete', in O. Krzyszkowska and L. Nixon (eds), *Minoan Society: Proceedings of the Cambridge Colloquium, 1981*, Bristol: Bristol Classical Press.

Castleden, R. (1989) *The Knossos Labyrinth: A New View of the 'Palace of Minos' at Knossos*, London and New York: Routledge.

Chadwick, J. (1976) *The Mycenaean World*, Cambridge: Cambridge University Press.

Chadwick, J., Killen, J. T. and Olivier, J-P. (1971) *The Knossos Tablets*, Cambridge: Cambridge University Press.

Chadwick, J. *et al.* (1986) *Knossos Corpus, Vol. 1*, Cambridge, Cambridge University Press.

Effenterre, H. van (1983) 'The economic pattern of a Minoan district: the case of Mallia', in O. Krzyszkowska and L. Nixon (eds), *Minoan Society: Proceedings of the Cambridge Colloquium, 1981*, Bristol: Bristol Classical Press.

Evans, A. (1921–36) *The Palace of Minos at Knossos*, 4 vols, London: Macmillan.

Graham, J. W. (1987) *The Palaces of Crete*, Princeton: Princeton University Press.

Haskell, H. W. (1983) 'From palace to town administration: evidence of coarse-ware stirrup jars', in O. Krzyszkowska and L. Nixon (eds), *Minoan Society: Proceedings of the Cambridge Colloquium, 1981*, Bristol: Bristol Classical Press.

Higgins, R. (1981) *Minoan and Mycenaean Art*, London: Thames & Hudson.

Hood, S. (1971) *The Minoans*, London: Thames & Hudson.

—— (1978) *The Arts in Prehistoric Greece*, Harmondsworth: Penguin Books.

Hood, S. and Smyth, D. (1981) *Archaeological Survey of the Knossos Area*, Athens and London: British School of Archaeology at Athens and Thames & Hudson.

Karaminas, P. and Petrakis, E. (undated) *The Phaistos Disk*, Athens: Helianthos.

Kean, V. J. (1985) *The Disk from Phaistos*, Athens: Efstathiadis.

McEvedy, C. (1989) 'Piltdown Man and his printing set', *The Independent*, 2 August 1989.

Palmer, L. R. (1961) *Mycenaeans and Minoans: Aegean Prehistory in the Light of the Linear B Tablets*, London: Faber & Faber.

Platon, N. (1968) *Crete*, Paris/Geneva/New York: Nagel.

—— (1971) *Zakros: The Discovery of a Lost Palace of Ancient Crete*, New York: Scribners.

Preziosi, D. (1983) *Minoan Architectural Design*, Berlin: Mouton.

Thomson, G. (1949) *Studies in Ancient Greek Society: The Prehistoric Aegean*, London: Lawrence & Wishart.

Warren, P. (1975) *The Aegean Civilizations*, Oxford: Elsevier-Phaidon.

—— (1987) 'The genesis of a Minoan palace', in R. Hägg and N. Marinatos (eds), *The Function of the Minoan Palaces: Proceedings of the Fourth International Symposium at the Swedish Institute in Athens, 1984*.

Whitelaw, T. (1983) 'The settlement at Fournou Korifi, Myrtos', in O. Krzysz-
kowska and L. Nixon (eds), *Minoan Society: Proceedings of the Cambridge
Colloquium, 1981*, Bristol: Bristol Classical Press.
Willetts, R. F. (1977) *The Civilization of Ancient Crete*, London: Batsford.

5 LIFE IN THE HARBOUR TOWNS AND OVERSEAS

Alexiou, S. (undated) *Minoan Civilization*, Heraklion: Spyros Alexiou.
Andel, T. H. van and Runnels, C. N. (1988) 'An Essay on the "Emergence of
Civilization" in the Aegean World', *Antiquity*, 62: 234–47.
Bury, J. B. (1951) *A History of Greece to the Death of Alexander the Great*, London:
Macmillan.
Cadogan, G. (1982) 'A Minoan thalassocracy?', in R. Hägg and N. Marinatos (eds),
*The Minoan Thalassocracy: Myth and Reality: Proceedings of the Third Inter-
national Symposium at the Swedish Institute in Athens, 1982.*
Castleden, R. (1989) *The Knossos Labyrinth: A New View of the 'Palace of Minos' at
Knossos*, London and New York: Routledge.
Catling, H. W. (1980) 'The Linear B inscribed stirrup jars of western Crete', *Annual
of the British School of Archaeology at Athens*, 75: 49–113.
Chadwick, J. (1976) *The Mycenaean World*, Cambridge: Cambridge University
Press.
Driessen, J. and Macdonald (1984) 'Some aspects of the Aegean in the late 15th and
early 14th centuries BC', *Annual of the British School of Archaeology at Athens*, 79:
49–74.
Evans, A. (1921–36) *The Palace of Minos at Knossos*, 4 vols, London: Macmillan.
Faure, P. (1973) *La Vie quotidienne en Crète au temps de Minos*, Paris: Hachette.
Guest-Papamanoli, A. (1983) 'Pêche et pêcheurs minoens: proposition pour une
recherche', in O. Krzyszkowska and L. Nixon (eds), *Minoan Society: Proceedings
of the Cambridge Colloquium, 1981*, Bristol: Bristol Classical Press.
Hood, S. (1971) *The Minoans*, London: Thames & Hudson.
—— (1982) 'A Minoan empire in the Aegean in the sixteenth and fifteenth centuries
BC?', in R. Hägg and N. Marinatos (eds), *The Minoan Thalassocracy: Myth and
Reality: Proceedings of the Third International Symposium at the Swedish Institute
in Athens, 1982.*
Hood, S. and Smyth, D. (1981) *Archaeological Survey of the Knossos Area*, Athens
and London: British School of Archaeology at Athens and Thames & Hudson.
Lehmann, J. (1977) *The Hittites: People of a Thousand Gods*, London: Collins.
Nixon, I. G. (1968) *The Rise of the Dorians*, Puckeridge: Chancery Press.
Platon, N. (1968) *Crete*, Paris/Geneva/New York: Nagel.
Warren, P. (1967) 'Minoan stone vases as evidence for Minoan foreign connexions in
the Aegean bronze age', *Proc. Prehist. Soc.*, 33: 37–55.
—— (1975) *The Aegean Civilizations*, Oxford: Elsevier-Phaidon.
—— (1982) 'The place of Crete in the thalassocracy of Minos', in R. Hägg and
N. Marinatos (eds), *The Minoan Thalassocracy: Myth and Reality: Proceedings of
the Third International Symposium at the Swedish Institute in Athens, 1982.*

6 THE RELIGIOUS LIFE

Alexiou, S. (undated) *Minoan Civilization*, Heraklion: Spyros Alexiou.
Cameron, M. (1987) 'The "palatial" thematic system in the Knossos murals: last

notes on the Knossos frescoes', in R. Hägg and N. Marinatos (eds), *The Function of the Minoan Palaces: Proceedings of the Fourth International Symposium at the Swedish Institute in Athens, 1984.*

Castleden, R. (1989) *The Knossos Labyrinth: A New View of the 'Palace of Minos' at Knossos*, London and New York: Routledge.

Chadwick, J. (1976) *The Mycenaean World*, Cambridge: Cambridge University Press.

De Quincey, T. (1821) *Confessions of an English Opium Eater*, London: the London Magazine.

Evans, A. (1921–36) *The Palace of Minos at Knossos*, 4 vols, London: Macmillan.

Ferguson, J. (1989) *Among the Gods: an Archaeological Exploration of Ancient Greek Religion*, London and New York: Routledge.

Graham, J. W. (1987) *The Palaces of Crete*, Princeton: Princeton University Press.

Graves, R. (1960) *The Greek Myths*, Harmondsworth: Penguin Books.

Hägg, R. and Marinatos, N. (eds) (1987) *The Function of the Minoan Palaces: Proceedings of the Fourth International Symposium at the Swedish Institute in Athens, 1984.*

Harrison, J. (1963) *Themis: a Study of the Social Origins of Greek Religion*, London: Merlin Press.

Hawkes, J. (1968) *Dawn of the Gods*, London: Chatto & Windus.

Higgins, R. (1981) *Minoan and Mycenaean Art*, London: Thames & Hudson.

Hood, S. (1971) *The Minoans*, London: Thames & Hudson.

—— (1978) *The Arts in Prehistoric Greece*, Harmondsworth: Penguin Books.

Marinatos, N. (1984) *Art and Religion in Thera: Reconstructing a Bronze Age Society*, Athens: Mathioulakis.

—— (1987) 'Public festivals in the west courts of the palaces', in R. Hägg and N. Marinatos (eds), *The Function of the Minoan Palaces: Proceedings of the Fourth International Symposium at the Swedish Institute in Athens, 1984.*

Niemeier, W-D. (1987) 'On the function of the "Throne Room" in the palace at Knossos', in R. Hägg and N. Marinatos (eds), *The Function of the Minoan Palaces: Proceedings of the Fourth International Symposium at the Swedish Institute in Athens, 1984.*

Nilsson, M. P. (1949) *The Minoan-Mycenaean Religion and its Survival in Greek Religion*, Lund: Gleerup.

Pendlebury, J. D. S. (1939) *The Archaeology of Crete*, London: Macmillan.

—— (1954) *A Handbook to the Palace of Minos*, 2nd edn, London: Macmillan.

Platon, N. (1971) *Zakros: the Discovery of a Lost Palace of Ancient Crete*, New York: Scribners.

Rutkowski, B. (1986) *The Cult Places of the Aegean*, Ithaca, NY: Yale University Press.

Trell, B. (1988) 'The Temple of Artemis at Ephesos', in P. A. Clayton and M. J. Price (eds), *The Seven Wonders of the Ancient World*, London and New York: Routledge.

Tzedakis, Y. and Hallager, E. (1987) 'A clay sealing from the Greek-Swedish excavations at Khania', in R. Hägg and N. Marinatos (eds), *The Function of the Minoan Palaces: Proceedings of the Fourth International Symposium at the Swedish Institute in Athens, 1984.*

Warren, P. (1982) 'The place of Crete in the thalassocracy of Minos', in R. Hägg and

N. Marinatos (eds), *The Minoan Thalassocracy: Myth and Reality: Proceedings of the Third International Symposium at the Swedish Institute in Athens, 1982.*
Willetts, R. F. (1965) *Ancient Crete: A Social History*, London: Routledge.

### 7 THE MINOAN PERSONALITY

Cadogan, G. (1976) *Palaces of Minoan Crete*, London: Barrie & Jenkins.
Chadwick, J. (1976) *The Mycenaean World*, Cambridge: Cambridge University Press.
Edey, M. (1975) *Lost World of the Aegean*, New York: Time-Life.
Evans, A. (1921–36) *The Palace of Minos at Knossos*, 4 vols, London: Macmillan.
Hawkes, J. (1968) *Dawn of the Gods*, London: Chatto & Windus.
Hood, S. (1971) *The Minoans*, London: Thames & Hudson.
—— (1982) 'A Minoan empire in the Aegean in the sixteenth and fifteenth centuries BC?', in R. Hägg and N. Marinatos (eds), *The Minoan Thalassocracy: Myth and Reality: Proceedings of the Third International Symposium at the Swedish Institute in Athens, 1982.*
Hutchinson, R. W. (1962) *Prehistoric Crete*, Harmondsworth: Penguin Books.
Jung, C. G. (1964) *The Collected Works, Vol. 10: Civilization in Transition*, London: Routledge & Kegan Paul.
Lawson, J. C. (1910) *Modern Greek Folklore and Ancient Greek Religion*, Cambridge: Cambridge University Press.
Lehmann, J. (1977) *The Hittites: People of a Thousand Gods*, London: Collins.
Marinatos, N. (1984) *Art and Religion in Thera: Reconstructing a Bronze Age Society*, Athens: Mathioulakis.
Miller, H. (1980) *The Colossus of Maroussi*, Harmondsworth: Penguin Books.
Nixon, L. (1983) 'Changing views of Minoan society', in O. Krzyszkowska and L. Nixon (eds), *Minoan Society: Proceedings of the Cambridge Colloquium, 1981*, Bristol: Bristol Classical Press.
Platon, N. (1968) *Crete*, Paris/Geneva/New York: Nagel.
Sakellarakis, Y. and Sakellarakis, E. (1981) 'Drama of death in a Minoan temple', *National Geographic*, 159: 205–22.
Starr, C. G. (1982) 'Minoan flower lovers', in R. Hägg and N. Marinatos (eds), *The Minoan Thalassocracy: Myth and Reality: Proceedings of the Third International Symposium at the Swedish Institute in Athens, 1982.*
Thomson, G. (1949) *Studies in Ancient Greek Society: the Prehistoric Aegean*, London: Lawrence & Wishart.
Tsipopolou, M. (1988) Lecture given at the Classics and Archaeology Department, Bristol University, 8 March 1988.
Tumasonis, D. (1983) 'Some aspects of Minoan Society: a view from social anthropology', in O. Krzyszkowska and L. Nixon (eds), *Minoan Society, Proceedings of the Cambridge Colloquium, 1981*, Bristol: Bristol Classical Press.
Warren, P. (1980–1) 'Knossos: Stratigraphical Museum Excavations, 1978–80, Part 1', *Archaeological Report 1980–81*, 73–92.
Wunderlich, H. G. (1975) *The Secret of Crete*, London: Souvenir Press.

# Index

(KL = Knossos Labyrinth)